Struggling Vines

A SOUL-CRUSHING JOURNEY TO LOVE

A Memoir

Melanie L. Hickman

Candida
Follow your heart
Melanie Hickman

Struggling Vines

A Soul-Crushing Journey to Love

Author's Note

Disclaimer:

The experiences within are the recollections of the author that aren't necessarily supported by anyone else. Some names and identifying details have been changed to protect the privacy of individuals.

For my husband, who has always supported my "crazy" dream to publish this story despite the fact that it reveals deeply personal details. He prefers to read the book after it's published and has promised to not divorce me after reading it (it's now in writing, Dear!).

Acknowledgements

I want to thank my editor, Lindsey Kesel, who took on this project not knowing how much work was ahead. I presented my writing as "just in case one day I work up the nerve to publish." However, the deeper she read, the more she encouraged me to tackle my fears of exposing our personal lives to the world. Her positive attitude, energy and support are a large part of why I decided to publish.

I want to thank all of my friends in Hawaii who supported and guided me through difficult times and decisions. Without them, I may have taken a different path in life and wouldn't be where I am today. Michele, for choosing the perfect restaurant for my birthday and changing my life. Sheri, for being my soul-sister through thick and thin. Your spirit is the most kind, beautiful and funny to boot! Liane, we are more like real sisters … the kind that argue, support and love each other endlessly through all of our disagreements. Darrell, for your spiritual guidance, even though sometimes I didn't want to listen/believe. Cynthia, for being amazing at what you do and encouraging me to face my fears. Jenna, for always listening to my stories before they were in writing (I know you want credit!). Dara, for all those soul-searching hikes and making me realize that what I thought was a weakness, was actually a strength. And for my friend who will remain nameless that has always been there for me to help me realize my dreams.

Finally, my mother for always supporting her "dreamer child", even when it isn't what she wants (and with me it rarely is). My aunt Diane for reading the horrible first draft and being able to see the story that lies beneath.

Tenacity. How do you know when this quality is a good thing or a bad thing? In my experience, concerning love, it has the potential to both create and destroy. In some of my past relationships, an abundance of tenacity has been my downfall. This instinctual drive caused me to fight to keep things together when I should have followed my gut, stopped doing what my mind was telling me was "right" and end the relationship. If I were to listen to my instincts in the first place, that little voice that told me not to go down that relationship road to begin with, I could have saved myself mountains of heartache. Over time, I've learned to listen to these voices and let them look out for me. Honing the skill of following your inner voice and knowing when to apply tenacity can serve as a powerful combination in life and love, but getting to this point takes a lot of soul searching, patience and sometimes pain. In the end, the long road to happiness is worth every step.

CHAPTER 1

October 13, 2007

As I was pouring the deep red wine into the glass of a random woman's outstretched hand, I glanced across the room to see his smiling face and purpling teeth. He's not a drinker, but tasting was part of his job. I was at the wine tradeshow voluntarily to help pour wine for the attendees in the wine trade. I loved the world of wine and relished in the distinct sense of comfort I felt from being a part of it. Derek was a sales representative for one of the largest wine distributors in Hawaii, and he was escorting clients to various wine vendors who were presenting at the event. Although he was spitting after each tasting, his enthusiastic wave and extra-wide grin indicated that the alcohol was penetrating his small stature. I indiscreetly waved back with a feeling of both joy at seeing his goofy, uninhibited antics and a hint of sadness. Why couldn't I stop thinking about the possibility of leaving this man? Something inside was driving me away from him and I had no idea why.

Derek was my best friend. We had been together for over two years and shared an apartment. He was the epitome of the word *aloha* — always friendly and warm, loving and generous. Our families were unusually close. Our mothers were so similar we joked that they had to be related somehow. We had talked of marriage and he had bought me a ring, but never seemed to plan anything. Recently, we had argued because I wanted to move out of his small one-bedroom apartment and buy a new home. He was totally against it, but I was stubborn and when I wanted something, I usually got it. I went out against his wishes and bought a two-bedroom townhome under my name. He agreed to move in with me, just to keep the peace.

We found each other under rebound circumstances. He had just left his wife and I had left my husband less than a year earlier. At first, this commonality kept us together. We deeply cared for each other and respected the fact that deep down we were both kind and good people. But as the relationship unfolded, it became clear that our lack of common interests was too great to ignore.

Not long after the night of wine tasting and my epiphany that I was second-guessing my situation with Derek, I found myself ending the relationship, but this time it wasn't because he was a horrible person or treated me poorly. I had my fair share of those in the past, but this breakup was different. Derek didn't cheat on me and he was still my best friend, but that voice inside told me he wasn't the one. There was something missing that I couldn't explain. He had a son who I had known and loved since birth, an amazing little *2-year-old* whom I had always treated as if he were my own. This amazing child made it that much harder to leave… but I had to take a leap of faith guided only by my intuition that there was someone else out there waiting for me, someone who was my perfect match. I had no idea who that person was or where I would find him, and at this point it didn't matter. I felt emotionally drained. I needed time to reconnect with myself, to get away and reestablish my priorities in life, to figure out who I was and what I loved.

Travel had always fed my soul and I had forgotten to make it a priority over the last few years. I truly believe that if you do what is right (which is often the more difficult path), the universe rewards you. In my case, the universe did just that. As I was making the phone calls to my friends to inform them of the very amicable separation with Derek, my girlfriend Michele invited me to join her on a business trip to Morocco. The timing was perfect, as it was right around my 32nd birthday in April, only four months away. We started making the preparations and as we were booking flight arrangements for the return flight home, we decided it would be fun to extend the layover in Madrid and celebrate.

CHAPTER 2

April 11, 2008

Michele and I arrived in Marrakech, Morocco, after a grueling 32-hour flight from Hawaii. We were staying at one of the newest luxury hotels in the area, thanks to Michele who had taken on the resort as one of her public relations clients. Morocco was a wonderful surprise that surpassed my expectations with its kind and welcoming people. We had befriended a taxi driver during our time there, Fatha, who ran a small tourism business on the side. He spoke English very well and turned out to be a valuable resource for us during our stay. Fatha recommended local restaurants and filled us in on all of the history of the area with enthusiasm; he was our local connection and seemed proud of his role.

The shopping in Morocco was phenomenal and in a sense refreshing, as nothing was made in China, which typically dominates so much of our material goods in the United States. As you walked through the marketplaces, or *souks*, you could purchase handmade silver goods, oriental rugs, leather goods, spices and foods with such brilliant colors and smells they that would send your senses reeling. I had never been to an Islamic country before and found myself in awe at the devotion of the people who would stop what they were doing when they heard the *adhan*, or call to prayer. It would echo across the land five times a day like clockwork, led by a *muezzin* who chanted in a haunting, yet mystifying voice over loudspeakers. The people were warm and friendly, and the young men seemed to be enamored with my light eyes and hair. For the first time in my life, I was considered exotic! When I would enter stores, the shopkeepers always had some weird fascination with wrapping me in a *hijab*, or headscarf. They enjoyed seeing the light-skinned American girl wrapped in their traditional cultural garb. I played along as it made haggling over prices easier. We spent days walking through the *souks* shopping, people watching and eating the local food. At one point we took a camel ride through the desert, trying to squeeze as many new experiences as we could from our short stay.

When the time came to depart Morocco, we didn't want our journey to end. However, what we didn't know was that for me, a whole different kind of journey was about to begin. We left the Arabian culture of Morocco and were transformed into a new cultural landscape upon touchdown in

Madrid. The beautiful old world of Europe with its historical buildings, culture, museums and the bustling metropolis of the capital city of Spain made my travel companion and me feel vibrant and invigorated, although we didn't seem to fold into the culture as we did in Morocco. The people didn't speak English, and the timing there was hard to grasp. We would read about a fabulous restaurant for lunch, search it out, arrive at the front door and there wouldn't be a soul in sight. We would arrive later in the afternoon to accommodate their bizarre eating schedule and still no luck. After a while, we tried adding two more hours on to our regular timetable, but all too often we still found ourselves standing out as obvious American tourists sitting in a restaurant alone while the locals trickled in around us.

Our second night in Madrid was my birthday celebration. Michele knew that besides traveling, two other things made me extremely happy — good food and excellent wine. She had done some research to find a local place that offered traditional tapas and an extensive Spanish wine list. Wine was practically the only thing I drank, so it was necessary to have a vast selection to choose from, which was 180 degrees from my roots in Ohio. Growing up, my four food groups were canned veggies, boxed carbohydrates, frozen dinners and Velveeta cheese, and it wasn't until I went away to college that I began to develop an appreciation for fresh food and fine wine. In college at Ohio State, I worked as a concierge in a local hotel and sampled all the local fare so I could refer guests to the best spots. I developed the habit of spending my menial income on nice dinners and wine that I couldn't afford and started to fall in love with gastronomy. A wine course in college had piqued my interest in the incredible possibilities of fermenting grapes, and I remember being shocked to discover that there were grape varieties outside of Chardonnay and Cabernet Sauvignon.

We ventured out for an evening of celebration through the labyrinth streets of Madrid. After searching for quite some time for what we expected to be a grandiose façade, we finally found the unassuming restaurant Taberneros tucked away into the small side streets close to the Royal Palace. It was a small, dim restaurant with heavy red tones throughout. There were a few small tables scattered around, but most of the seating was bistro style, which essentially indicated you'd be crammed up against the people next to you. As we stepped inside, the waiter said something in Spanish and it was clear that we could sit at any table we liked — of course we could, because despite our attempts to embrace the culture of locals, we were still the first to arrive. We choose a larger table that could seat four people to the left of the door.

I was excited to try a glass of red wine from Rioja, one of two DOCA's (Denominación de Origen Calificada or Qualified Designation of Origin) in Spain and perhaps the most famous of the two. The waiter came over to take our drink order and to my disappointment, they were not serving a Rioja by the glass. I took our waiter's recommendation for an alternative Spanish wine region and we started our evening. The waiter had taken so long to bring our drinks that the restaurant started filling up around us. No sooner did we settle into our surroundings, take a sip of wine and order our food before the waiter interrupted us asking us to move to a smaller table to accommodate a larger group. We were promptly escorted to a *very* small table just inches away from guests on either side. I was comfortable at our first table and didn't really feel like squeezing into close quarters, but reluctantly agreed. The only thing that seemed to brighten the situation was the fact that behind my seat was a large wine cellar visible through the glass wall. I walked over to it with curiosity, pressed my hands against the glass and proceeded to make a noise akin to Homer Simpson seeing a Duff beer. There were hundreds of bottles just calling my name.

Michele and I are both petite in stature, just barely breaking the 5-foot mark, yet we each possess the ability to eat large amounts of food. As plate after plate of *tapas* arrived, I shared my disappointment with Michele about the fact that Spaniards don't seem to be as friendly as Moroccans. I told her we needed to make friends with some locals so we could get a true feel for the city, similar to our experience in Morocco. She rolled her eyes at me as she shot my comment down: “Melanie, Madrid is a major city. It’s ridiculous to expect to find a complete stranger to show us around the city. That’s about as realistic as visiting New York City and finding a local there who is interested in playing tour guide to two perfect strangers.” I always loved a challenge and told her that anything was possible, but I didn’t argue the point because it certainly was valid. Rather, I’d make a game of looking around the room to see who appeared most normal and would know the city the best, entertaining Michele with my elaborate descriptions of various groups of people and how our evening with them might play out.

I’m not one to stay out much past 11 p.m., but I wanted to spend my birthday living up to the reputation of a true Spaniard. I entertained the thought of partying at a *discothèque* until 4 a.m. The idea of having a partner in crime on this mission was quickly stomped out when Michele made it clear that she had no intention of joining me for such debauchery. In all actuality, the chances of my idea coming to fruition were slim to none, as I didn’t have the first clue where to go. While Michele isn't much of a drinker, I, on the other hand, was already on my third glass of wine and feeling quite pleasant. I noticed that the table next to me must also be in good spirits, since the woman and her two male companions were finishing up their second bottle of Champagne. I overheard the man sitting diagonal from me order a third bottle of Champagne for his table. I joked with Michele that we needed to become friends with our neighbors, as they seemed to drink well and in quantities that I could appreciate. As the waiter dropped off the last bottle to their table, I stared in disbelief. The next thing I knew, my eyes turned to the man who ordered the bottle. I gave him a look as if to say, "Wow, three bottles of bubbly? I'm impressed!" That was the first time our eyes met and, in that very moment, my life changed dramatically.

There was something different about him. For a fleeting second, I felt a strong indication that I knew this man somehow. He was brawny with wide shoulders, handsome with beautifully shaped eyes and had a distinguished look with salt-and-pepper hair. Suddenly aware that we were engaged in a "moment," I quickly looked away. Michele and I went on with our dinner, finished up with dessert and were about ready to leave when I overheard salt-and-pepper man, clearly a Spaniard, ask the waiter for two additional glasses. I had been trying to learn some Spanish to get us by on the trip and was able to pick up things here and there. I had told Michele over dinner that my goal over the next year was to learn Spanish as I've always hated being the typical American limited to just English. I tried to be nonchalant and whisper to Michele what I think I heard. She rolled her eyes at me, no doubt thinking, "Here we go again." I was beside myself that I understood him correctly and asked her to be patient.

A few minutes later the waiter dropped off two champagne glasses at our table and, in broken English, attempted to explain that the glasses were at the request of the table next to us. The waiter poured Michele and I a glass, and I was delighted to accept the gesture and intrigued by the possibility of getting to know our new friends. In an attempt to engage our benefactors, I turned to the man and woman on my immediate right. I assumed them to be a couple and hoped that Mr. Salt-and-Pepper across the table was a single friend. The woman introduced herself as Vanesa and spoke with the clearest English of the three. We quickly learned that they were colleagues finishing up a work meeting and that David (*Dah-VEED*), salt-and-pepper man, was a wine maker in Rioja and Iñagi, the other gentleman, was a winemaker as well. Vanesa was serving as host of the dinner, as she was employed by their distributor in Spain.

While the conversation proved challenging, often slow and with a lot of hand gestures, the trio were all very friendly and we ended up hitting it off. They asked us why we were here and, for a brief moment, modesty seemed to escape me and I felt compelled to share that we were celebrating my birthday. They offered to treat us to another cocktail at the restaurant or to take us out to another bar. I wanted to soak up every possible opportunity on my one night celebration in Madrid, so I cleared it with Michele and opted to experience another nightspot. Vanesa was the most familiar with Madrid and recommended a little place only a 10-minute walk away. Buzzing with the excitement of new friends (and expensive Champagne), the five of us headed off through the streets of Madrid. I found myself walking next to David, who was very inquisitive and doing his best to form sentences asking me about my travels and my life. As I spoke, he listened so intently as if he was not only trying to interpret the language, but also attempting to figure out who I am as a person. He watched me so closely as I spoke, seemingly not wanting to miss a word and I found him very endearing. He was so full of questions that it became a difficult task to attempt to turn the conversation to him. When there was a pause in question firing, I started to ask of few of my own in the slowest

English I could muster about his work and where he was from. He explained that he lived in northeastern Spain, Rioja, the infamous winemaking region that I knew much about thanks to my love of the drink. He was only in Madrid for one night on business, and the following day he would present his wines at a tasting in Madrid and return home in the evening. When David shared that he was a winemaker and a vine-grower, I made some gestures as if working the soil and made a comment about him being a farmer. It took him a few seconds to translate the word and then, with satisfaction, he looked at me and said, "*Sí.*" I felt rewarded that we were able to establish that fact… or had we? I wasn't one hundred percent sure that he understood. Despite the fact that the communication between us was bumpy, I felt extremely comfortable walking next to him that night. He had an energy about him that I had never experienced before, and I couldn't wait to hear more.

We arrived at the next spot, but to our dismay, there was no wine to be found. David approached the bar and asked me what I would like to drink. I asked him what he was having, a gin and tonic, and told him to make it two. Even the gin and tonics here were pretty, served in a glass similar to a wine glass with ice cubes that were perfectly square cubes, not chips as I was used to in the States. Our conversation continued, and I noticed David being very quiet, yet observant. I could tell that even though we weren't speaking much to each other, he was as acutely aware of my presence as I was of his. I find it interesting how when you realize you are interested in someone, whether consciously or unconsciously, it can cause you to focus less on them in conversation. Somehow, it felt much easier to speak with everyone other than David. He seemed to do the same and didn't go out of his way to engage me at that point either. I had no intention of checking in early that night and I was trying to convince the group to continue on with me and make it a late night, especially since I knew my partner in crime had already made it clear it wasn't on her agenda. I would not go out alone, but I had a feeling that regardless of what the group decided, David would join me until the bitter end.

My hunch was correct — I couldn't convince anyone to join me. But when the question was posed to David, his answer was an enthusiastic, "Why not?" When I thought David wasn't looking, I asked Vanesa if it was safe to go with David alone. With a reassuring smile, she responded, "David is more than safe." I take this as a very good sign and hope that it doesn't mean he's gay. We say our goodbyes, and David and I jump into a taxi headed to a posh discotheque, Gabana 1800, that Vanesa recommended in the Salamanca district. When we arrived, there was a velvet rope to guide people entering the club, however, the only person by the door was the doorman — not the best sign. When we entered, the spot was half empty, which led me to believe that not all of the stereotypes of Spaniards are true and while the people may go out and stay out later, they don't all necessarily party until 4 a.m. on a school night. As we entered the dimly lit club, my eyes focused on an elaborate bar stretched along the entire right wall, filled with liquors and a plethora of what I would soon learn is the Spanish aperitif of choice, gin. We approached the bar, ordered our drinks and began to converse as best as we could with the language barrier. He noticed my camera and asked to see photos from my travels — perfect! — an opportunity for nonverbal communication. I shared pictures of our trip to Morocco and my house in Hawaii that I had just purchased less than one year ago. I found it amusing how carefully he listened to everything I said, observing every movement and gesture. He offered me his business cards in an attempt explain a little more about his work and where I could contact him.

We decided to move our conversation and take a seat next to the dance floor. The music was loud yet we seemed to communicate despite the distractions, and I managed to sort out that he liked playing rugby, but was dealing with some ongoing injuries that required him to visit a masseuse or physical therapist of some sort. He also told me he was planning a business trip to Chicago in July, and I gave him some pointers on things to do as I had lived there for a few years before moving to Hawaii. His eyes remained so fixed on mine during our conversation, as if he was searching to find something deeper in me. Our eyes connected again, and this time I wasn't scared to return his gaze as he dropped a bold confession on me: "Melanie, I know I like you when you have no one, no two, but three glass red wine." We laughed, and inside I was completely amused by this comment because I knew that if he was serious, I was definitely the one for him. Little did he know, my liver had been perfectly pickled over the last few years, just in time for his arrival.

David had a brawny build that could be intimidating, but his eyes were much more revealing, undeniably soft and kind. Through our language barrier, we were trying to discover our histories and in the midst of a rather tangled interpretation, we kissed finally. Everything about him was sensual: his strong but gentle touch, his soft lips, the taste of his mouth. It felt as if time had stopped and the world around me fell silent. I was like Jell-O in his presence, a little girl who needed rescuing from the harsh world outside. *Did that just happen?* I thought to myself as a shockwave seemed to travel through my body spurred by his touch. We were so wrapped up in learning everything we could about each other that time seemed to pass in a flash, and the next thing we knew, the dim candlelight of the club was replaced with bright white light, a clear indication that our night was over. I had achieved my goal of 4 a.m. but was nowhere near ready to say goodbye to the surprise twist of events that had unfolded that evening.

As we exited the discotheque, David planned on hailing a taxi for me and would tell the driver the name of my hotel to ensure a safe delivery. We would keep in touch, hoping to see each other again one day, but I feared that plan was lost in translation. I had given the business card with the hotel address on it to Michele so she could find her way home after the bar. The idea didn't seem like a bad choice at the time, because I figured I could simply tell the taxi driver the name of the hotel and arrive safely. But when David asked me for the name of the hotel and I replied, "Hotel Laura," he gave me an odd look and relayed the hotel to the driver, who also gave a blank stare and mentioned that he wasn't familiar with the hotel. I read a look of concern on David's face and knew he wasn't about to send me off in a taxi with no destination. He asked me to move over and joined me for the ride. In transit, he continued to prompt me for the "true" name of the hotel and I continued to repeat, "Hotel Laura" as slowly and clearly as I could. He seemed simply perplexed at such an elusive location, as neither he nor the driver were able to identify the hotel, and I was at a loss as to how I could further clarify the location. I knew it was a newer hotel, yet it seemed odd that despite searching through books and interpretation tactics, no one could identify this hotel. I finally told the driver to drop me at the shopping area next to the Plaza Major. Michele and I had walked so much of the city the day before that I knew the streets would look familiar from there. David and I got out of the taxi and I immediately took off in the direction of the hotel, with him at my heels. The streets were empty at 4 a.m. in the morning and I was delighted to see the signage of the hotel in the distance. As we approached the large banner signifying the name, I pointed to it and victoriously proclaimed, "See, Hotel Laura!" His eyes seemed to bulge for a second in disbelief. He then smacked his forehead with his hand and said, "Melanie, it is not Hotel Lora, it's Hotel *LAU-ra*!" in his perfect Spanish accent. I couldn't believe what I just heard him say… could this misunderstanding be blamed solely on a slight mispronunciation? I defensively responded, "How was

I supposed to know how to say it with a Spanish accent?" in a frustrated tone as if we had been married for 20 years. Our faces were both serious as we looked at each other, exasperated by the situation, then we simultaneously paused. As the absurdity of the events that just unfolded started to set in, we both immediately started laughing hysterically at the fumble and our reactions. Had I simply written it out for him, we would have been there an hour ago.

He walked me to the front door of Hotel *LAU-ra* and took me into his arms and held me in a tight embrace. His strong arms felt safe and warm, and I could've remained there for a lifetime. These were arms that had no agenda other than to hold me close to him. I didn't want to leave this man that I had just met, a man whose heart appeared as big as his stature. He reminded me about his upcoming trip to Chicago and we decided to keep in touch and make plans to meet there during his visit in July. He gently kissed me good night and turned away. The next day I returned to the U.S. with a head full of amazing memories and high hopes that I would see this man with amazing, calm energy again.

CHAPTER 3

April 17, 2008

When I left for my trip I never expected to return with such a story. I would jokingly tell my friends that I had met my future husband in Spain — a kind, handsome winemaker with deep eyes — and describe how one day I would live on a vineyard in one of the most famous wine-producing countries in the world. I would add that my liver had been properly pickled for this man, as he loved me because I had not one, not two, but three glasses of red wine. Everyone knew how much I liked wine, so they all agreed that he was my perfect match… in a fantasy world, of course! I thoroughly enjoyed reliving all of the magical details of my short time with David and speaking of how I foresaw a grandiose future with him. The story sounded so dreamlike and I relished in the joy of embellishing the details about our future love affair because, truly, I didn't really know if we would ever see each other again. I very much wanted to gaze into his eyes again, but I was also aware of how fickle men can be, so I just had a good time verbalizing my dreams with my friends and laughing about the possibility of what was to come… expecting nothing and secretly wanting everything.

A few weeks later, I had an in-home appointment with my massage therapist, Darrell, who is also a close friend. One of his many gifts, besides massage, is his uncanny ability to use intuition on his clients, so I would often chat with him during my massages to see what kind of information was coming through about me. I decided to share the story of meeting David. I spared him no expense and told him the ambitious story that I had been sharing with all of my friends, describing an idyllic life with my future husband. Rather than rolling his eyes at me, which was fully what I was expecting, he seemed intrigued by the story and asked to see a photo. David had recently sent me a picture of himself in his vineyard, so like a giddy child, I quickly ran upstairs to grab it. As I handed it over, his response made me almost jump out of my skin: "Melanie, this man could very well be your match. And look, this is interesting, you have very similar hands." I had no clue what matching hands had to do with anything, but I couldn't believe what I was hearing! I continued speaking to Darrell as if he were being obtuse, reminding him that I live in Hawaii and that this man — *this stranger* — lives in Spain, as if that would change what he was telling me. "Distance doesn't matter in love," he responded. "You should keep in touch with him and see what happens."

David and I did just that, continuing to communicate over email for the next few months in an attempt to get to know each other further. Our back-and-forth seemed so interesting at times, because while we were from such distinctly different backgrounds, we seemed to think a lot alike.

While our geography and culture had few similarities, I had a feeling that our childhoods were somewhat similar. He was from a small village called Elvillar in the Basque region of northern Spain with a population of 200 people. I grew up in a small rural village in Prospect, Ohio, where the total population was about 1,000. We both lived very simple lives in our youth; neither of us came from wealth, so we hardly traveled, and agriculture was the driving force of the economies in the areas surrounding us. I grew up around fields of corn and soybeans, and he grew up surrounded by vineyards, so we were both clearly connected to the earth. We were both children of divorced parents, and in Spain 30 years ago, divorce was very uncommon. The one major difference between us was that I came from a very large family of full, half, and step siblings, while David was an only child.

He was always so inquisitive about me and who I was, so I shared a little bit about what I liked in an email before a work trip to Maui. His endearing broken English response reaffirmed that despite our different cultures, we seemed to have a lot in common.

Hola cariño,

I Hope that you enjoy in Maui.

Now, i go to the Jerez de la frontera (andalucía) to the horse´s fira. I will send you pictures because is very pretty this region.

I think that you and me have more something in shared;
i love travel (but until today i cant travel more, because my proyects and my works put the travel for another day) ,
i love to have a laugh whit friends, I love play rugby,
i am passionate wine (is my life), i would like drink a bottle of red wine... or 2... or 3 with you.
i like the dogs (above all my CUTE dog) :)
and of course i love to eat (sure too too much!).

When will you have holidays?

Would be nice to kiss you again

Un beso mi niña,

David

We continued to communicate through emails for a few months. I knew he had plans to go to Chicago, but he still hadn't invited me to join him, so I started to think he had changed his mind about seeing me. If he really wanted to meet up, wouldn't he send me the details months in advance so I would have plenty of time to request time off and book airline tickets? Maybe his plans had changed.

With a little more than a month's notice, he finally got around to asking if I would join him in Chicago. It was about time! I couldn't believe what was happening. I happily accepted his invitation and started making travel arrangements for July. I asked him how long I should stay, among other questions, and he always seemed to have the same answer, "As you wish," which confused me because everything can't be "as I wish." I took my best guess and decided to spend seven days with him. He was going to be there longer, but I didn't want to interfere with his work. As the date drew closer, reality started setting in and I was getting really nervous about what all this meant. I had made so many jokes about my "future husband" because, while my heart found truth in those words and told me I would see him again, my mind couldn't wrap itself around the idea. It was clear that we are both interested in each other, but what would happen beyond this trip? I was driving myself crazy overthinking the situation and decided to just go, have fun and keep everything light. Plus I had probably freaked Darrel out with all of my future talk, and he gently reminded me to not scare David away with my intense hopes and dreams and suggested I try to stay in the moment and enjoy the ride. I promised myself that I would go in with no expectations and kept repeating, "Keep it light!" out loud in order to solidify the idea in my mind.

The week before my Chicago trip, I traveled to Ohio to get in some family time. My mother was in disbelief that I was about to meet up with a man that I had only spent one evening with. She said I needed to be careful that he might be crazy, and then made a comment questioning my mental state for agreeing to meet him in the first place. I had always been the black sheep in the family, so really none of this should have been such a big shock for her. I sarcastically reminded her that if his aim was to harm or rape me, he would have done so in Madrid instead of spending money to fly to the United States to commit the crime.

I was getting nervous, as I had asked him multiple times about details of his arrival and where he was staying, only to receive the bare minimum — his flight landing time. I spent the night before his arrival at my friend Anne's house in Wrigleyville, and since he never asked me to stay with him in his hotel, and I had no idea if I would be invited to do so, or if I would feel comfortable staying with him for that matter. I decided to leave my luggage at Anne's house just in case. She offered to drop me at the airport so I could greet him when he landed. In addition to the accommodation question, I didn't know which hotel he had reserved or if he had actually even boarded the flight! It seemed he had a way of only answering select questions, or maybe it was the language issue… I couldn't be sure. There I stood outside of the international gate waiting for a man that I had spent one night with in Madrid and attempted to get to know over emails. Even though he had sent pictures, would I recognize him? Over an hour had passed and I started to wonder if I was in the right location, or if I had missed him, or if maybe I was losing my mind! Had he walked right by me and I didn't even notice him? Or perhaps he changed his mind and never got on the flight. My heart and mind were racing. It didn't seem normal to wait so long for someone to arrive. Then I saw him and my heart leapt out of my chest. He was shorter and stockier than I remembered, but more handsome. We made eye contact and he cracked a smile as if to acknowledge the look of relief on my face. I ran up to him and gave him a long hug. There we stood, two perfect strangers with no idea what was to come over the next week, brimming with anticipation. Would we revel in every moment or count the days until it was over? Both the excitement and tension were practically palpable.

We jumped into a taxi and were off to his hotel in downtown Chicago. The cab pulled up to The Whitehall Hotel, a smaller hotel with a lot of charm, which was located on Delaware Avenue in the Gold District walking distance from Michigan Avenue. Through nervous chatter, I tried to explain that I grew up in Ohio and that Delaware was a city close to my hometown, and I was just there visiting family. He looked amused but not quite clear as to what I had just said. We checked into the room and he started unpacking, and I thought it strange that he never once asked about my plans or my luggage. I took a seat on the bed and watched him in awe. I was amazed at how perfectly his clothes were folded. Based on his actions, I gathered that he was quite the perfectionist, carefully hanging his shirts and putting everything exactly in its place. I assumed that in his work, the quality of perfectionism was a perfect fit. He told me that he needed new shoes and it was obvious that if we didn't leave the room at that point, he would have fallen asleep. So apparently, we were going shopping together.

We decided to walk down to Michigan Avenue and stopped into a Sak's Fifth Avenue to see what we could find for him. I remember riding the escalator in front of him to the second floor of the store. He gently touched my back and I swear I felt sparks shooting through my body. It reminded me of that night in Madrid, how his touch was exhilarating and made me want more. He gently pulled me closer to him and I knew that as soon as we reached the top of the escalator, the moment would end. I was holding on to each second begging time not to pass. We stepped off and got down to business. He was asking for my opinion on various items, and his quest for shoes quickly turned into shorts and anything else that he could find. As we headed toward the dressing room, I pointed him to one of the changing booths and decided to wait in the hall outside. I heard him call my name, so I began to retrace my steps back. I was startled by the fact that he hadn't shut the door and was standing there in his underwear as if it were totally normal to be half naked in front of me! He seemed so comfortable with his body. There was just something about this man and the way he carried himself that intrigued me beyond words.

After we finished our shopping, we walked down Michigan Avenue so I could show him some of the tourist spots in a feeble attempt to keep him awake. We decided to head to the top of the John Hancock building to have a cocktail and enjoy the view. Verbal communication wasn't easy for us; we had to carry Spanish – English dictionaries around for those times we got stumped, which was often. This was before smartphones and I had a feeling the dictionary would be our best friend over the next week. I could tell he was getting tired and I was too, so we headed back to the room. He still hadn't asked one question about my luggage or where I planned on staying. And since I am notorious for having my whole entire life practically planned in advance, the uncertainly was killing me. But I was enjoying my time with him and decided I wouldn't stress about the luggage and just let the night unfold.

We returned to the room and decided to watch TV in the bed. I curled up in his arms and felt so relaxed, so at home that I fell into a deep sleep. The next thing I knew he was waking me up. I wondered if I had overstayed my welcome and he was ready for me to leave. As I opened my eyes, I saw him standing there with a huge smile on his face and a hanger in hand. In broken English, he asked me if I planned on sleeping in my dress. Like a child with half-open eyes, I lifted my arms above my head and he pulled my dress off and hung it in the closet. The next morning I woke up safely in the arms of a perfect gentleman.

Now that we had the room situation figured out and I knew that I would be staying with him, the next morning we headed up north to Wrigleyville to retrieve my luggage from Anne's house. I decided it would be easier to get ready at her place, so I left her to tend to David while I got ready. She knew that David's English was very limited, plus he was rather shy and quiet when he didn't know someone, so she asked him if he would like to watch TV and turned it on for him. The next thing I knew I heard Mexican soap operas on Telemundo — her attempt to try to make him feel comfortable — and I found myself laughing inside. I couldn't imagine that he was enjoying the program and eventually decided to intervene. I walked into the living room and through uncontained giggles reminded her that for one thing, he knows how to work a remote (regardless of the country of origin, he is a man!) and two, He's Spanish, not Mexican. He, of course, never complained and offered me look of entertainment. As I headed back to the bathroom to finish getting ready I heard the channel change and giggled again when I heard what he had chosen — cartoons! Apparently, he was a big fan of "Family Guy."

David and I left Anne's house and headed out to explore Lincoln Park and the zoo with a plan to eventually feast on my favorite pizza in Chicago, Pequod's Pizza. On the long walk to the park, he started to ask me about my age. I told him there are two things you never ask a woman — her weight and how old she is. Pretending not to hear a word I had just said, he repeated, "How old are you?" I groaned and admitted that I was 32. "Oh, older than me," he stated. I knew this wasn't the case since I remember him telling me he was one year older and we started to argue over the issue, yet he wouldn't show me his ID to prove his point. I was self-conscious about the fact that I was getting older and didn't particularly enjoy him teasing me about my age. He seemed to delight in the banter and I knew he derived some sort of twisted pleasure in getting me amped up.

It had been a long day of walking and exploring and by the time we arrived at Pequod's, we were thoroughly exhausted — not only from the walk but also from trying to communicate all day through dictionaries and exploring the basic levels of each other's native tongue. Thankfully, the language difference didn't stop us from understanding each other. If certain words proved difficult to translate, we found ways to communicate through intuition, through touch and looking past our surface reactions; we had to look into each other's soul. When you don't have the connection of language, it's similar to losing one of your senses, for instance, your sight. Weakness in one will make all of your other senses stronger, more acute and aware. We took a seat opposite each other in a booth and ordered a pizza. There came a point during the dinner when conversation wasn't needed and the lack of conversation felt completely natural. We simply enjoyed our dinner without words, observing each other without expectations. I looked up at David as if I could read his mind. He seemed surprised that the silence was so comfortable, so finally I broke the silence and said, "There is a term for this in English, it's called 'comfortable silence.'" He smiled gently, repeated it out loud and replied, "Yes, I like very much. It is beautiful expression." We finished our dinner with few words, soaking in every moment, and I felt very connected to him in that moment, with the distinct feeling that the universe had been plotting to bring us together all along.

Prior to his arrival, I had brainstormed with Anne about

what I could do to entertain David while we were in Chicago. She recommended riding bikes along the lake, which was something that I really wanted to do, but I figured he would be too macho for that sort of thing so I didn't even suggest it. Instead, I booked an architectural cruise and tickets to a Cubs game with friends. David had asked me ahead of time what restaurants I wanted to try but I let him choose, and he booked a couple of dinner reservations at two of Chicago's best restaurants. We seemed to enjoy many of the same things, so it was easy to be together. In our exploration of Chicago, we had run across many signs advertising bike rentals. David noticed them and asked if I was interested in riding. I looked at him in awe and wondered what the odds were of him suggesting the one thing that I wanted to do but never spoke of. I agreed and the next day we had a glorious day riding bikes alongside the lake. David was shameless in his quest to make me laugh. Riding behind him, I teased that I could see a little bit of his butt crack when he leaned forward and suggested he pull his pants up. Let me tell you, translating the words "butt crack" is not easy! Once he finally realized what I said, rather than fixing the problem, he decided to pull his pants down even further, his backside in clear sight for all to see, and proceeded to slow down to ensure that everyone knew I was with the man with the exposed butt crack. At one point, he was so focused on showing off that he almost fell off his bike into a mound of sand! His childish games amused me to no end. As we continued on, he seemed to be constantly snapping photos along the way. We made a stop at Navy Pier, parked our bikes and decided to walk to the end of the point. When we arrived at the end, David pulled me close and looked deeply into my eyes, and we were standing there nose-to-nose. I could feel myself melting inside. We moved forward to kiss when suddenly David quickly pulled out his camera and snapped a photo. I relished in the fact that he wanted to capture every moment of the trip and I, too, wanted to freeze and hold on to every little detail with my mind and, as it turned out, also with my heart.

The more I learned about David, the more I worried that my plan of "keeping it light" was headed towards disaster. The more time we spent together, the more I was taken by this guy. He was a man of few words, yet his actions spoke volumes — a concept that was foreign to me. In all of my past experiences with men, they would promise the world and skip the most important element, the delivery. David was different. He seemed to read my mind and be more in tune with my emotions than perhaps I was, so much so that at times it made me self-conscious.

We had found a comfortable pattern in our days, which consisted of awaking early every morning but staying in bed and making love until 10 a.m. or later. He was a passionate and unselfish lover, constantly concerned with my enjoyment. His sensual side was evident in his touch, which can only be described as heavenly. By the time we would emerge from the hotel room, after hours of our morning "exercise," we were starving. I wasn't familiar with the downtown breakfast eateries, so my friend Anne had given me the idea of eating at a seasonal restaurant on the beach. One morning, as we were heading out to satiate our hunger, I suggested a breakfast spot that was a good distance from the hotel, so by the time we arrived we were famished. To our chagrin, the restaurant didn't open for another 45 minutes; it was only open for lunch. I have a tendency to be indecisive and this was definitely one of those times. I couldn't decide if we should stay and wait or try to search out another restaurant. David asked me to choose our course of action, so after much deliberation (with myself), I decided we should head back from where we came and see if we could find another option for brunch. The only problem was I had no idea where to go and I could feel David's patience thinning as his hunger grew. I was leading us aimlessly through the side streets of Michigan Avenue, hoping and praying that something would cross our path, and still nothing. David started to ask questions about where we were going and how long it would take us to find a place to eat, and I could sense a shift in his tone and demeanor. He had never been impatient with me and it didn't sit well. I started to feel very anxious and frustrated, so my pace quickened and my mood changed to mirror his. Rather than enjoying the moment, I was stressed and feeding off of his negative energy. The smile melted off my face and I was on a mission to get to the next destination. After about 10 minutes of no communication other than the obvious nonverbal frustration, he stopped me and asked, "What is this?" looking at the expression on my face. I quickly responded, "You are obviously hungry and I'm trying to find a place to eat!" He stepped in front of me in order to disrupt my focus and I noticed that the impatience in his eyes had been replaced with a soft gaze asking for forgiveness. "I don't want this," he said apologetically. "I want to see you smile again... please?" He kissed me on my forehead. I never forgot this moment because I had never had anyone act so acutely aware of my emotions. It was so important for him to see me happy that it caused him put his feelings aside. I remember thinking that if I lost him, I would never find anyone so deeply connected to me again.

After breakfast, we walked along Michigan Avenue

shopping and getting to know each other more deeply. Every day, we talked about waking up and going running, yet it never happened because we were more interested in sexual exercise than any other physical activity. David seemed to be enamored with this joke, and would occasionally pull me into sports stores to ask if I wanted to run. I never quite understood why he found that so funny until one night later in the week when out to dinner with my friends, my buddy who lived in Spain for a short time made a comment about how the Spanish use the same verb *correr* to describe both running and having an orgasm. Then it all made sense why he seemed to find such humor in asking me if I like to run.

On the average day, David was always full of questions for me, but this time it was my turn. He wasn't one to talk about himself, but when I broached the subject of family and asked about his parents, I could feel his energy diminish. He said his father left when he was 13 years old and they haven't spoken since, and that he only had his mother. Even though his physical appearance didn't reveal any emotion, I could tell that inside he was hurting. I hugged him and told him I was sorry. In this case, his body didn't respond to my touch, as if he didn't want sympathy or to even acknowledge vulnerability. I decided to change the topic to a safer subject, and inquired about his work instead. He explained that he was starting a new project featuring wines from his family vineyards with vines that were almost 100 years old. His connection to the land was undeniable. He spoke of his vineyards and winemaking philosophy as passionately as if he was speaking of his children. He shared that he followed biodynamic principles in his vineyards and explained how the philosophy goes beyond organic and sustainable, encompassing the environment in a holistic manner and incorporating all systems including the cosmos. He explained that he preferred to utilize concrete "eggs" to ferment the wine, since concrete is a form of stone and it allows the wine to breathe. I was amazed by the intricate details of his process, by how he put so much thought into every step. The more I learned about this man, the more he impressed me. He had a boyish charm, and while he was confident, he would gradually reveal insecurities that made him more real to me. As we passed by a window that displayed the character Shrek, David stopped and pulled me back to look at the poster and declared, "I am Shrek," referring to his burly structure. He turned to look into my eyes, kissed me and continued to say, "and you are my princess Fiona." I responded, "Not the fairytale I was thinking of, but hey, I'll take it!" as we both laughed at the silly comparison.

That night we went to dinner at Alinea, one of the

hottest restaurants in Chicago with its art-like nuevo cuisine. The front of the restaurant was so unassuming that if you were to walk by it on the street, you would never know the gem that lies inside. We entered the building and walked down a narrow grey corridor. About halfway down the hallway, I jumped a little as the walls on the left side parted to reveal the restaurant. A host immediately greeted us, as if they were expecting our entrance at that exact moment. To the left sat a small dining room and to the right was a glass wall exposing the kitchen, with a small staircase straight ahead of us. David peered inside and said, "Wow, 11 people in the kitchen!" I wondered how he was able make an accurate count in a matter of seconds, so I counted everyone to see if he had just pulled a number out of the air, but he was correct. David looked at me and stated, "You are nervous?" Without thinking, I defensively responded, "I'm not nervous!" speaking before I actually took the time to connect with my emotions. I loved fine dining and felt that I had been to my fair share of restaurants, but this spot was cutting edge, and suddenly I felt intimidated. I realized that David, once again, was so acutely in tune with me that he processed my emotions before I was even aware of them. It was exhilarating, yet frightening to some extent, and I felt instantly vulnerable. We took our seats at the table and were promptly introduced to a spectacular culinary evening.

People typically reveal who they are in many different ways, but that night during dinner I discovered how very sensual David could be. He was aware of everything in the room — me, my emotions, the people around us, the waiter, the food and how it paired with the wine. Every course that arrived was like a work of art, and the waiter explained what each dish was and the best way to eat it. David seemed to live in the moment, savoring every second. He even noticed the woman next to us who was dining solo and commented that seeing her alone made him sad. He felt this restaurant was an experience that was meant to be enjoyed in good company. Every moment that passed confirmed that I was falling in love with a perfect stranger. Why was it that when he looked into my eyes, it was so different from any other person's gaze? I could feel him seeking deep insight into my soul, his long and profound gaze searching perhaps to find himself in my eyes.

As we arrived at the hotel that night, I was overwhelmed with emotion. Internally, I was struggling. I wanted to tell him how I felt, to spell it out for him, and everything in my heart was telling me it was safe to share my feelings with him. But my head was in complete opposition, screaming that taking that route would be crazy and only end in disaster. Plus, I had promised myself that the week wouldn't be heavy, that we would just have "fun," and that no matter what, I wouldn't have expectations of this man after our time was over. Once we arrived in the room, all of the emotions and thoughts swirling around in my head decided to come out when he touched me. Out of nowhere I began to cry. I couldn't seem to control it, and no matter how hard I tried, the tears continued to flow. Embarrassed, I tried to look away but he insisted on looking into my eyes while I unsuccessfully tried to fight the tears, which just made them flow even harder. He was asking me why I was crying, but I couldn't tell him that I was scared to death, scared that I was falling in love with someone who lived a half a world away from me. The situation could have made him uncomfortable and pushed him away, yet for some reason he seemed pleased with my disturbing display of emotion. As the tears poured from my eyes, he did something that took my breath away — he stuck out his tongue and licked my tears. It was his primal way of communicating, as our words were from two different worlds and seemed insufficient. Yes, he could taste my feelings and I could feel the compassion in his soul… but I never told him how I felt about him. He had said to me numerous times, "*Carpe diem*," but I didn't understand his context nor did I have the courage to ask for clarification.

The following day we had plans to attend a Cubs game with three of my close friends. My friend Sam spoke Spanish, and while we communicated effectively on many levels without words, it was a nice break to have Sam there to interpret. Not to mention, I knew nothing about baseball and Sam was more than happy to offer David an education on baseball in his native language. We ordered beers and peanuts to give David the authentic American experience, which he thoroughly enjoyed. As the beers went down, I started getting sassy and decided to challenge David. As I raised my beer, I asked Sam to tell David in Spanish that I would "drink him under the table." Sam translated for me and the next thing I knew, David looked at Sam with a pleased look on his face, then turned towards me and said with a big smile, "*Sí?*" clearly assuming it was a sexual reference. Sam exploded into laughter and told me that he didn't think that term translated very well in Spanish, and the rest of us burst into laughter simultaneously. David fit right in with my friends, as if he had always been part of our group. After the game, we met up with a few more friends and visited some old hangouts in Chicago. There was no tension with David, he just rolled with the punches. On the drive back to the hotel, David said to me, "Your friends, they love you very much. I can feel it." He could've said many things about my friends, that they were "nice" or "fun," and yet he chose the words that meant the most to me — he could *feel* that they loved me. It was his soulful way of speaking about their character and mine, his message to me that he felt the rightness of what was happening.

The days quickly slipped by, and I dreaded our time together coming to an end. I couldn't even think about it without welling up. On our last day we decided to take a walk to a nearby park. David was always full of questions, but on this occasion he seemed to be stuck on one question in particular. He wanted to know my nationality due to the uniqueness of my last name, Labudovski. I had tried to tell him many times it wasn't the name I was born with and that I was divorced. I had married my college sweetheart of 6 years out of duty rather than true love when I was in my mid 20s, and any marriage based on anything other than love is doomed from the beginning. When we split, I was young and embarrassed. I didn't want any attention brought to the matter, so when I switched careers in the middle of the process, I decided the best way to stay under the radar was to keep my married name and avoid the questions. I thought I made it clear to David that I was previously married, but he was having trouble grasping the concept of the word "divorce." I sat down and carefully explained it to him so he understood that I had been married before. My heart sank as I realized that when it finally clicked in his mind, I could see the disappointment in his eyes. He couldn't understand why I had kept my ex-husband's name. I went over the reasons for not changing my name back to Hickman — the insecurity, frustration and embarrassment I experienced, but he perceived it as me holding on to my ex-husband on some level. I suddenly felt as if I had betrayed David somehow. I knew in my heart I hadn't kept my husband's name out of love or a desire to hold on to the past. I had ended the relationship, and while it was one of the most difficult things I had been through up to that point, it was one of the best decisions I had ever made. For the first time in years, I had been able to be myself and not feel controlled by what had felt like an ever-judgmental watchful eye. It was freedom in the truest form. To David, none of this mattered, not the reasons why or how, and I saw conflict in him for the first time. The game had changed for him and his energy seemed different, almost disheartened, at least from my perception. We returned to the hotel walking in silence.

My departure was fast approaching and it was time to work out the logistics of transportation to the airport. David had work in Chicago after I left, so he would be staying for a few more days. I asked if he planned on coming with me to the airport and he said he would on one condition — that I not cry. He explained how he hated goodbyes and became firm, almost stern, in his direction of no tears. I agreed, knowing that it would be difficult to keep my promise. There were so many questions unanswered, so many things left unsaid, and I was stuck on the one thought that kept playing over and over in my head, *Do we have a future together*? On the way to dinner the previous night, I asked him when I would see him again. He responded, "Do not worry, *preciosa*, we will see each other again one day." The uncertainly of his answer was eating a hole in my heart, but there was nothing I could say, and for some reason I believed him. I couldn't control the future, or this man, so I just lay my head on his chest and prayed that his words would come true. I tried to translate the word "soulmate" for him and told him I was sure he was mine. I hoped he would look up this term at a later date and feel the same, because this was not a word I regarded lightly or had ever used to describe anyone else. I could tell he was trying to be strong at the airport when we were saying goodbye. He held me and kissed me, but made it clear by not getting too emotional that he didn't want me to cry. We had one last final kiss before I turned and walked towards security, holding back the tears with every ounce of my strength. I glimpsed over my shoulder as I heard him start to say something, "Melanie, do not cry when I'm gone… I will feel it." I tried my best but there was no fighting it. Once I turned my back, the tears flowed and they continued for the duration of the long flight home to Hawaii.

CHAPTER 4

July 13, 2008

I had lived in Hawaii for seven years when I met David, and it was the one place that I had ever truly called home. I grew up in Ohio, but for some reason, I felt constrained and frustrated to no end. I remember in high school longing to discover what lay beyond the sprawling fields of corn. That longing in a hormonal teenage body sometimes bubbled up in anger and resentment towards my roots, and I perpetually felt trapped. After graduating from Ohio State University, I moved to Chicago hoping to feel freed by city life, but after only a few short years, I once again felt landlocked by its close proximity to my roots and the similarities of the Midwestern lifestyle. However, once I moved to Hawaii, everything was different and it was home for me in my heart. When I lived on the mainland, I would come and go and never felt an attachment or yearning to return to those places. Yet the first time I left Hawaii after moving there, I remember feeling sadness as I boarded the plane to depart, and when I finally returned, I was overwhelmed with excitement to be home. Hawaii had an energy that just fit me. Here I felt happy and content.

After meeting David, all of that changed. When I landed in Honolulu from Chicago, I stepped off the plane and the intoxicating positive energy that usually greeted me was gone. I was suddenly numb to Hawaii's pleasures. The rush of warm air that once would recharge and rejuvenate me upon arrival felt cold against my skin. The beautiful fragrance of plumeria that once reminded my senses that this was my home suddenly smelled different. Every step was heavy with tears and seemed only to take me further away from him. I wanted to run back to the plane and insist they return me to David, as he was now the place in my heart that felt comfortable to me… like home. I sobbed the entire walk from the gate to my car, stuck in my own world and unconcerned with others' opinions of my public display of emotion. I regretted not staying with him longer in Chicago, I regretted not setting solid plans to see each other again and, most of all, I regretted not telling him how I really felt.

The next few days were painstakingly difficult. I tried to focus on work and other distractions that would lead me back into my normal routine, but all efforts were futile. I had become the person whom I loathed in the past, heartbroken and weak. I had a tendency to get emotionally caught up in my previous relationships, but when it came down to the finish line, I could always just turn off that switch, walk away from the relationship and not look back. I had mastered that mechanism of defense. But this time it was different. The wall that I had maintained in past relationships, the one that protected me from getting hurt, was missing in action. I was vulnerable, owned by my feelings. From a rational standpoint, if I were outside judging the situation, I would think the whole idea of falling in love with a stranger after one week together was absurd, but actually living this experience seemed to effectively strip me of all rational thought.

David was in Chicago for another week after I returned home and due to depart the following day. I had just finished getting ready and was about to walk out the door when my phone rang. My heart skipped a beat when I saw his name on my phone. I tried to pull myself together before answering, took a deep breath and, upon hearing his voice, instantly felt tears welling up in my throat. I desperately tried to push them down in a feeble attempt to make this a light conversation. He was with some fellow winemakers and told me that he was thinking of me because they were on their way to Pop's, a Champagne bar I had told him about in Chicago. We had talked about going when I was there, but time didn't allow. He said he wished I could be there with him and then in broken English said, "Melanie, I very much enjoy our time together. The bed in the hotel still has your scent. After you leave, I call housekeeping to ask them not to change the sheets. I will remember you when I return to Spain." With those words, I could no longer contain my tears. Sobbing, I thanked him for everything and told him I would never forget him either. I was certain my heart could stop at any moment, and the pain was unbearable. "Don't cry my *preciosa*, everything will be OK." He thanked me again and we said goodbye. I didn't want to say that word to him... *goodbye*. I lay on the floor, curled into a ball and cried until my head hurt. Another human being had never so profoundly touched me in my life. He was a beautifully deep soul, full of passion and love. I had not tasted his wines, but knew that a man of such depth, devotion and meticulous attention to detail could only produce wine equally as soulful and profound.

David was headed to South Africa after Chicago for another business trip, so I knew contact would be scarce over the next week. I was on Kauai for work and had some downtime before dinner, so I decided to start shopping for David's birthday gift. I wanted to send him a present that covered all the senses, as he was such a sensual person.

During our time together, David had told me that his bed in Spain was a futon made of teak. I was looking at a number of artisan shops when I came across a wooden candle carved into pieces that fit together to form the symbol of yin-yang. When I inquired about the piece, the woman told me it was made of teak and coconut. It felt like the start of the perfect gift — not only was it made of teak, but it was also complimented by coconut, which I felt was representative of me and my life in Hawaii. The yin-yang mirrored the connection of our energies; while so different, they seemed to flow together and form a perfect harmony. The gift would communicate the notion that together, we achieved balance.

Over the next week, I found additional gifts that either represented me or served as reminders of our time together: a Shrek birthday card, a box set of Family Guy DVDs, wasabi nuts and *li hing mui* to represent the unique tastes of my home, and a Michael Bublé CD, which I would belt out in the car at the top of my lungs thinking of David the entire time. The final gift was a poem that I wrote to David on the flight home. I found a card that had the Chinese character representing double happiness. During my time with him in Chicago, I discovered that he had a tattoo on the back of his neck. When I inquired about why he chose that symbol, he simply shared that at one point in his life, he fell into sadness. Once he pulled himself out of his internal darkness, he had the happiness character tattooed on his body as a reminder that happiness is the way. I tucked the poem inside the card, a token of gratitude for our time together:

In this life, many people cross our paths.
Some just for a moment while others remain.
Regardless of the length of time, every encounter is a gift from which we are meant to learn; every interaction serves a purpose.
You were placed into my life and for that I am grateful.
I do not know the purpose, or how long you will remain, but what I do know is that I learned from you.
I learned about the true beauty of a human soul, beauty expressed in kindness, acceptance, passion and laughter.
You are a blessing and you touched my heart in ways I didn't think were possible.
Thank you.

I boxed everything up and walked down to the UPS store to send it out with nervous anticipation. I shipped the package well in advance, knowing it would take some time to reach Spain. David planned on spending his birthday on Mallorca with his friends, and I hoped he would receive the gift upon his return and contact me immediately.

July 25, 2008

I had to get something down on paper about all that had happened with David. I had to record the most profound moments in my journal for fear that I might forget the impact they were having on my life:

He thinks of me like a bottle of wine. He wants to know everything about it — the winemaker, the grapes, exactly where the vines were planted, the blend and the history behind the making of the wine.

Now it all makes sense — his need to know more, his analytical nature, the way he sizes me up and tries to figure me out. When he looks into my eyes, it's as if I'm a glass of wine that he's checking for color and clarity. He's trying to sort out the complex nature of my soul.

When I cried, he licked the tears from my eyes. It was the most romantic thing anyone has ever done. A gesture to show me if I'm hurting, he will drink my tears. He later commented that he liked the taste of me — he liked the taste of my tears. What an amazing man."

David sent me an email from the airport in South Africa letting me know exactly when he would return home on Saturday. We planned on connecting via Skype and I was giddy with the anticipation of seeing him and hearing his voice. It had been two weeks and I was counting down the moments until I would hear his voice again. The next morning I logged onto Skype and waited for him. Every second seemed like a lifetime and I started to wonder if he would show. Once again, he waited until the last minute. I was wide awake with excitement and eager to catch up. He, on the other hand, was exhausted after a long trip and it was clear he wanted to go to sleep. I tried to empathize with his situation and communicate compassion, but I was deeply disappointed that our talk was so unbalanced and short.

The next morning when I checked Skype, there was a download file waiting for me. I accepted it and what I saw took my breath away. David had sent me a photo from his camera that I had not seen before. It was the picture from Navy Pier in Chicago, taken from the side, he and I gazing into each other's eyes with our noses touching. It was beautiful beyond words and I was touched. He was a true romantic. I only hoped this type of behavior wasn't routine, that I was special. A week later a CD of all the photos he shot in Chicago arrived. On the CD he wrote, "*fotos desde Chicago con amor, que no me olvida*," which means "pictures from Chicago with love, so that you don't forget me." When I looked through the images, I found one that was telling about the romantic in David — he had snapped a picture of the bed in the hotel room.

David's birthday came and went. I suspected he was home from his vacation, yet I hadn't heard from him. I had worked so hard to pull together the perfect gift and fully expected him to reach out to me as soon as he received it. We hadn't set any parameters about our relationship, but in my mind a simple acknowledgement was at the very least the polite thing to do. I started to wonder if this was a one-sided relationship. Was I waiting in vain for this man? Was our time together just another week for him? Once he returned home, back to his regular routine, had he forgotten me? My once stable emotions seemed beyond my control. I didn't feel like myself. I started to write in order to purge all of these feelings that felt so uncomfortable:

August 8, 2008

This is all very hard for me. Today is his birthday and he has not responded to my package. The connection and trust I felt when I was with David has started to fade with the sharing of our story. The questioning of his integrity from my friends puts doubt in my mind. They expected that he would be in contact with me more. We would talk on a consistent basis, but that wasn't the case. Is this storybook romance too good to be true? I find a man who loves to travel, is passionate, feels connected to me and deep in spirit, yet is still a little boy inside. I want to tell him how I feel. I want to share all my uncertainties, questions and fears. I want to be honest with him like I've never been with anyone in the past, but at the same time I'm scared to death. When I think of my future, I picture myself living with David in Spain on a vineyard. It has always been an easy visual for me, something my soul recognizes as home. There are many things that need to happen before that takes place: 1) change my name, 2) see David's home, 3) connect with my confident inner being who has a strong enough constitution to handle a life change so severe.

About two weeks after his birthday, David and I connected again on Skype. I had to ask him if he received my gift, at which point he thanked me. I was hurt that he didn't bring up the gift or reach out to me sooner. I put my heart and soul into the perfect gift for him and I get a thank you *after* I asked. Maybe I was being foolish pining after this man, yet I could not quit. Every day was a roller coaster. Over time, I stopped enjoying sharing the story of David and me because it seemed that in my heart, the love I felt for him never died, but for him it was different. The more days that passed, the further he felt from me. Our communications seemed to be spread further and further apart. A pattern started to form with us — as soon as I felt that I was fighting a losing battle trying to hold on to this man, I would force myself to try to let him go. Without prompting, he would surprise me and reconnect once again.

One morning I spent time with a good friend, Kerry, and what a wonderful soul she is. She was the perfect person to talk to because she's a no drama kind of girl. We were on our morning walk down to Kahala beach when I couldn't contain myself and started to tell her about David and the birthday gift and how he didn't say thank you until I asked. He had recently sent another text saying that he tried the *li hing mui* and it made him think of our dinner in Chicago. She responded, "What else do you need to hear?" Simple but true… why do I feel that I need constant reinforcement from him? I should just have the confidence and respect to just let it be. She also said if it's meant to be, it will be — this is something I know, I just have a hard time integrating it into my thought process. But it is so true. If there was such a connection between David and me, then it won't die. It will remain and thrive, if that is what the universe wants. My soul has always known the right path, the right style and what's best for me. I just needed to be more connected to this concept and have faith. And I needed to remember that, should my soul be wrong in David, then it would for a reason, and it would be out of my hands. Everything takes time and patience, cultivation and growth. I knew that I still had a lot of growing to do in order to truly be ready for someone to truly love in the way I wanted, and to be able to receive that which I so deserved.

August 15, 2008

A thought kept lingering in my mind from the awkward moment when David discovered that I hadn't changed my name back to my maiden name. The conversation that day signaled a dramatic twist in our time together. Had that conversation not occurred, our visit would've been almost too perfect to recount. That discussion enraged the insecurities inside me and served as a constant insinuation that reality was very different from my time with David in

Spain — a brutal reminder that maybe it was too good to be true. It made me have even more regrets about my decision to get married previously. I had tortured myself over that fact on a regular basis prior to ever meeting David, and now the sinking feeling of deep regret had returned and seemed almost unbearable. Why did I make such a poor decision when all signs pointed to ending the relationship, not marriage? Why didn't I have the courage to leave my ex before we went through with the marriage? It was too late now and there was nothing I could say to David or myself to deflect the consequences of that bad decision. I couldn't change the past, no matter how hard I wanted to. In all of the times that I explained to friends about why I hadn't changed my name, not once did anyone ever feel that I was holding on to my ex-husband. I totally disagreed with the notion, as I was the one to exit that relationship. But it did make me wonder if holding on to his name would hinder me from moving on in my life. On some spiritual level, would keeping his name hold me back? Would the universe never allow a new beginning due to some small connection to a time past, or was I subconsciously not ready to move on? I had let go of the past, but maybe I wasn't truly open to another person at that point. I had so many questions, but deep down something told me it would be cathartic to go through the seemingly grueling exercise and put Labudovski to rest and start over as Hickman. I was at a totally different point in my life now and I didn't care what anyone thought about my marital mistakes. Well, most anyone. I did worry that this information was a game changer for David and it deeply hurt me. These thoughts swirled around in my mind and I knew that it was time for a new beginning and reconnection with the person inside me who was dying to come to life again.

I started the process of changing my name with the state, my passport, driver's license, my company, credit cards, you name it. To my surprise, going through all of the work this time around was invigorating. I felt a huge weight being lifted and I was happy to take this part of my life and put it in my past, where it had always belonged. I decided to change my email address and inform my friends and family of the name change as well in a group email. David was included on that distribution. I didn't know how he would respond, or if he would respond at all. After a short time, he did address the email and his response was once again short — "I am very happy with your decides" — which should have been enough, but once again he left me wanting more of an explanation about his choice of words. I wanted to ask why it made him happy.

September 14, 2008

Tonight I look up at the moon and think of you. I wonder if you do the same. Do you fit me into your thoughts? Or do you look up at the moon and only think of your passion for your work and have no time for me? Are you such a grounded person that thoughts of me don't plague your mind, like you do me? It has been two months since I saw you and I still think of you every day. I long for your touch. I want to feel that connection with you as if two souls would meet again regardless of time and place, yet you don't reciprocate. Your contact, while thoughtful, is distant and scattered. You still bring me to tears when you enter my mind. When you called me from Chicago to say goodbye, you told me you would remember me. Will you keep your promise? I've tried to fill the void of not having you near me, but nothing seems to replace you. I compare everyone to you. No one stands up to your depth, soul or character. I don't believe you say things for no reason... I believe everything is thoughtful. David, my soul yearns for you.

"Yin-yang. Perfect fit?" I was speaking with my friend Anne about a guy she went on a date with and it made me think of David. She was telling me how they were different, yet together the differences seemed to complement each other. It was good to hear her voice, and she gave me the ego boost I needed. Instead of providing the standard cheerleader rhetoric, she said things that I appreciated so much more, like describing me as humble, generous, good hearted… everything I aspire to be but often fall short of.

October 1, 2008

One day while chatting on Skype, David and I started looking into the cost of flights to Hawaii. The time was early October and he explained that he was in the middle of harvest season, his busiest time of year. However, he said things would start to slow down in December, so the only time he could get away was over the holidays. I couldn't believe it! Was I hearing him correctly? Was I going to get to spend Christmas with this man? He had expressed some concern about the cost, but otherwise it seemed all systems were go. He said he would look into flights, so I immediately started making plans for his visit. My faith was restored! I was so thankful that I wasn't completely crazy, pining for this man for months in vain. I had spent many mornings heartbroken, in tears, missing David, all the while thinking that I had completely lost it for holding on for so long. I had stopped talking about how wonderful our time together was, or how I couldn't get past the feeling that my soul had known him before, for fear that my friends would think I was crazy too. But now I could put all of that behind me and start planning our time together.

I called my mom and told her I wouldn't be coming home for Christmas again this year, but would love to have her here for Thanksgiving. My mother has always been wonderful when it comes to fixing up my home. She never shied away from hard work, and I had a list for her in order to get my house ready for my company, David Sampedro. I still couldn't believe he was actually coming to visit!

In seven years, my sister had never been to visit me, so she decided to come with my mother. Time had flown by and they were expected to arrive the following week. Everything was confirmed and I was ready. But I was getting very nervous because communication with David had been sparse since he told me he would come visit and he had a habit of not responding to my messages. When we did talk, he still hadn't confirmed his flight. My stomach was in knots and I knew that if he didn't book soon, I would never hear the end of it from my mother.

Another week came and went and still no confirmation from David. My family arrived and we were still proceeding as normal, expecting communication at any moment regarding his itinerary. We were hard at work preparing for his arrival — painting, shopping for furniture, moving rooms around so the house looked presentable. I had four days of vacation that I decided to save for David's visit in December, rather than spend it while my mom and sister were here. Not one to keep opinions to herself, Mom was clearly disturbed by my choice to save my vacation for a man that, as she would say, "may not come through." Her words before I dropped her at the airport seemed to be etched into my brain: "Melanie, I sure hope you are right about this guy and he does come to visit, otherwise it's going to be a lonely Christmas for you. Next time put your family first."

From what I had gathered so far about David, he wasn't one to plan things well in advance, nor communicate those plans until the very last minute. But while he could come off as aloof, I had the feeling that he was a man of his word. He knew I had planned this vacation for him, and he knew my mom was coming out to help with the house for his arrival… or did he? Our communication was difficult at times, actually most of the time. Had I not made it clear about my expectations and did I misunderstand him? I was struggling inside and couldn't share my true emotions with anyone. I was hurt, and to add insult to injury, I felt like a fool for not listening to the advice of my friends and family. I remembered some particularly impactful words my friend Darrell had once spoken: "When you hold someone's hand, you don't have to squeeze. Energy doesn't flow with tension." But tension was all I seemed to feel. My only outlet was to write:

December 7, 2008

I think I have finally let go. To feel a relief lifted off of my chest. To saturate myself in worry, longing, doubt was killing me. I have to know in my heart that what is meant to be in my life will be. If my wonderful David isn't the one, there will be another even greater than he. I think that if he doesn't come, I am finally going to write him a letter telling him my feelings and how he changed me and how grateful I am to him for that. It will go something like this...

David,

My friends have always told me that I should tell you how I feel about you. I figured that you are so intuitive, that I don't need to tell you, that you already know. However, everyone likes to feel appreciated, so now I will share with you my heart-wrenching journey. Let me start by saying that even at our first encounter, there was always something about you that intrigued me. Something in your calm demeanor, your attentive presence, that stuck with me. The night in Madrid when everyone else wanted to go home, I knew you would stay with me. I remember even on that first night how wonderful it felt when you looked in my eyes. I remember telling my friends there was something about the way that you held me (a perfect stranger) that felt so comfortable when we were saying goodbye in front of the hotel. Your embrace was different than any I had felt before. When we left, I knew I would see you again. When I returned home, I shared the wonderful story of meeting you, the most wonderful birthday gift I've ever received! I joked that I had met my future husband in Madrid, and how our fated experience was too perfect. The independent American girl who loves adventure, travel, culture, wine, and romance meets the passionate Spanish winemaker who is humble and grounded yet travels the world. How perfect! As I would share the story of our fated first meeting, people would comment that it sounded to good to be true. When we actually made plans to meet up in Chicago, the joking ended and I took a whole new approach. I decided that all I wanted out of our meeting was a new friendship and we both could learn to speak a different language. Little did I know that spending a week with you would deeply affect me more than I ever dreamed. Everything about you felt right. How you, too, are independent, hard-working and serious, yet when the time is right, the little boy in you comes out to play! I loved the bike ride along the lake, how you didn't care what anyone else thought and delighted in making me laugh, and how you fit in so well with my friends, as if they were your friends, too. Your awareness struck me, you commented on everything. For example, when we were eating pizza, not saying anything, then you mentioned that the silence was "good." When I explained "comfortable silence," you liked the phrase.

I finally heard from David a few days later. He informed me that he would not be coming to visit me… and I never sent him the letter. I spent the holidays alone.

CHAPTER 5

January 6, 2009

2009 will be a good year. It has been six months since being with you and I have to admit, you still enter my thoughts everyday. However, I have to learn to let you go. It will be freeing and healthy... There were days when I ached for you so badly. It was all very strange for me to feel this way. No man has ever affected me the way that you did. For not "knowing" you, I felt so comfortable with you. I still can't figure out why I was brought to tears so many times while in your presence. It was as if you stirred something in my soul. I still feel very connected to you. But the world is a funny place and I can now accept the fact that that our meeting was probably more meaningful to me than it was to you. Because we are not in contact very much, I don't know where you are in life. I only catch little glimpses here and there. I think a small part of my soul will always love you. I had a dream the other night and I can't shake it trying to figure out the meaning. I remember being in the house I grew up in and there was food around as if it was a holiday, but I was alone in the kitchen. The next thing I knew, I had family around urging me to get ready for dinner out at a local Indian restaurant. In order to prepare for dinner, we all had to get naked. It was a little weird but in some way it felt natural. We left and there was a man. It wasn't your face in the dream, but a representation of you because he felt like family; he had your familiar energy. From there I remember walking up the stairs still naked, and I noticed that when we left the house, others had suddenly become dressed. The part of this dream that really stuck with me was your face; there was so much sadness and as I carried you up the stairs, you told me you loved me. Not just any old "I love you," but a deep, heartfelt love that yearned for the same response from me. I looked down and said with all of my heart and soul that I loved you too, and then I awoke. I wondered if I could feel your sadness from halfway around the world. Was I supposed to send you a letter exposing my true feelings for you? Was that why I was naked and vulnerable? The thing that stuck with me the most was that the vulnerability felt comfortable in the dream.

I would occasionally reach out to my intuitive friend Darrell, not for a reading, but because he seemed to have a calming demeanor and was a good listener and guide of sorts.

As I droned on about how I didn't like the way I felt, he suggested a book for me to read, '"The Alchemist" by Paul Coelho. He felt our journeys were on a similar path said it would help me connect with David's energy. The book would also guide me to sort out some of the internal struggles I was experiencing. As I started to read the story, I was struck by the similarities in the life of the boy in the story and myself. The main character, Santiago, was determined, headstrong, and curious to learn about the entire world. A recurring dream drove Santiago to pursue his dreams. He longed to travel and have new experiences in order to find his destiny. While I was reading, I couldn't help thinking about the dream that had haunted me for months. The dream had many versions, but one thing was always the same: I couldn't talk because I had so much chewing gum in my mouth. I would attempt to take the gum out of my mouth to no avail. The gum was lodged between my teeth and the more I attempted to pull it out, the more the gum seemed to flow from my mouth. I was embarrassed and frustrated because no matter how hard I tried to speak, the gum stifled my words with its ever-flowing presence. Santiago, like me, seemed lost. In the end, after many journeys and life lessons, he returns to his home… in Spain. I closed my eyes and dreamed of returning "home" to David.

January 10, 2009

Dear David,

Something inside me keeps telling me to write you and tell you how I feel, so I must follow my guide. Initially, I wanted to send you letters in Spanish so I could practice, but being that I will be speaking from the heart, it is too difficult for me to translate my feelings into Spanish. I have stopped myself from writing these letters for many reasons. I am scared to be so vulnerable, to expose myself to someone, scared that you don't feel the same. But I decided to take a look inside myself and one thing I know about me is that when it comes to my friends, I am very generous with love. I give love and try to expect nothing in return. I know that this is the way love is supposed to be given. Why, then, is it so hard for me to truly express how I feel for you? I consider you a friend. I would do anything for you just as I would any of my other friends. But I know why, it is because my feelings for you run deeper than friendship, which means I have to put my ego aside and knock down that wall that we all build to protect ourselves from others letting us down. I guess I am choosing this point in time to tell you because I feel like I have nothing to lose. You didn't come to see me in Hawaii over the holiday and now I know you are coming to the United States for work but are not incorporating me into your plans. I'm not judging you for this because I have no idea what is going on in your life. I've tried to reach out to you, but your life is busy and I must respect that your priorities are focused on other things. The only thing I would have appreciated from you was a simple communication earlier that you weren't coming to visit over Christmas. I was looking forward to seeing you and was disappointed that you waited until the last minute to tell me.

It has been hard for me since seeing you in July. I didn't expect to feel so strongly about you. I knew when I met you in Spain, there was something different about you. I felt it in the way you held me outside of the hotel that night. And the way you looked into my eyes. I knew I would see you again. Then, of course, we met up in Chicago and the experience was unlike anything I had ever felt before. I think it was in part because I was so comfortable around you. I was truly myself.

Once again, I never sent the letter. I decided to stop reaching out to David. My communications weren't genuine anyway. I was hurting inside and trying to pretend that I was fine with his decision to not come and visit me for Christmas, to wait until the last minute like he did, to selectively respond to my emails. I wasn't strong enough to be honest with him and the situation was killing me inside. I needed to stop focusing on him and start focusing on myself. I wasn't interested in dating. There wasn't one man who caught my attention. I wanted to be alone but this doesn't always go over so well with friends. They feel that you should "get out there."

I had been spending time with my coworker who had recently met a guy, and he had "a friend" they wanted me to meet. I resisted the idea of being set up, but somehow the four of us always conveniently ended up together. Her friend was an attractive guy, nice, successful, a "catch," but the problem was I didn't want to be caught. I felt empty inside. One night, a group of six of us decided to have a barbecue. My friend had made me promise I would at least consider Jim, the friend, as a potential love interest, so I tried. I tried to find conversation, to be interested in him and his world. I needed a little help, so I employed a few glasses of wine to assist me. The night ran on and by the end of it, we kissed. I forced myself to go through with it and I will never forget the way I felt afterwards. Here was a man whom most women would kill for — good-looking, ambitious — and yet I felt nothing. Actually, I was trying to visualize David as I closed my eyes, but it didn't work. It was clear that he was not the one for me and that part of me really was reaching for something, anything, to fill the void inside. This situation only appeared to make the void more cavernous and obvious. I felt stuck; the events of the evening confirmed that I needed to deal with whatever this was alone. I knew I had to let my emotions run their course and lead me where they may. I needed to suffer in silence.

For the next few months, I tried meditating, practicing yoga, anything I could to calm my mind. Work was going well for me, so I threw myself into that. I had switched careers a few years back and was working in pharmaceutical sales. It wasn't my calling, but it worked for me for the time being. I had a wonderful boss and a good team of coworkers and really liked and respected a majority of the doctors I called on. It always seemed that when everything else was failing around me, my work was there to remind me that my angels were looking out for me, allowing me to suffer in silence without having to worry about being dependent on anyone other than myself.

My once stable life seemed to be more of a rollercoaster after meeting David. No sooner would I start to feel a little better and move him out of my mind, when somehow the universe would find a way to bring him to the forefront again. As I walked through the aisles of the grocery store close to my house, I nearly dropped the items in my hands when I saw one of his wines on the shelf. I couldn't believe what I was seeing — his wines had made it all the way to Hawaii. I wondered if he knew that his wines were being sold in here. He had mentioned to me in the past that he was looking at different distributors in Hawaii and apparently he had found one. I took a photo and emailed it to him, grabbed a bottle and headed home to drink it. As I opened the bottle, I tried to imagine the work that David put into making it, as if drinking a glass of his wine would somehow bring him closer to me. I started to keep my eyes open and noticed his wines were popping up more and more around Hawaii. Of all the places to sell wine, I wondered why he would be in such a small market like Hawaii. It didn't make sense.

One morning I reached out to Darrell. I needed his help; I was struggling to find serenity, wrestling with the advice that Darrell had given me regarding David. He had told me multiple times that David didn't know how I felt about him and I should write an honest letter telling him the truth. I started getting defensive and increasingly annoyed about his advice, wondering why he suggested such things repeatedly. It seemed that a vast majority of my friends advised me to let David go and steer clear of him. They seemed to be protective of me, while Darrell always pushed for me to reveal the truth to David. Although I knew Darrell was intuitive, I started to believe his intention was to see me hurt. Maybe he wanted to teach me a lesson of some sort, otherwise, how could he ask me to do something so bold that could risk my heart completely? And besides, it almost felt better not knowing the truth, that way I could hold onto my fantasy that David felt the same way about me. Over time, my interactions with Darrell became less frequent because I was not ready to acknowledge any hint of truth in his advice.

April 2009

Two of my best friends, Anne and Kelly from Chicago, were due to arrive in April and I was looking forward to having them close. Anne had been with me from the beginning of the whole David situation, and while I didn't share half of the suffering that was inside of me, she knew I was hurting. This had made her quite protective of me, and her way of supporting me was to portray David as a villain. During her stay in Hawaii, she repeatedly told me that I needed to forget about him, painting vivid mental pictures by going into great detail about how he probably has women all over the world.

She told me that his actions made it clear that he cared nothing about me, otherwise he would respond and communicate with me, instead of doing everything on his terms. I didn't want to believe her, but if I didn't go through the experience myself, I probably would have said (or at least thought) the same thing. A year had passed since I met David and I knew something had to be done, but the only thing that seemed to make sense was the notion that I needed to let him go.

The weather during Anne and Kelly's visit was wet and rainy, which is very atypical for Hawaii. We were doing things that involved shopping, eating and drinking, probably a bit more than we should have. We decided to stop in to the Macy's on Kalakaua Ave. on the way to The Cheesecake Factory for *pupus* and drinks. I was at the sunglasses counter when I heard my phone ring. Not thinking anything of it, I looked down and saw a text from David. I immediately felt a rush through my body and started to shake. It had been months since I'd heard from him. He had sent me a message telling me that he was in New York City and would like to speak with me. I looked up at Anne and asked what I should do. She immediately responded, "Absolutely nothing! Do NOT reply to him, do you understand me?" My friend Kelly yelped in disbelief that after all of our conversations about him, he decided to text me at that very moment. Her disbelief was short-lived and she jumped on the bandwagon and insisted that I ignore the message as well. It was Saturday and they made me promise not to respond to him until they told me to. I hadn't listened to anyone at this point and it certainly hadn't served me thus far, so I figured I would start now since I was under intense pressure anyway. It took every ounce of my strength not to reach out to him as I had always done in the past. If he contacted me, I immediately responded… always! David, on the other hand, was very selective in his responses. There were many times when I reached out to him and he didn't answer my question or didn't respond at all, which always hurt me. I had to hold this thought tightly in my mind and avoid giving into the temptation. I repeated all of the negative assumptions that Anne and Kelly made about his character in my mind. It was the only thing I could do to fight off the urge; yes, I would convince myself he was a bad guy, a player who would only continue to break my heart.

We left Macy's and crossed the street to enjoy a late lunch at The Cheesecake Factory, starting with a few drinks at their bar. A few turned into many, and after a couple hours Anne decided to head back to the hotel. The bar was packed and as soon as Anne got up to leave, a man immediately took the seat next to me. He was alone and extremely chatty, sharing stories with Kelly and I for what seemed like eternity. He had moved here only a few months ago from Redondo Beach and was having a really hard time finding people with whom he connected. I understood his perspective because Hawaii is a notoriously hard place to break into. He explained that he had moved here for a job opportunity and to clear his head after a recent divorce ended his 20-year marriage. The more we talked, the more he made it clear that he wanted to become part of my circle of friends. I felt empathy towards him as I remembered how difficult it was to make friends when I first moved to the islands, and he seemed quite harmless. I gave him my number and promised to introduce him to some of my friends. I tended to hang out with an older crowd and he shared that he was in his late 40's, plus he was quite the personality so I figured he would fit in just fine. Kelly and I said our goodbyes and decided to call it a night.

The next morning arrived, and I was at their hotel informing the girls I had held up my end of the deal and was ready to respond to David. Like rabid dogs, they came at me insisting that I not waste my time on him, especially while they are visiting me. They said *he* could wait for me this time. The first thought in my mind was, *If I wait too long, he will return to Spain and I may miss this opportunity*, but I succumbed to their pressure and agreed to wait one more day. The next thing I knew, my phone chimed — David again, telling me he's worried because I failed to reply to his message. Then he told me that he was in a hotel in New York City, missing me. He was watching TV and a commercial came on that made him think of me. I felt that twinge in my heart; it was such an internal struggle for me… here was the man that I had dreamed about for the last year, the man that I felt was my one and only soulmate, yet he continually hurt me by making it clear that I was not on his list of life priorities. He was awaiting a response from me and I just let him hang. I hated it when he did that to me, and now there I was, under the pressure of my friends, giving him a taste of his own medicine. I hated playing games, but the last year left me so hurt and vulnerable that I felt I had no other choice.

The three of us hopped in the car and decided to drive around the island. About an hour into our drive my phone rang. It was Joel, the guy from the bar at The Cheesecake Factory, inviting us to come out for a ride on his roommate's boat. It was easy to say no to this man (not like my struggle with David), but I told him we could meet up next week and hung up the phone.

The girls and I decided to make a stop on our circle island tour to visit two of my friends, Jen and Matt, on the north shore. I purposely left my phone in the car so I wouldn't be tempted to sneak into the bathroom to text David and tell him how much I missed him and that I was thrilled to hear from him again. I guess I hadn't properly prepared my urban friends for what they were about to experience in the country. Jen was a coworker of mine who had recently retired. She was a throwback to the 60s, a former flower child, a love with a heart of gold. As a product of her time, unhindered by age or experience, she definitely danced to the beat of her own drum — and the aluminum-laced marijuana grow room situated under the house was further proof of her unconventional lifestyle. We pulled into the driveway and there she was with her big welcoming smile and large, braless breasts. I could feel my friends' weak attempts to be politically correct and not stare. Jen was always a very gracious host, and she and her "teddy bear" (nickname for her husband Matt) had fired up the grill and prepared some barbecued chicken. To call Jen an animal lover is an understatement; when I worked with her, she was known for always keeping a bag of dog food in her car in case she spotted a stray or any animal in distress. She and Matt had two dogs and eight cats and, yes, they lived in the house.

Obviously uncomfortable in their new surroundings, Anne and Kelly made feeble attempts to settle in after the experience of meeting Jen had them in an initial state of shock. Matt ran down to grab the chicken off the grill, although I knew my companions had lost any appetite that may have accompanied them prior to entering the “House of Animal Hair." We were all sitting around the dining room table, which was adorned with a most unusual centerpiece — a fat cat licking himself and staring back at us as if *we* were disturbing *him*. I could read my friends’ minds and sensed they were praying that the food would not end up on the same table as the cat. We heard Matt climbing the stairs to the house and, in what seemed like slow motion, he placed the food on the table directly in front of the cat, almost as if to taunt the feline — and my friends. The fat cat was intrigued by the food and poked his head shamelessly into the pan. I could see the disgust on my friends’ faces, which grew deeper when Matt held the meat with his hands to cut it, licked the barbecue sauce off his fingers, and then placed them back on the chicken. Needless to say, we didn’t eat much that day. Actually, my friends ate nothing and I politely accepted a piece of chicken out of guilt alone. Beer seemed safe, so we enjoyed a few and were on our way. It was the first time all day that I hadn’t thought of David and it felt wonderful. We said our goodbyes and headed back to the car, only to find that David had called me when we were inside. This was a first; he never called me! And he didn't leave a message. The pain in my heart was instantly reignited. When I returned home, I sent him a message telling him that I had been entertaining friends all weekend and would be available to talk on Monday. I'm not sure what it was — fear, insecurity, my friends feeding me information all weekend about the man who would break my heart — but suddenly, at the perfect time, just when the opportunity to be honest was staring me in the face, I somehow listened to all forces outside of my heart and found the strength to blow him off.

Monday morning, like clockwork, David and I were communicating. I made it clear I expected him to do the calling, and he did. I was walking into one of my doctor's offices for a meeting, and normally my work would have waited for him, but this time I answered, told him that I was into the middle of work and asked him to call me back at a specific time. I figured I would never hear from him again since he had made these promises in the past and I always ended up waiting, and in the end I suffered disappointment. For the first time in over a year I felt like I was taking care of myself, looking out for my needs and not making David

Sampedro the priority in my life. A small part of me felt relief that I could be strong. I felt like such a doormat over the last year. I was that poor, pathetic girl who keeps going back to the man that continually breaks her heart, and I hated who I had become. I yearned to be that strong female again — the woman whom no man could affect, the woman who could walk away from any situation and never look back. I asked him to call back at 5 p.m., but I wasn't going to make plans around his call because he had burned me too many times in the past. Instead, I made dinner plans in Waikiki with Kelly and Anne at one of my favorite sushi restaurants. We were waiting in line for the restaurant to open when my phone rang. It was him! For what felt like the first time ever, he kept his promise and connected with me when he said he would. I looked at my friends, who offered a few hard looks and coaching words about how he's a dog and had women around the globe. "Don't be weak!" they said. I answered the phone with an indifferent tone. We attempted to communicate over the phone, which always presented a challenge due the language barrier. I was hurt that he was in New York and failed to contact me beforehand. I would have come to him… didn't he know that? Had I not made that clear? The next thing I knew, he was trying his best to tell me in English that he missed me. He spoke of how he could not forget my eyes, my nose, my lips. He told me that he was planning a trip to California but I wouldn't take the bait. I was trying to be hard, but deep down I truly missed him with all my heart and soul. My mind had taken over at that point and I started to believe everybody except him. They loved me and were looking out for my best interests. He was full of flattery and unfulfilled promises. If he wouldn't be direct and ask to see me in California, it was over. I didn't want to fall into his trap again, so I didn't reciprocate and excused myself in order to get back to my friends. Conflict was raging inside of me, but I decided to put a stop to it once and for all. I needed to end this one-sided relationship. I felt drained; I had nothing more to give.

A few days later, I wrote David a very emotional email. I told him I wasn't at his beck and call, that I wasn't his good-time girl whom he could call only when he was lonely in a hotel room in the U.S. I explained if that's what he wanted from me, he should never reach out to me again. Even though I knew his English was weak, I figured if he were a good man, if he didn't understand and he actually cared about me, he would ask for clarification on the email. If he did understand and wasn't interested, I would never hear from him again. Over time I received the confirmation I dreaded — no response at all.

The following week I heard from Joel, the chatty guy from the Cheesecake Factory, who wanted to meet up. I had made a habit of saying no to opportunities and decided to say yes this time and see what happened. We decided to have dinner at a small restaurant in Hawaii Kai on the water. Until this point, I had never met a man who talked more than me. He was funny, but it was obvious he was hurting inside. He droned on throughout dinner and by the time we finished eating, I was emotionally exhausted by the conversation. Yet for some reason I wanted to hang out with him again. My subconscious was screaming no but a void inside me was desperate for attention, and on some level he reminded me of David — his facial hair, the fact that he spoke fluent Spanish. So rather than doing what was right and running for the hills, I decided to follow through on my promise and introduce him to my friends. I arranged a night to meet two couples at a little hidden gem in Honolulu called Ward Rafters. My friends Lorena and Don had told me about this place and been there before but Keli, Vic and Joel had not. The location was spectacular, situated on the top floor of a house in the Diamond Head area. The owner had a connection to the jazz scene, and if anyone of caliber came into town, they were sure to make an appearance at Ward Rafters to entertain the underground scene of Honolulu. Joel pulled up in front of the house to pick me up, and as I looked out at him, I remember thinking that he was quite handsome. It then occurred to me that I hadn't had this thought about any man in over a year. I wondered if my letter to David had actually worked. Would I be able to move on with my life? Regardless, that wasn't what the evening was about. It was about introducing Joel to some like-minded people whom I was sure he would get along with... at least this was my honest intention.

We arrived at the venue with wine and *pupus* in hand. The music was wonderful and I could see that the unique atmosphere thrilled all of the newcomers, especially Joel. We were all laughing and having a good time, and the next thing I knew I felt Joel pulling me closer to him. My friends were aiming their cameras and he was more than happy to pose, swinging his arm around me with what I guessed was a sense of pride. Suddenly, rather than being with two couples, it started to feel like we were a group of three couples. I was unsure about how I felt, as things seemed to take an immediate turn.

Joel was an attractive man, but he was not relationship material. He was fragile, hurt and confused. Everything inside of me said to stay clear of him, but sympathy and the void inside me ultimately won and we continued to see each other. But it was a very bizarre "relationship" because at times I felt like his counselor. Over time, he shared with me that he had lied about his marital status, he was separated not divorced, and his age. He was actually 54 years old, which didn't seem possible seeing as how Joel had a body that most men in their 30s would die for. Whether he was a product of Redondo Beach or just plain vain, it worked for him, so for the wrong reasons, I didn't let his age bother me. I liked him, but I wasn't really planning our future together. He was great at motivating me to get back into shape. We spent countless hours at the gym — a nice boost for my self-esteem, which had dwindled with the extra weight I had put on during my pity party over the last year. He and I had a very strange relationship, and at first it seemed we might start something greater. We made the mistake of being intimate once, but the guilt of his unresolved marriage didn't sit well with either of us. We decided that intimacy wasn't appropriate until he was divorced, yet the lack of closeness seemed to make us both a bit crazy. It was clear to me that he wasn't over his past situation, and I didn't want to complicate what we had with a physical relationship. We were left with a friendship and a lot of sexual tension. He was Latin and very affectionate, so we always looked like a couple when we were out, even though we were "just friends." We both served as a strange kind of crutch for each other: I was his confidant (counselor at times), young (so I looked good at his side), and his only friend in Hawaii. He was an avenue for increasing my self-esteem and getting my feet wet in the world of dating again.

Joel and I spent a lot of time together and spoke almost every day, and I thought we had it all figured out until he told me that his wife and mother were coming into town and that he would have to stop all contact with me. Suddenly, I was extremely bothered... but why? Technically, we weren't in a relationship. Then it dawned on me — he was using me much more than I was using him. When he needed something (which was often), I jumped to help him out. He, on the other hand, was available only when it was convenient for him. How had I missed this until now? The only time he would jump to help me was with repairs around my house, but even that was for his benefit. He would constantly tell me how he missed his home and all of the projects he had worked on over the years. Starting projects in my home gave him a sense of purpose; he felt needed. Being a single woman and owning a house can be scary at times. Things happened, large and small, and I typically had no clue where to start. For the first time in my life, at least in regards to my residence, I felt safe. For anything that came up, Joel would be there in a matter of minutes. But it was all a big lie.

The weeks came and went. I didn't call, and I hadn't

heard from my "friend" Joel. He finally called and it was clear he felt like an ass. His "family" (i.e., his mother and wife) was in town and, as predicted, it made things worse between us. I realized he was just another selfish man, like David, who only cared about himself. I was tired of dealing with selfish men. The following week I traveled to Miami to visit my best friend from college, Nicole, and her family before heading to Peru for vacation. I told her the whole story and used the week away to escape from my relationship woes. I remember feeling confused because in the process of sharing my Joel story, I felt as if somehow I was losing David all over again. I couldn't figure out who I was mourning the loss of since more often than not, it felt like a replay of the experience with David… but hadn't I already put that situation to rest? It didn't make sense. Emotionally, nothing made sense at this point in my life.

CHAPTER 6

June 15, 2009

It was perfect timing for a vacation. Michele and I had planned another trip, this time to Peru. We would spend a few nights in Lima and then venture east, eventually visiting Machu Picchu. This was the land of spirituality and intrigue, and I would use this time to reconnect with myself.

The first few days in Lima were all about shopping and my poor attempts to speak Spanish with the locals. I loved trying, and they seemed to appreciate the fact that I tried so hard. Every morning, we would eat breakfast in the lounge and I would grab a local paper and try to read it. If I got stuck, I would ask the manager to help me with the words. I think he enjoyed this game as much as I did. One day we decided to take a tour around the city. One of the stops was at Parque de Amour, or "Lovers' Park," named for the huge sculpture of a man and a woman laying down, kissing and holding each other in a loving embrace. I stared at the massive and mesmerizing stone carving in awe. As I reveled in the artistic beauty of the piece, I felt a distinct yearning for that kind of love in my life. My subconscious was begging me to find my soul's connection and depart from all selfish men that I seemed to encounter. I took a photo so I could always remember this image. I made a declaration to Michele that I was going to attract my soulmate into my life. If it wasn't David, then my true soulmate would come to me, I was sure if it.

When I traveled, one of my favorite things to do was to purchase décor for the house. When I returned home, the items would serve as a constant reminder of my travels. As Michele and I shopped around the various markets, I was looking for something unique for my bedroom. I believe that the way you decorate your home influences the energy in the room and I needed a painting that represented love. After browsing the local artwork, I knew what I wanted but it was nowhere to be found. I was searching for a painting of a man and a woman, but the traditional paintings in Peru were of families or villages. I was determined to find exactly what I sought before the trip ended.

The landscape of Peru was breathtaking. The altitude in the city of Cuzco was over 11,000 feet, and the narrow cobblestone streets reminded me of Europe. Michele and I visited beautiful Catholic churches, toured a salt mine and hiked Machu Picchu and the countryside learning about the history of this land. We decided to visit an historic agricultural destination called Moray, a circular site that wound down deep into the earth. The stairs to descend were made of ancient rocks that protruded out of the earth, so you had to watch your step. Michele started to feel uncomfortable and decided to stop halfway down. I wanted to continue, so she said she would wait for me at the top. At the bottom of the site, I could see a family being led by a guide, and it appeared they were doing some sort of ceremony. I had heard so much about the spiritual side of Peru and it was a large part of the reason for my visit, but I hadn't yet come across any opportunities to partake in an authentic cultural tradition. As I approached, the participants started the ceremony. I tried to respect their space and quietly do my own thing. The mother turned around and, in Spanish, asked me if I would like to join. I gratefully accepted and the leader handed me coca leaves and told me to follow along. The leaves were for my wishes, which I had to state aloud in front of this family: I asked for health, success and happiness. The mother and one of the sons wished for love. It made me sad that so many people, including me, were searching for their soulmates, and I lamented that so few actually find that person. Most people end up settling and I silently prayed that I wouldn't be that person.

Machu Picchu was breathtaking and offered the perfect opportunity to just sit and reflect. I felt so fortunate to be in the midst of such beauty. In the tranquil surroundings, I remembered a conversation that I had with my friend Darrell about a year before when I acknowledged that I seemed to have luck on my side. He corrected me and said, "You're not lucky, luck comes and goes, you're blessed and that quality remains." Sitting there looking at this ancient site, I knew he was right.

The next day Michele and I headed back to Lima. I still hadn't found my painting, which meant I had to find it in Lima. We walked through the city and stopped in a gallery that we had visited when we were here before. I started searching everywhere, and then, as if it were calling my name, the painting found me. In it stood a man and woman in traditional garb who were both looking off into the distance. The man was positioned behind the woman, extending flowers to her, perhaps asking for forgiveness. The background was interesting as well — there was a pillar in the middle of the painting that separated two identical landscapes. Both subjects were looking at the scene on the left, seemingly focused on the same goal: a life together. I knew I was supposed to forget about David, but it made me think of him, of us. I dreamed of him contacting me and telling me he was sorry for all of the hurt he had caused. I purchased the painting that night and we left the following morning. I was hoping that the items I carried home would one day bring me the comfort I was looking for inside.

My life back in Hawaii continued as normal. I started to get really into my spin class and was going at least three times a week. It was a great way to focus my energy, which I seemed to have an abundance of. This is where I met the next guy who entered my life, Keahi, and thankfully this visit was short-lived. I've always felt that you can learn from every experience, but I still have a hard time understanding why he came into my life, or perhaps more importantly, why I let him into my life, even if it was only for a short time. I met him while waiting for my spin class to start… a local guy who was friendly and seemed sweet and engaging. I had never seen him in my class before and suddenly he was always there offering to help me set my bike or put it away after class. Very chivalrous and seemed harmless enough that eventually we met outside of the gym over coffee. He inched his way into my life by taking this same chivalrous approach in my personal life, helping me with things in order to pass time with me. From deep-sea fishing (which he claimed was his work, but I later found it was a hobby, not a job), to teaching me how to cook, and fixing things around my house. Time soon revealed that he was a manipulative man with major emotional issues (I suspected bipolar disorder, among others) and while he would never admit it, it was clear that he was addicted to Xanax, or any other "downer" that he could get his hands on. He had a long, sketchy history of drug use that now translated to prescription drugs, but he justified this behavior because the meds were prescribed by a doctor — a doctor who just happened to be one of the psychiatrists I called on, who typically treated patients with severe mental illnesses. I didn't want to judge him for this, as many people see a psychiatrist and I wanted to believe he was a nice guy, but my gut told me otherwise. He didn't truly have a job and was always prepared with a victim story if something fell through in his life. He lived with his mother and they seemed to have a fair share of rather bizarre issues that made my skin crawl at times. I remember leaving town for a business trip once and asking him if he wanted to stay in my house and watch my dog, Hapa. I figured it would help me save money on a dogsitter and help him escape his mother. The night before I left, I told him he could stay at my house. I gave him the code to get into my home and I would meet him there later that night after a work dinner. I returned to a man with dilated pupils on the floor cleaning up diarrhea after my dog.

My instincts went into full drive. I knew he hadn't done anything bad to Hapa, but my pup was a sponge for emotional baggage, which often translated into an upset stomach. This man was too much for him. I immediately called my old dog sitter and begged her to watch Hapa in the eleventh hour. She agreed, so I could travel without worrying about my dog dying or my house catching on fire.

You would think this would be the last straw with this man, but I tried again to find the good in him and kept him in my life. My optimism ended when one day I found an empty prescription bottle in my cabinet. When I was going through my divorce, my doctor had given me a prescription for Xanax and I had one pill left over for years at this point. While I didn't need it now, I figured I would save it for a rainy day, just in case. One day I was in my bathroom and something told me to look in the prescription bottle. It was empty and I knew that I hadn't taken it. I asked him if he had eaten the pill, knowing full well he had. He denied it and decided to personally attack me, saying that because I went looking for the missing pill, I must be addicted. I was sick of his games, how he forced himself into my life, the way he insisted on meeting my friends when I preferred to keep them in separate corners. I asked Keahi to leave and never return. I should have followed my gut from the beginning with this one. I could only stand to be around him for a little over a month, and it was a month too long. He drained all of my energy and left me feeling horrible. The experience only reaffirmed my belief that it's better to be alone than to be with the wrong person. Joel had been crazy in a narcissistic, materialistic California way, but Keahi was a certifiable, full-blown wacko.

Towards the end of my relationship with Keahi, if you can even call it that, I started to think I must have serious issues if I allowed a man like him into my life. I was constantly doing self analysis, but after him, I wanted help and decided to seek out a professional counselor. While the first therapist I saw was nice enough, it quickly became obvious that we weren't a good fit. I needed a specific action plan. I wanted to be told, "OK, 'X' is your problem and here is how you fix it." But that wasn't her method, and I suspected it was probably not how most counselors operated, either. The only time that she did offer direct advice was during one of the few sessions that I had the nerve to bring up David. Rather cavalierly, she said, "He sounds like a better fit for you, why don't you reconnect with him again?" I felt I had enough issues at this point and it was no use explaining the entire David situation, so I never returned to her for therapy.

September 23, 2009

I must be putting bad energy out to attract the men I do. I can only pray that my energy will adjust to match my "one," whom I feel is David Sampedro. I feel I still have more to learn. I am still growing and I need to be comfortable just being me. I need to make sure I am not lonely being without a man. The mind is an interesting thing with me. If I listen to my mind and not my gut or heart, it puts fear in my path. My soul tells me if I grow, I will be aligned with my "one." I need to learn to not control and be patient. The universe will bring me that which is mine when I'm ready, so that I will not make the same mistakes again. I know I am getting closer. I feel different from before. I shouldn't think of the last guy as a setback, but rather as a lesson.

I was in search of something that would feed my soul and get me back on track, when an opportunity seemed to fall into my lap. A friend of mine, the manager and wine buyer at a wine bar/restaurant that I would frequent every now and again in Kailua, told me he was going to start a new business where he would offer wine education classes every Saturday morning for two months. Knowing that I loved to learn about wine, he asked if I would be interested in signing up. It wasn't cheap, but I figured it would be a good way to spend my free time doing something just for me. I gladly accepted, driven to advance my knowledge of the world of wine. Becoming a true wine aficionado seemed to be an elusive task, as the wine world not only has a long and very detailed history, but is also constantly changing and growing at a pace that only a true professional can keep up with.

There were a few challenges I faced in order to be a part of this course: For one thing, it took place at 10 a.m. every Saturday, which meant no late Friday nights for me. And the location couldn't have been more inconvenient, as I lived in the Kahala area on the opposite side of the island. When you live on an island, you gain a very different perspective of distances. When I lived at home in Ohio for a few months during college, the thought of driving one hour to campus and back every day was no big deal. But after living in Hawaii, a 25-minute drive over the Pali Highway once a week seemed like an extremely daunting task. The only saving grace was the magnificent beauty of the mountains that divided the windward and leeward sides of the island. The drive began at sea level with views of the Pacific Ocean, and within minutes I was in the midst of clouds surrounded by chiseled mountains that often featured small lines of waterfalls on a rainy day, only to then descend back down the windward side, greeted again by the turquoise waters of the sea. It didn't matter how many times I drove through those mountains, each trip felt magical.

The class lasted for an hour and a half and consisted of extensive education and wine tasting. The tasting portion had always been the most difficult for me because tasting (not drinking) wine requires you to stop your mind and focus on every intricate detail of the liquid — its viscosity, mouth feel, acidity, tannins, color, smells and flavors. It really is an art, and once you find yourself in the moment, taking in the full effect with multiple senses, you then actually have to be able to associate it with something that will register with you at a later time. Eating a blackberry and registering the taste in your memory is one thing, finding that flavor in a wine as one of many is a whole different skill set entirely. I'm often able to pick up flavors that dominate, but the subtle tones, the ones that only whisper to you, those require a quiet mind free from perceived judgment. Those require a skill set similar to following the little voices of conscious in your head.

I was thoroughly enjoying the much-needed opportunity for me to develop my wine knowledge, connect with like-minded people and make new friends. There was an older quiet man, Dean, who, over time, started to feel like family. He, too, was attending from the other side of the island. In fact, I discovered he lived only a mile away from me when he threw a wine class reunion at his home. During the course of the party, news had gotten around that a wine certification program was going to be offered in Hawaii for the first time. Dean, Paul (another friend from class) and I and were up for the challenge and decided to form a study group to prepare for the certification. We met up every Wednesday night to continue our studies and taste wines based on the region we were studying for that night. If we studied Greece, we would bring Greek food and wine. We were a very mismatched group, yet we spent many nights drinking and laughing until tears formed. It's amazing how something like wine can bring people from totally different walks of like together on common ground. Needless to say, our study nights may have been a little too fun, as Paul was the only one who passed the test. Regardless of the outcome, I enjoyed learning, so when I heard that an Introductory Sommelier course was going to be offered the following year on Maui, I signed up immediately.

I wasn't dating and was feeling much better, yet my mind never seemed to stop and it drove me crazy. I would go to yoga and try to meditate. Hell, I even took that vacation to

Machu Picchu hoping that something would calm my mind and give me solace, yet inner peace still seemed to be the unattainable goal. I decided if I couldn't locate serenity on my own, I would hire someone to find it for me. Friends of mine had told me about this guy they knew who offered services to teach you how to meditate, in the comfort of your own home. So for the next two months, I paid for Holokai to come to my house every Tuesday evening and show me how to meditate, how to connect with my inner self. Many nights I sat there with him telling me to visualize something, and when he would ask what I saw, my answer was always "nothing." It seemed that no matter how hard he coached or how intently I focused, my third eye was determined to stay shut. After numerous sessions repeating the same frustrations, he decided to attempt some energy work on me to see if he could clear my blockages. He had me lie down on the floor to check my seven *chakras* (Sanskrit word for energy points in the body). He held a small pointed object from a string — when held above a certain chakra, if it circled clockwise, it was an indication that energy flow was good in that chakra. He started at the very top of my head… so far so good. He moved down one more chakra, all was well there, too. Just as I started to get comfortable, he paused above my throat chakra and proceeded to inform me that a significant energy blockage seemed to be coming from this area. Why was I not surprised? He started asking me questions and then delivered a diagnosis. Apparently, I had something that I needed to say or get off my chest, and the blockage would remain until I did so. He told me it would be therapeutic for me to state what was on my mind to whomever was causing the blockage, and this act would restore a healthy energy flow. The only problem was, he was asking me to do the impossible.

October 2009

I had heard about a wine dinner at Formaggio's in Kailua and asked my friend Deb to join, so she agreed to go and keep my company, even though wine wasn't her thing. The Director of Sales from the Quintessa Winery in Napa Valley was there to present the wine selections that were being featured for the dinner. He was running through the flight of wines, sharing information on the winery and the soils of the vineyards. As he detailed how this particular winery follows the biodynamic concept, my ears suddenly perked up and my heart skipped a beat as my mind slipped back to Chicago, eating lunch on Michigan Avenue with David and our conversation about his belief in the biodynamic philosophy of winemaking. It had been months since I sent David that emotional email and I was in a much better place with it all. While the thought of David made me miss him, I felt much stronger now and had even sent him a birthday card recently. I had decided that regardless of my feelings, I would always keep him on my birthday and Christmas card list. I quickly pushed the thoughts of David out of my mind and attempted to focus on the presentation at hand. The presenter continued on about the different nuances of the various wines, why certain food pairings were chosen and so on. Then, the final wine was poured. While explaining the production process of the wine, he shared with the group that it was fermented in concrete eggs, and once again I stopped in my tracks. This, too, was how David preferred to ferment his wine. I couldn't help thinking that it was a huge sign. Uncertain of what I was supposed to do with this message from the universe, I decided to sleep on it and worry about it in the morning.

I had stopped logging in to Skype months ago because it was too painful to see David online, especially when he never reached out to me. I didn't use Skype to communicate with anyone other than him, so what was the point? But this particular morning, something told me to log in to my account, so I did, and wouldn't you know, David's account was active… he was online! Six months had passed since writing the letter. I proceeded to type a heartfelt apology for my overt display of emotion. I also told him how the night before, I had been to a wine dinner featuring Quintessa, where they fermented the wine in concrete eggs and it made me think of him. I wished him well and immediately shut my computer and left for work. The next morning, I opened my computer and noticed a photo download request from David. I opened the file and saw a picture of David standing next to a concrete egg. He was online as I viewed the photo and proceeded to ask me if I knew where the photo was taken. When I responded that I didn't have a clue, he said that it was the concrete egg at Quintessa. How many times can coincidences like this happen with one man, especially when we lived half a world away from each other? He thanked me for remembering his birthday, and little did he know, I couldn't forget it if I tried. He would be on my birthday and Christmas card list for the rest of my life. I'm not sure why, but I had decided this in the past and promised myself I would never sway on this decision. David asked for interpretation of the birthday card, but it was many months ago and I had forgotten what I had written in the letter. We caught up for a bit and then I needed to start my day, so we said goodbye.

I felt strong and secure when speaking with him this time, not needy. I seemed to have found myself again after all the internal struggles I had gone through after we met. I was finally ok with the fact that we may never be together in this life, but I knew I would see him again on the other side, and for some strange reason, this gave me peace. I was willing to take peace however I could find it, and this worked for me. I believe that we are all spirits inside a human shell and our purpose on earth is to learn, and if you don't learn your lesson in one life, you will return until your soul or spirit has grown and fulfilled its goal. However, when it comes to matters of the spiritual world, I cannot speak with certainty as no one knows the absolute truth. Too often, rigidity leads to disagreements and conflict rather than a natural, beneficial flow. I prefer to stay open minded about the potential of the spirit world and remain flexible to changing my beliefs.

CHAPTER 7

January 1, 2010

Another year had passed and the holidays were fast approaching. I decided to go home for Christmas and spend the time with family in Ohio. It was busy as always, yet nice to be with my loved ones. I left my family early on New

Years Eve, and with the six-hour time difference, I was expecting to be home to spend New Year's Eve with my four-legged family in Honolulu, my dog and cat. That was the only thing I really wanted out of the holidays.

I was also supposed to be using this free time to write a toast for my best friend Keli's wedding, set for New Year's Day. I had tried working on it many times, but nothing was coming to me. She had been clear about wanting me to speak about both of them, not just her, but this proved challenging as I struggled internally to find a genuinely good guy in him. I was like the mother who knew too much, and that knowledge caused deep distrust and worry for my friend. How, then, was I supposed to formulate a meaningful toast?

I had a layover in Minneapolis, and when I landed I discovered that my flight was delayed. After seven hours of waiting in the airport, my flight was canceled, so there I was, stuck in Minnesota on the last day of the year. The airline offered accommodations for all of the stranded passengers and loaded us into transport vans headed to a hotel. As we drove by a local bank on the way, I saw the temperature outside on their display, zero degrees! I couldn't think of a worse way to spend the transition into a new year. When I entered the hotel, I noticed a sign for live jazz music at their restaurant. I loved listening to live jazz, so I decided to head down to the bar and utilize the food ticket the airlines had given out. The sympathy on everyone's faces when they saw me sitting alone on New Year's Eve was almost humorous. I enjoyed the music, the people watching and the strange looks I was getting from those around me. I left the bar before the clock struck midnight. I didn't need to ring in the New Year with strangers, so I headed to my room and fell asleep.

My flight left early the next morning and I still hadn't written the toast. There is something to be said about how stress can really shift you into gear. I had to get it done on the flight because I would only have an hour or so to get ready for the wedding when I arrived in Honolulu. Thankfully, the words flowed on to the paper. I was able to find a sincere way to craft a toast to this union that I feared was a mistake: I spoke not of his character, but rather of the love he felt for her.

As I suspected, it was a whirlwind getting to the wedding and by the time I arrived, I was exhausted. Keli had sat me at a table with a friend of hers, Dan, who she had spoken of many times, but I'd never met. He was nice, a bit nerdy and formal, but nice. He attempted to make small talk, but I was so exhausted that it was hard for me. The next thing

I knew, it was my time to get up. The adrenaline that comes with standing in front of a group of people is quite effective in shaking off jet lag. I stood up and delivered my toast, and I could tell by the look on Keli's face that she was pleased. That was my goal, to make her happy, and I had succeeded. I was content knowing that I had come through for her because, God knows, I had really struggled to find the right words.

When I returned to the table, her friend Dan was full of compliments about my delivery of the toast. His comments made me wonder if he thought I was a box of rocks before he saw me hold my own in front of a group of people, but I figured I was just delirious from the long day and a bit oversensitive. He seemed to enjoy talking about himself. He told me about his job as a pilot and mentioned that he would love to take me for a ride in his small two-seater plane. I wasn't impressed at the time, but he seemed harmless enough, so I said yes and gave him my number. He was going to be out of town for the next couple weeks and would call me when he returned.

After weeks of convincing myself to give this guy a chance, I started to get excited to meet with him again. I hadn't heard from him and called Keli to ask if he was back in town yet. He seemed way too benign to be a player, so I assumed I misunderstood him. He took longer than expected, but eventually got in touch with me and we set a date. He was a member of the Outrigger Canoe Club in Waikiki, so we made plans to have dinner there. It was a beautiful location right on the beach with a stunning view, but Dan's affinity for talking about himself put a damper on the experience. I think it was an insecurity thing, and I wondered why I seemed to attract narcissists lately. By the end of the night I knew Dan was an overachieving workaholic. He had two full-time careers as an attorney and a private pilot for a wealthy businessman. Between my travel schedule and his, we would be lucky to spend four days a month together, but we decided to give it a shot.

He would call me when he was away on business and was always very sweet, but the conversations never seemed to flow, at least in my mind. I would barely get the word "hello" out of my mouth and he'd be rambling on about the details of his day or, God forbid, politics. He was a staunch Republican, the type who can't even understand a moderate perspective, which I considered myself to have. He viewed anyone outside of his opinion as an idiot, so the idea of discussing politics was less than appealing. His energy would become prickly if it was a hot issue and, for him, everything in politics was a hot issue. He was a good guy underneath it all, but he wasn't the best when it came to emotional issues — which is fine in the beginning of a relationship because typically you don't need to address those kinds of things during what my mother called the "honeymoon stage." Dan was most comfortable discussing ideas of the intellect rather than personal or emotional subjects.

He took awhile to get used to, but eventually I did. His travel schedule was intense, but this wasn't an issue for me because I had a busy social life of my own. On paper, we fit together fine. But then his tendency to overcommit began to cause a rift in our situation. On one hand, he would brag about how he made his own schedule and could do as he pleased, but on the other hand, he would frequently call at the last minute to cancel our plans, stating that he underestimated his workload. This was a pet peeve of mine since I believe if you commit to something, you should follow through. I started to clarify this with him and in his "rational" lawyer brain, his way to rectify the problem was to stop committing to plans. Rather, he would *try* to meet me at such and such time, but he couldn't promise anything. Don't get me wrong, there were good things about Dan too, like despite his lack of time for a personal life, he seemed very smitten with me and was very kind. When we were together, he was so polite, almost as if he was nervous to touch me, and for some odd reason I found it endearing. We enjoyed doing a lot of the same things. He was an ocean lover and lived right on the water, so whenever possible, we would try to meet up right before sunset so we could watch it together. He was definitely a man with toys, and in addition to his plane, he had a sailboat that always made for a great time. While we never seemed to figure out a time to go up in the plane — which I find ironic because that was his first offer when he met me — we did spend a good amount of our time together on his sailboat enjoying the tranquil waters of Waikiki.

Dan and I continued our relationship and while the "sparks" were absent, he was stable. I started to analyze my past relationships and decided maybe stability was just what I needed. I knew he wasn't the cheating type, and loyalty was definitely a draw. He was intelligent, had good morals and was family oriented, so why not? He had introduced me to his parents after a few months, and they both were very sweet, kind and best of all, normal. At first blush, he seemed like a catch. He had shared a couple of stories about women he had dated in the past, and from what I gathered, they used him for his money; they didn't really have goals and aspirations of their own, so they were willing to deal with his fickle nature in order to reap the benefits (i.e., his money). I then realized that this was typically the kind of women he attracted. He didn't have much to offer in the way of dynamic personality. He was more sweet than charming, so he wooed women by entertaining them with his big, expensive toys, and I started to wonder if I had fallen into the same trap. Was I becoming that woman who overlooked his many flaws because there was potential for a "good" life? Maybe, but I could already tell that something was amiss and I was starting to tire of his empty promises.

A few months into the relationship, I had earned the honor of President's Council for ending the year in the top two percent of sales and a won an incentive trip to Maui. I asked Dan to come along, but of course, he couldn't commit fully, but instead offered to fly over for a night in his plane and take me to dinner. I invited my mother instead but agreed to let him join us for a night. Most of the evenings were to be spent with coworkers, so I was a bit nervous about introducing him to everyone. I was worried that he would either talk about himself the entire night or talk politics, which never went over well, but we never got that far. He kept pushing back his arrival date based on some excuse until eventually it was too late. He was in the middle of purchasing the apartment next to his, which was one of the excuses have gave me. Between the apartment, work and planning for his next flight, it seemed he didn't have time for much else.

A few days later when I had returned home to Oahu, he invited me over to look at the apartment he had just acquired. He showed me photos from his camera of the unit before some of the work was done, and one of the images revealed a group of people posing in his new place. Knowing that he had just bought the unit a few days before when I was on Maui, I asked him when he found the time to have people over. He played it off, stating it was just some people from the office. The point wasn't who it was, rather the fact that his definition of "too busy" to come see me on Maui was partially due to the m,fact that he had chosen to invite friends over to show off his new purchase. As any good lawyer would do, he argued his case. When I didn't accept his answer, he pulled his classic Dan move — he got defensive and started telling me how I have unreal expectations. He said it would have cost too much for him to fly to Maui, even though he was the one who offered to do it in the first place. I was tired of trying to explain my feelings to a man who seemed to have none. I told him of my frustration over the fact that I never seemed to make his priority list.

Trips to Maui seemed to be a hot button issue for us,

but I thought I'd give it another try. A friend of mine was having his 50th birthday party on Maui and I asked Dan if he wanted to join me. He agreed this time, and even offered to fly us over in his plane. In his normal fashion, a few days before the party, he told me he couldn't make it and I would have to purchase a flight at the last minute. While I knew a handful of people over there, I would have rather not gone alone, but I had no choice. It seemed I was constantly making excuses for his absence. In the end, I had a great time with my friends, and I managed to make some new acquaintances and reconnect with an old friend. Luke was a former co-worker from my time at Castle & Cook Resorts, the private owner of the Island of Lanai, a beautifully rustic and unique island that sits off the coasts of Maui and Molokai. Luke wasn't actually at the party, but a mutual friend who also used to work for them was there, and when we started reminiscing about the old days, he came up in conversation. At 1 a.m., in what I believe qualifies as a "drunk dial," we decided to call Luke and see what he was up to. It was wonderful to hear my old friend's voice after all these years. He mentioned how he traveled to Honolulu for work, and suggested that we grab a drink the next time he was over. I happily agreed, as I had fond memories of Luke. He was always a good friend to me, but over the years, as our lives grew apart, communication had dwindled. At the close of the trip, I realized the evening was probably best spent without Dan, as I was able to catch up with people that I hadn't seen in years.

When I returned to Honolulu, Dan and I had another argument about his unreliable nature. I gave a hypothetical situation visualizing a future with him, pointing out that his life and work would always take precedence over me and wondering where that would leave me if I needed to travel for work. Without defensiveness or anger, he simply agreed and stated that I wouldn't have to work at all. Then it all became clear to me: he was attracting that type of woman, because that was exactly the type of woman he wanted — someone at his beck and call where he would be the provider. He wanted a passive-aggressive dictatorship, and I wasn't interested in being the oppressed party, even if it would have meant I'd be financially secure.

The following weekend I headed to Seattle for a meeting. I needed time away to think, so I decided to extend my trip and spend a few days with a friend in Oregon. We went to dinner and, of course, enjoyed one of my favorite pastimes, wine tasting. We spent an afternoon visiting the wineries scattered amongst the hills of Willamette Valley. It was a nice, relaxing weekend. I had spoken to Dan a few times over the phone but the conversations felt forced and unnatural. My subconscious knew to cut the line at this point, but tenacity held it's ground hoping something might change with our dynamic.

It came time to depart Portland and return back home to Hawaii. I had picked up a few wine magazines to read on the flight home, but upon boarding I noticed the movie selections were good, so I didn't get around to looking at the magazines until the descent into Honolulu. About 40 minutes outside of home, I cracked open the issue of Wine Enthusiast and found myself searching the back section where the wine ratings were located. I perused the Spanish wine section to see if any of David's wines were listed, thinking to myself as I searched that old habits die hard. To my surprise, there he was, his everyday wine listed with a high rating! It wasn't a story, but rather a brief mention of his wine, and I was happy for him. I said a little internal prayer for his happiness and wished him the best. While David technically was out of my life, he always held a place in my heart, and I had come to terms with the fact that part of my heart will always be his. I never told anyone this, and at times it made me feel guilty because I expected more from the men I dated; I expected them to give me 100% of their heart when I couldn't offer them the same in return.

I hadn't ended it with Dan yet, and I knew he wasn't the one for me, but my work was going well and we had plans to go to wine country in Sonoma in a few months for another incentive trip. I knew it was the wrong decision to keep him around for this reason, but with our schedules we never really seemed to spend much time together anyway and it just seemed easier to not have to find someone last minute to go to Sonoma with me. I thought this was the easy way out and wondered how I got myself into these situations. The flight landed and I turned on my phone. The first message to appear was an email from David and all it said was "How are you?" I looked up at the roof of the plane as if looking directly into the eyes of God and said aloud, "Seriously?!" I was starting to wonder if God was playing sick jokes on me. How could David's timing be so impeccable? I hadn't heard from him in months and suddenly I read his name in print and he reaches out to me? I decided not to answer until I was in a good place emotionally. I knew the next few days would be telling with Dan and I needed to focus on my current situation, not some fantasy man halfway around the world.

My worries that it would be difficult to come to terms with ending my relationship with Dan were quickly erased and he made it extremely easy to walk away. When I got home, I asked if he had scheduled the time off for California. He had a very long, convoluted answer that in the end was a very short no. If he'd only backed out earlier, rather than worrying about the repercussions, my life would have been much easier. I was tired of dealing with his work priorities and was ready to get out. The man bragged about not having taken a vacation in nine years (by his own choice), as if this made him above most people on the planet, and this was not for me. Dan was one of the easiest men to leave, no tears, no guilt, no wondering if I was doing the right thing. I was finally learning to listen to my gut, and when I followed it, rather than taking the so-called "easy" way out, it felt wonderful. He was disappointed in my decision but wasn't willing to compromise, and no compromise meant I was leaving. He knew this and showed little emotion upon hearing that we were finished. Perhaps he thought it was a negotiation strategy on my part, but it wasn't, I was done. There was a reason why he was such a successful lawyer, but these are qualities that don't transfer well into relationships. I immediately started making phone calls, and my friend Keli was more than happy to join me for an all-expenses-paid vacation to Sonoma.

CHAPTER 8

May 12, 2010

In a couple of the offices that I called on for work, the people were more like family to me than work acquaintances. I had become friends with one of the office managers, Jenna, who enjoyed hearing my stories of the ups and downs of being single. Jenna hadn't spent much of her young life single; she had a child when she was still in high school and got engaged in her early 20s. She was young in age, but an old soul, and she found my stories to be quite entertaining. She had referred me to a chiropractor/kinesiologist in her office named Cynthia, saying she could help me both physically and mentally. Jenna claimed that Cynthia was amazing at her line of work and could perform miracles. I was doubtful, but what did I have to lose? I set up my first appointment and was in awe of Cynthia's ability to tap into my emotional and physical blocks. I started to see her on a regular basis, and every time I left her office after a treatment, I felt like I was walking on a cloud. She knew I would be surprised by her abilities, so she humbly stated from the beginning that she wasn't a mind reader. Through muscle testing, she could read my body, and if something was off, whether I was consciously aware of it or not, she would recognize the blockage, go down a line of questioning and make chiropractic or homeopathic adjustments accordingly. The reverse was true as well, as she was able to gauge when a thought was good for my energy and would ask me to pursue it and see what happens. She knew the story of Dan and without me uttering a word, she said, "Wow, walking away from him was easy for you! This is a good sign that you're making progress." We both had a laugh.

A few times during our adjustments, I had brought up the deep, dark secret of David, but I always downplayed the stories and would quickly move on so as not to invoke too many questions on the matter. This time she wouldn't allow it, catching me off guard: "You've brought this man up a few times during our visits, but you've never really expanded on the situation. Can you share more with me?" I told her how I was reluctant to share the story in detail because it is so old, and at this point, extremely embarrassing. I proceeded to fill her in on our meeting, the reunion in Chicago, the heartbreak that ensued and all of the strange coincidences that occurred over the years. When I finished, she looked at me for a moment and then asked if he knew how I felt about him (the question I loathed). I gave her an uncertain answer, explaining how I suspected he was so intuitive that he most likely already knew I had feelings for him. She looked at me point blank and told me I needed to write to him and tell him honestly how I feel. I quickly responded, "Absolutely not! He will think I'm CRAZY after all of these years, no way!"

"Melanie, this is the only way you will ever have closure with this man," she said. "He is still very much in your energy. What do you have to lose? He lives in Spain and you live in Hawaii. Think of it as a way of either confirming your feelings or releasing them. You will never find the right person if your heart is always holding out for David."

I remembered years ago in one of my many sessions with Darrell, how he told me the exact same thing, urging me to tell David how I felt and to do it in writing, paper and ink, as it is more personal. I had vehemently opposed then as well, but maybe they were both right. Maybe it was time to stop listening to my ego and listen to my heart. Plus, for the past two years, I was still having the reoccurring dreams about chewing gum getting stuck in my mouth. I've addressed this with a therapist, Darrell, a meditation guide and now Cynthia, and they all propose the same interpretation — that I have something stuck in my throat, something I need to say, something I need to get off of my chest. I stopped and processed everything for a moment and, for the first time, actually considered writing to him.

Cynthia continued to do some adjustments and suggested that I put him out of my mind for a few weeks and only write to him when I'm in a good place. She said I should be extremely honest and clear as possible, so he understands the meaning. She found it odd that her intuition was telling her I should use pen and ink to engage David, being that we live in a world of instant communication, but that's what my body was expressing and she was just relaying the message. I laughed to myself thinking how I had heard the same thing from Darrell, yet at the time refused to believe it. I always secretly worried that one day I would run into David years down the road at a time when we both would have moved on with our lives, maybe even married others, and that seeing him again would rekindle the fire in my heart for him. Oddly enough, this scenario caused me anxiety not for how I would feel when it happened, but rather how those feelings might hurt the person in my life at that time. I feared that no matter who I was with, if David wanted my heart at any point, he could have it. I hoped and prayed that writing this letter would put that fear to rest. I wouldn't have to worry about him not knowing how I felt about him any longer. If I ever did run into him, it would be with a clear conscience.

June 4, 2010

David is back in my energy again. His presence is and always has been so strong within me. I've decided that on June 17th, I am going to write him a letter telling him everything inside my heart. I am not as scared as I was before and I need closure with him. I need to either be with him as a couple or truly purge him out of my energy so that I can move on. However, I always have these vivid visions of everything working out between us. I really feel he is my soulmate. I've been feeling like I want to settle down lately, and I have this overwhelming urge to share my life with someone, to have someone "add to" this wonderful life I have created. I also keep feeling the energy of a male child near me. I am scared to think that he's ready to come into my life so soon. I've always envisioned being with my "one" for a good period of time before children, so I hope he can wait just a bit longer so I can spend time with my love first.

I have changed so much since I first met David. I think I am a better and a more solid individual now. I guess I had to go through my dark nights of the soul to land here. I always knew that it was happening for a reason, but it was just so hard to deal with at the time. I am really excited and scared to death to see what my future holds. I know that I will make a wonderful wife and mom, but it has to be with the right person or it doesn't work. He has to appreciate me, to be my best friend and love me with every ounce of his being, to be the one who would have only my very best interests at heart. He would be my champion and I would promise to do the same. I need passion and adoration, trust and love. I can't wait to see him again (or meet my "one" for the first time). I want to go to Spain and be with David. I will leave these details up to my angels to decide what is best for me.

June 7, 2010

I managed to pull David into my dreams again. This time we were in a small dark room, almost like a recording room, with a couple of chairs and a garbage can. I start to talk to him and discover that my mouth is full of gum. I want so badly to speak to him, so I lean over the trash can in the room and try to remove the gum from my mouth, but it keeps coming out and I can't seem to find the end. When I look into the trash, I see a woman's disposable underwear and bra. I manage to form the words to ask him about it. He gives me some lame answer, making it clear that there is another woman in his life. I feel hurt but realize I have no room to talk. I apologize and tell him it is not my place to ask. He says that we would speak about it later when we figure things out.

WHY do I have these reoccurring dreams with the gum? They are so real that I've often had a hard time confusing the dream with reality. It's no wonder that in my last dream I said to myself, "See it wasn't a dream. This occurrence is real." I'm now trying to remember how long I've been having these dreams... I think since I met David, which would make sense because I've never told him how I truly feel about him. I wonder if the dream will stop once I let this secret out. I think this will be the case. Let's hope a better dream takes its place!

I spent the next two weeks trying my best not to think of what I was going to write, and instead focused on taking care of myself. I was working out, mediating, writing and doing anything and everything so as not obsess over what I would say. The day had arrived, June 17, 2010, and I felt I was ready. I had found a beautiful, handmade tablet with dried leaves and bamboo on the front and a gold sticker that had the Chinese character for "double happiness," as I always felt that together our happiness would be multiplied. I attached the sticker to the inside cover of the tablet above the handwritten date I had included. Perhaps it was a little much, but I figured my heart on paper was worthy of a beautiful container. I sat down in my living room and the words started to flow…

David,

I feel like I have told you how I feel about you a million times. And on occasion, I feel that I don't have to tell you how strong my emotions are, because you already know. Regardless, I am writing to you so I have peace of mind to know I did everything I could to clarify how special you are to me. I don't want to look back on my life and one day wonder if I wasn't clear enough with you or if my ego took priority over my heart. So, as embarrassing and scary as this is, I'm going to write to you totally without ego and completely from my heart. And if I find that you don't feel the same way about me, at least I will be ok knowing that I was honest and conveyed to another person (i.e., you!) just how much you are loved (even if it is from afar). So here goes my heart (yikes!)…

To put all of this into perspective for you, even after two years, as I write these words I can't seem to hold back my tears. It is all VERY strange to me that I feel so strongly about you after two years of relatively no contact or communication on your part. However, I've finally come to a place where I don't get upset or hurt anymore (ok, maybe a little hurt). I just accept it. I hate to admit this, but I still think of you almost every day. I know it sounds crazy!! It is crazy, and I just can't explain it but I feel a strong connection to you. Maybe it is all in the hope that you feel the same way about me. I've never experienced anything like the time I had with you. I felt so comfortable with you, like you were my best friend and my lover. I felt as if I could trust you. I believed everything you said to me.

When we were in the car on the way to dinner our last night and I was so eager to know when I would see you again, you told me not to worry and that we would see each other again, and I believed you with all of my heart and soul. I held on to your words as a place of comfort, knowing that we would indeed be reunited. I would love nothing more than to be with you again. I want a relationship with you. I want to see if you really are the person that I believe you to be. You seemed so kind and loving, honest and passionate, funny and adventurous... all things that I see in myself, yet I felt you were more solid in those attributes than I was. You did so many things that I can't forget. Like the way you looked into my eyes as if you were trying to look into my soul. It was so beautiful to me. And the way you seemed to bring out my sensitive heart, which lies underneath a very strong and tough outer shell. Never before had I broken down in tears in front of someone I technically didn't know. Yet when I did, you licked my tears. I think you had my heart from that moment forward. I can only attribute the tears to the fact that the man who fed my soul, the one whom I loved, was a half a world away from me. I couldn't tell you that at the time. I was too scared and perhaps unsure as well.

To me, that week in Chicago with you was spiritual; everything just felt right. So of course I was heartbroken each time I would reach out to you and you wouldn't respond. It brought up so much fear and need on my part. It was such a difficult thing for me to feel so needy, and I struggled with these emotions for a very long time. I now call it my "dark night of the soul." I think I cried every morning for a year. It was one of the worst things I've ever been through. I knew the only one who could end my misery was me. I had to get to a place where I didn't "need" you anymore and see how that felt to me. Wanting to be with someone, rather than needing someone is such a healthier place to be. That is where I am after two long years. I don't need to be with you; I want to be with you. When I close my eyes and think about my future, I picture it with you. I would love to get to know you better. If things worked out, I would love to share my life with you. I know you could never leave Spain, but I have nothing keeping me in Hawaii. I love it so much here, it is such a wonderful place to live, but if I discovered my soulmate elsewhere, I would move to you. I don't know what I would do there, but I've been blessed with success so far and I'm sure that would follow me regardless of where I call home.

I could go on and on but I won't. I don't know how you will react to these words. I hope that you will let me know if you don't feel the same, but not getting a response from you would be as clear of an answer as any. On the other hand, if you want to see me again, I would love to meet you. I would like to return to Spain, but it doesn't have to be there. I'm willing to meet you anywhere in the world. One day I will visit the town of Avila to see where St. Teresa lived. She was an amazing woman of spirit and strength.

When I look at the moon, I think of you, David — why?

Beautiful music makes me think of you. I wasn't going to

send you music, but one day recently this song came on and it spoke to me. The words are a reflection of my feelings. It brought tears to my eyes.

I hope you appreciate my heart in ink. Melanie, the hopeless romantic who wants the fairy tale. She wants to be a princess beside her Shrek.

Now the question is...

Will you let me in?

Love,
Melanie

Thank you for everything, David!

I included a copy of the song "Gravity" from Sara Bareilles. The lyrics captured our story so perfectly:

Something always brings me back to you, it never takes too long.
No matter what I say or do, I still feel you here 'til the moment I'm gone.
You hold me without touch, and keep me without chains.

I've never wanted anything so much, than to drown in your love and not feel your pain. Set me free, leave me be... I don't want to fall another moment into your gravity.
Here I am and I stand so tall... just the way I'm supposed to be.
But you're on to me and all over me.
You loved me because I'm fragile, when I thought that I was strong.
You touched me for a little while and all my fragile strength was gone.
I live here on my knees as I try to make you see that I think you're everything I need, here on the ground.
But you're neither friend nor foe, though I can't seem to let you go.
The one thing that I still know is that you're keeping me down.

I walked the letter over to the same UPS store that I had used to mail his birthday gift years earlier. I worried that I might get the same response this time around — a thank you after inquiring if he received it, a text months later telling me that he was enjoying another part of the gift and was thinking of me. However, this time it was different. This was the last letter I would ever write to him. If I didn't hear from him, that was my answer and I would be forced to move on. I was hoping that Cynthia was right, and even if he didn't respond in kind, that simply writing the letter would purge him from my energy and allow me to move on once and for all. I would then be able offer 100 percent of my heart to someone, not only just the portion that wasn't reserved for David.

I didn't tell many of my friends about the letter. I was too afraid of what the answer might be and how humiliated I would feel if he didn't respond. I had a friend whom I always met for hiking named Dara. The trail that we hiked seemed to be my thinking trail and I had explored many internal battles there with Hapa, my four-legged hiking partner, by my side. I had contemplated many life situations and made many decisions on this route, so I felt it was only right to share my story with Dara on this very trail. She knew all about David from the very beginning and was always intrigued by the story. I knew this could be the last time I spoke of David with her. I was unsure if it was a story of closure or new beginnings, and I was scared. I told her everything, and when I finished she looked at me in awe and said how much she admired me. I was shocked as I was expecting something else, perhaps a look as if to say "stupid girl." Instead, she told me that I was inspiring and strong, and said she would never have the courage to put herself out there for someone the way I did. She was amazed that I wanted to send it in the mail, no tracking, no electronic confirmation, nothing. I told her that if he was meant to receive the letter, he would. Then he could choose to respond. If he never received the letter, I wouldn't hear from him and that would be what was intended to happen. I needed to hear her words of awe and respect, devoid of judgment or fear. At that moment, I felt a wave of gratitude for my friends and how their words always seemed to help me when I needed it most.

A month came and went and I didn't hear a thing from David. I wanted to see if he had read the letter, and I promised myself that if he had, I would move on. I went to see Cynthia to try to make sense of it all. Cynthia closed her eyes, felt my energy and said, "He's received it, but there is something else going on in his world right now." Disappointed by what I had just heard, I avoided asking any more questions. I had my answer. It was time to move on.

CHAPTER 9

July 9, 2010

A few weeks after sending the letter to David, I heard from my old friend, Luke — the guy whom I had reconnected with on the phone while attending the birthday party on Maui a few months back. It should have been no surprise that he would come through on his promise to call me, since he was one of the few good guys out there and it was apparent in everything he did that he "walked the talk."

I had met Luke when I first moved to Hawaii 9 years ago, and he became one of my very first friends in the islands. We worked together for the Island of Lanai for about four years and always got along very well. I was in the marketing department and he was the resident golf professional, and we would often collaborate for photo shoots and entertain media representatives who would visit the island. We always enjoyed each other's company, but had slowly lost touch over the years after I changed jobs. He used to frequently call me to meet up when he was on Oahu, and even after Lanai, we spent a good amount of time together. At one point in our friendship, I got the feeling that Luke was interested in something more, but he was such a gentleman that he never pursued anything, which was good, because I wasn't in a very healthy place after my divorce. I needed a friend, no complications. He sensed that and silently respected my wishes.

I had completely forgotten about our conversation when Luke called. Hearing his voice again had been music to my ears. He was from Georgia and even though he had lived in Hawaii for 20 years, he still had a little twang. I didn't like southern accents, but it was cute coming from him. He told me he was staying at a friend's house down the street and wanted to take me out for dinner. I gladly accepted.

Although it had been a few years since I had seen Luke, he looked the same: tall, built like a golfer, blonde hair, light eyes and bright red skin from the sun. He was part Irish, so a tan was never part of his repertoire. It was as if no time had passed and my dear old friend was just as easy to talk to and laugh with now as he had been in the past. He picked me up in a taxi and we went out to dinner at a Japanese restaurant in Honolulu. We were sharing all of the details about the years past that we had both missed out on, chatting about everything from our families to dating and work. Since the last time we talked, both of our careers seemed to have improved significantly. When I left Lanai, I was the marketing manager and Luke was the director of activities. He told me that he had recently been promoted to executive vice president of marketing, a well-deserved role. It was clear whenever he spoke of the island how much he loved Lanai. I enjoyed hearing about the place, as it had always been my favorite island in Hawaii. It was small, special and seemed to have a distinct energy from any other island that I'd been to. I had spent many mornings walking through the Japanese garden behind my regular hotel, The Lodge, in awe of the tranquil grounds. Over the course of the conversation, I told him how I was itching to travel again, and that my travel partner Michele was forgoing trips this year due to home improvement expenses. He quickly responded, "I'm headed to Cape Cod in September. Come travel with me!" I looked at him as if he were crazy and replied, "Luke, I haven't seen you in three years and now you want to take a vacation with me? I'm sorry, but no, that is absolutely ridiculous!" He pleaded his case over the course of the evening, reminding me that we've always gotten along well and that we've traveled successfully as friends in the past. I countered with the argument that our previous trip to

Maui may not be a good indicator for how we would fare on a cross-country endeavor.

Apparently, Luke's friend John owned a house on Cape Cod and he went for a visit out there every year. I told him I would think about it and we left the restaurant to continue the evening with another glass of wine at Formaggio's. I noticed a distinct glimmer in Luke's eyes that told me he was interested in more than being just my friend. I had seen this look in the past and it made me want to run, but this time the instinct to escape remained dormant. I didn't know what I wanted, but I knew he was a good person with a good heart. I knew that after all the time that had passed, he still respected and adored me as I did him, but for me it wasn't in a romantic sense. As we walked to the next location, he grabbed my hand. I thought it was cute, so I allowed it. It felt like we were two childhood friends together again, but I knew there was so much more behind it. We crossed the street and as soon as we reached the other side, he kissed me passionately. I was in shock, but it wasn't awkward. Immediately following the kiss, we looked at each other and laughed. His face revealed sheer pride, and reminded me of a child who had accomplished a goal.

We continued on to our next destination hand-in-hand,

as if what had just happened was a normal occurrence for us. We had another drink and continued to talk about anything and everything. After an hour or so I started to feel tired, so we decided to end the night and grab a taxi. As the cab pulled up in front of my house to drop me off, I could feel Luke staring at me. I looked over to see his eyes firmly fixated on me, pleading for some sort of validation. "Melanie, I like you," he said.

"I know, we are good friends," I responded.

"No Melanie, I really like you. I always have."

He kissed me and said goodnight, and the taxi pulled away.

The next morning Luke called and asked if he could come over to see me before he left for Lanai. He had changed over the years — this time he wasn't scared to ask for what he wanted — and I rather liked his assertive confidence. I asked if we could meet for coffee at the Starbucks next to my house.

When I saw him at the coffee shop, I could tell I had unleashed something in him, as if his attraction for me in the past was fuelling the fire for me in the present. It was clear that he was looking at me as the girl who had gotten away all those years ago and he wasn't about to let that happen again. When I talked he seemed to listen to every word. I could do no wrong in his eyes. I trusted him, but the problem was, I didn't trust myself. He told me he wanted to see me again the following weekend. If he were anyone else, I wouldn't have understood or believed his feelings for me as it was too soon, and I wouldn't have been so presumptuous and skeptical. But this was Luke and I knew I wasn't ready for whatever this was. The last thing I wanted was to hurt him. "Luke," I said, "I can't really explain but I'm not ready to rush into anything. I'm not sure what your intentions are but I just need you to know that."

He gave me a funny look and laughed: "Melanie, can't we just hang out? I mean, we both enjoy each other's company, right? Well, then let's not make a big deal of it and just spend time together." I figured I was overthinking it, as I tend to do, and agreed to just go with the flow. I really did enjoy spending time with him.

Luke called me every night to check in and we always found something to talk about. It seemed effortless to have him in my life again. He was so easygoing, drama free and had such a happy demeanor. The days came and went, and the next thing I knew it was the weekend and I was picking him up from the airport and heading out to dinner. He knew how much I loved food and wine and was always willing to go along with whatever made me happy. He immediately started in about making our flight arrangements to Cape Cod, but I still wasn't sure if I should be going. Everything was moving so fast and while I trusted him and enjoyed his company, part of me was holding out for contact from David, hoping he would acknowledge the letter.

Time passed and that confirmation I sought so desperately never came. I started to wonder what was wrong with me. Was I sadistic? I had a man right in front of me who was a good person of sound character — kind, sweet and adoring — who adored me even after all of these years. In essence, he was safe. So why on earth was I still renting space in my head to a man who never responded to my messages, was full of empty promises and obviously cared very little about me? In my mind, the choice was clear, and I refused to waste another second of my energy on someone who would never come through. I told Luke I would go with him to Cape Cod. After that, we were "on." There wasn't a lot of physical attraction with Luke, but I figured as you grow to love someone, this aspect loses its importance and what is truly important is what lies beneath. I was older and hopefully wiser now. Smart enough to know that the man that I had great chemistry with had left me high and dry. My priorities had shifted. I wanted to share my life with a friend whom I could trust and respect completely, someone who cared deeply about me and loved me, perhaps even more than I loved him. I cared very much for Luke now, and I knew over time I would grow to love him after all of my wounds had time to heal. I had hoped for more alone time to allow for the healing process, but in this case time wasn't on my side, so I had to make do and try my best to put the past behind me.

The next month was full of planning and traveling between islands. I loved going to visit Luke on Lanai. It was such a spiritual place for me, the one place that I could actually relax. He had a small plantation home tucked into the woods away from everything. An oasis of peace. In my eyes, Lanai was close to heaven, a small island with a little over 2,000 residents. There are no stoplights, only one school and a little town square surrounded by a handful of local shops and restaurants. A majority of the island is privately owned, uninhabited and extremely rustic. There are two luxury resorts and one 10-room hotel in Lanai City that features a small restaurant frequented by locals and tourists.

Luke would take me around the island and show me all of his projects — the orchid gardens, improvements to the land, changes on the golf courses. He seemed to know everyone, and it was clear that he was well liked. He was actually pretty hard not to like.

Luke knew I loved the outdoors, so one day he decided to surprise me with an excursion to a side of the island that I had never been to. He had packed a picnic lunch for us in his ATV and we headed out on a hiking trail. I loved that he knew the island like the back of his hand. He was constantly stopping to share little-known facts about the surrounding environment. I was on the back of his ATV as he maneuvered trails in the mountains that often had steep cliffs. When I questioned my safety, he told me to hold on to him, and when I did, I felt safe. My arms were wrapped around his waist. I held on tight and pressed my face up against his back, and I knew he would do anything to protect me. I hadn't felt this way in a very long time and it made my heart skip a beat. We climbed the mountain, rambled through desert to rainforest, and descended back into desert. On the other side of the mountain, there was a stretch of beach that led to a place known as "Club Lanai." It was fascinating. Apparently, in its heyday it was a tropical oasis only open to the elite few. I had never seen anything like it. We walked along the fallen coconuts and explored a few abandoned buildings that used to host parties and guests. There was a pier that overlooked Maui, and you could feel the energy that this place once held. I begged him to revamp this site, as there was nothing else out there like it. We decided to lay out our towels and enjoy our lunch on the beach. It felt like a perfect day. I had struggled for so many years, but today everything felt right. It seemed I was finally happy again.

September 2010

Another month slipped by and it was time to head out to Cape Cod. We made a stop in New York City on the way, soaking up the city and dining with friends. I made it a ritual to visit my cousin every time I was in New York, plus I wanted her to meet Luke. He got along with everyone and I knew she and her husband would be no exception, and they weren't. We also met up with a friend of his who worked in the financial district. It didn't matter whom we were meeting with, it always seemed natural and easy for us to introduce each other to friends or family.

I had been to New York many times but Cape Cod was new for me and my excitement was overflowing. The scenery was beautiful and September was the perfect time for two people from Hawaii to visit the Cape. It was a little chilly, which felt good to us, and there seemed to be a lot less people on the island, so getting around was easy. Luke was right, I absolutely loved the company of his friend John who owned the home. As Luke promised, he was a perfect host and we all got along fabulously. We would ride bikes around the Cape, make extravagant dinners consisting of *foie gras*, fresh-caught lobster and wine, or simply relax on the balcony overlooking the ocean. It was one of the mellowest vacations I've ever experienced, and it couldn't have come at a better time. I needed to decompress after all of the emotional ups and downs I had recently endured. Here I felt there was no pressure; I was able to do what I pleased, when I pleased, no questions asked. This was part of Luke's character coming through. He was a confident person and that translated into a very easygoing demeanor. I had been so nervous about our trip, worried that it was happening too soon or that I might not enjoy myself, or that it would be awkward for Luke, but evidence of this being a bad decision never presented itself. We traveled well together, just as he had predicted. Maybe this was what I needed all those years ago, but I just wasn't ready for him back then. I couldn't appreciate Luke for who he was, but now I was able to see through all of the superficial nonsense. I started to wonder if I was being fair to him by not sharing the reason why I wanted to take things slow, but I figured it was too much irrelevant information. The intention of the letter was to either finally get closure with David or move forward with him. To bring him back into my life or let him go once and for all… and as things progressed with Luke, I thought maybe it was time to let him go.

Our return flight home was painfully long. We had to drive from the Cape back to NYC to catch our flight, and from there we had the grueling nine-hour flight back to Hawaii. I was sitting in the middle and felt pinned into my seat with people on both sides, Luke being one of them. About halfway through the flight, I could feel myself growing irritable. Hours passed and the irritation crept from the strangers surrounding me to Luke. I had lumped him into every other annoying person on the plane. I didn't want to talk to him or look at him. His smell bothered me, and even his laughter about the movie started to get on my nerves. At one point I snapped at him, telling him his laughter was disrupting other passengers. I just wanted to be home alone. He was planning on spending one night with me before heading back to Lanai and I secretly wished I could just have my space for the night. When I became aware of these feelings, they scared me. How could I have such awful thoughts about this man? I convinced myself that once I got off that god-awful plane, my emotions would return to normal.

We deplaned and the sheer thought of returning to my animals put a smile on my face. Finally, we arrived at my house and I rushed in to let them know I was home. Hapa was always quick to forgive and showered me with immediate affection. My cat, on the other hand, seemed to hold a grudge when I left him for long periods of time. He walked by me with attitude and proceeded to demonstrate his disapproval by promptly biting me on the hand. Luke was always telling me how he didn't like my cat, which doesn't earn points in my book, and soon as my cat bit me, Luke seized the opportunity to yell at Kitty and scare him. My immediate reaction was defensive and I yelled back at him. The cat was oddly standoffish with Luke whenever he was around, and after the incident, he ran into the closet and hid in safety. He had never reacted like that to any person before. The situation probably would have been minor had I not been coming off of 15 hours of traveling, but now my temper was flaring. Kitty wouldn't come out of hiding and I was ready to go into hiding. I unpacked and went to bed with a chip on my shoulder.

The next morning I took Luke to the airport. After a couple of hours of him being out of the house, the cat came out of hiding, but it was clear that Kitty was giving me the no-go signal with Luke. He had acted so strange around him, and I knew from experience that my animals' reactions to people were quite telling. I was concerned.

The next night of solitude was sorely needed. I curled up in bed with a book and fell asleep. The following morning I awoke and rolled over to see the time. I had an early start planned because I had to catch an 8 a.m. flight to Kauai for work, and 5:30 arrived way too soon. I grabbed my phone to read emails, which was part of my morning routine in order to get me going. I couldn't believe what I saw — an email from David with the subject "Hello from Spain" that read:

Hello Melani,

I'm sorry for not answer before, but i read your letter only two weeks ago.
I'm harvesting in Spain, in diferents areas and i would like have more time for sit in my office and write you.
for the moment i want that you know that i never forget you, but the life is very fast and you know that i need work all the time. My friends said me that I'm "wokholic"...

If you want, you can answer this mail and you can return the comunicate with me.
(sorry for my english, it´s the same bad than two years ago)

kiss you

David Sampedro Gil
Viticultor & winemaker

Proceeding the initial shock, the first emotion I felt was anger. I poured my heart out to this man and this is what I get in return two months later? A few lines stating that he never forgot me and that I can email him back if *I* want to! Thank you very much, David Sampedro, for telling me that I'm not absolutely nuts, but based on the email there was no need for me to respond, so I didn't. I wasn't going to uproot my life for a response from him that was totally indifferent, FORGET IT! His reply was so typical. I figured if I didn't send an email back, I would never hear from him again and my life would be much simpler.

I got ready for work and within a few hours I was on Kauai. I walked into one of my doctor's offices, a favorite of mine thanks to an adorable yellow lab named Ginger. I was sitting in the reception area with her waiting for my doctor to come out when I felt my phone vibrate. It was David again. He always surprised me, but this time I couldn't believe what I was seeing — another email already?

Hi Melani.

Are you ok? I hope that you are happy. I thinking that I would like visit you to finally this year or first to the new year. I'm working all days and I think that when finished the harvest and make the wine I'll go holidays and for learn english. What do you think?
Thansk and kiss

David

Persistence was not a quality that David had ever shown me. He had given up on me multiple times. Our entire relationship thus far was due to my tenacity; I was always the one reaching out to him, remembering his birthday, remembering him during the holidays, remembering *us*. Did I want to do endure the same emotional roller coaster again? But something was different this time — he was asking to come visit me. I couldn't answer right away. I needed time to think about the implications of my actions. Luke was in my life now and my decisions could potentially affect him. I sent David a quick response telling him I was fine, just busy, and would respond when I had more time.

That weekend I was babysitting my friend Kerrey's teenage daughter Rose. We decided to rent movies and eat pizza. Rose picked out two movies at the video store, but since I knew I had work to do that evening, I paid little attention to her selections. We got back to my house, devoured the pizza and started the movies. I picked up my computer and start plugging away with work. About 45 minutes into the movie, something drew my attention and I looked up and started watching the movie. The scene involved an old woman with two young adults pulling into a vineyard. They stopped to ask questions in Italian, inquiring about a man from the older woman's past, when around the corner entered a handsome older man on a white horse. The elderly woman was nervous, breathless at the sight of him. I immediately took interest in the movie and start asking Rose about the details up to this point. She was annoyed at my disruptive questions, and with her sassy teenage attitude, she told me I should have paid attention before and if I'm interested I can watch the movie tomorrow. I picked up the case checked the name of the movie — *Letters to Juliet.* It's about an old woman, Claire from England, who falls in love with a *viticultor* (vine grower) from Italy in her youth and decides to search for him again in her later life. She finds him and they marry, and what captured my interest most was the fact that she spent her whole life thinking of her love but never had the courage to act until she was an old woman. Coincidentally, this was one of my greatest fears with David. The next day I watched the movie in tears, as every scene seemed to call out to me. At the end, they reveal the heart-wrenching letter that was sent to Claire later in her life from the Sisters of Juliet encouraging her to once again pursue the love from her youth:

"What" and "if" are two words as non-threatening as words can be. But put them together side by side and they have the power to haunt you for the rest of your life. What if? What if? What if? What if? I don't know how your story ended, but if what you felt then was true love, then it's never too late. If it was true then, why wouldn't it be true now? You need only the courage to follow your heart. I don't know what a love like Juliet's feels like, a love to leave loved ones for, a love to cross oceans for. But I would like to believe if I ever were to feel it, that I would have the courage to seize it. And Claire, if you didn't, I hope one day that you will.

Wow. It was all about second chances to find true love. At that point I knew there was no way the timing of this movie was a coincidence. Even the words “to seize” struck me as I recalled David on numerous occasions in Chicago looking into my eyes and saying to me, “Carpe diem, Melanie,” *seize the moment*. I didn’t know how to interpret his meaning of the phrase back then, but now it was clear to me. I looked up through the ceiling to the heavens and said, “Ok God. Fine! I get it. I will write to him.”

After a few days, I accomplished my mission:

David,

I want you to know that I never felt that you intentionally hurt me. You have made it very clear that at this point in your life, your career is your priority, and I respect that. And more importantly, I no longer take it personally. When you didn't respond to my letter and after waiting two years to see if you felt even an ounce of the love that I felt for you, I had to let the idea of us go. I started to picture myself at 80 years old, all alone, telling my friends that I am still waiting for my soulmate from Spain to come find me. Haha!

So you ask if I'm ok. The answer is yes. I'm in a very good place now and happy with my life. If you would like to come visit me, you are and always will be more than welcome.

My biggest fear about sending that letter (aside from you thinking I was crazy!) was losing you as a friend. Even though we don't communicate much and the term "friend" is something I usually reserve for someone who is an active participant, I still feel some sort of bond with you and ALWAYS wish you the utmost happiness and success. So your holiday is your decision and as long as you are ok with seeing me as a friend, I welcome you here. If you are looking for something more, this may not be the right time. I realize now that we are different... I can't give you 100% of my heart for one week and 0% after you leave. I don't work that way. I can, however, offer you the same love I give my friends. And let me tell you that love is nothing to balk at... it's pretty darn good love. ;)

Let me know what you decide. Also, I'm sending you lots of good energy for your harvest this year! When should I expect the case of wine to show up at my doorstep?

Love,

Mel

Suddenly, the man who never responded to anything was responding immediately. David said he still wanted to visit me and downplayed it as an opportunity to learn English. He explained that it was difficult to discuss his emotions with me over email, that he wanted to explain everything in person and he didn't want to hurt me. The part that stood out the most was the fact that he said he felt something for me as well, but wasn't sure if our future was together. He said that when he saw the moon, it made him think of me. I had said this exact same thing in the letter that I had sent to him. Was he playing games with me? I didn't know if he was speaking the truth or reiterating my words in order to win my favor again. My faith in him was on the verge of collapse.

Throughout all of these new occurrences in my life, I couldn't forget the reality that I was now faced with. I was in a relationship with a man who was a wonderful person and treated me very well. I wondered how I was going to tell Luke that a "friend" from Spain was going to come and stay with me for a month. Luke was amazing and trusting, but this was going to be hard to explain. I worried whether or not I was doing the right thing, but I just kept telling myself that David was only a friend and there was no harm in that.

Another week passed and the weekend arrived. I was in my regular Saturday morning routine heading to spin class when David contacted me via Skype. I quickly responded that I was headed to the gym and would be back in an hour. After making arrangements to talk a couple hours later (which I thought for sure he would fall through on), we spent three hours together. After about 20 minutes, we decided to use video chat since we hadn't seen each other in years. I picked up his call and discovered he could see me but I couldn't see him, but as soon as I heard his voice, I knew that all attempts to pretend he was just a friend would prove futile. I missed him instantly. It was as if no time had passed. I felt flush and his voice seemed to wrap around me like an embrace. The sound of his voice was strong and kind. I knew I was under his reign once again, but this time I wasn't scared. I felt secure and warm when we talked. We were sharing, laughing and connecting again in that same beautiful flow that we had experienced a few years ago.

I updated him on my life and showed him around the house. Everything felt perfect until we ended the call and this time reality really struck. I couldn't even lie to myself now about thinking of him as just a friend. I knew that if I couldn't convince myself, there was no way that I could or would even want to convince Luke that he didn't mean more to me; it would be a flat-out lie and I couldn't do that. I knew things had to change, but I didn't know how to go about the transition because, from Luke's point of view, everything was fine. We spoke briefly everyday and I still very much cared about him as a person, so my demeanor hadn't changed… only my heart had changed, or rather, reverted back to its natural state.

As soon as I got off Skype with David I knew I wasn't being honest with myself and I had to come up with a new solution. I was at a loss as to what to do. David was planning on coming in January and my relationship with Luke was plugging along. It was only October, and if I selfishly waited to see what happened with David in January, it wouldn't be fair to Luke, yet it was a huge risk to end a relationship that had such potential. A relationship with a man whom I truly cared for and in whom I found few flaws, no less. I knew David wanted to explain his situation and feelings to me, and that he preferred to do it in person, but I couldn't see waiting until January. I knew Luke and I would progress, but David was reaching out for me now, and if I allowed it, that too would progress. I could barely handle one relationship, let alone juggle two. A solution came to me: I would go visit David soon, but there were a lot of variables that needed to fall into place before that happened. For one thing, he had never asked me to visit him. It would be interesting to see if the universe would shift to accommodate this new plan. I was stiff with stress and decided that I needed a massage and maybe some guidance by way of my intuitive friend.

The next morning, Darrell arrived at my door with his massage table. I was so tense I couldn't wait to release my stress. I lay on the table and felt reservation about sharing the updates with Darrell, but I did it anyway. He was happy to hear that after all this time, I finally had the nerve to be honest with David about my feelings — something he had encouraged me to do years before. I continued to elaborate about the conflict in my heart, about not hurting Luke, who was a very safe option. On the other hand, David was a huge risk halfway across the world and he had disappointed me numerous times in the past. I told Darrell that I worried about what might happen if I waited to see David in January, and that part of me wanted to see his home before inviting him into mine. Darrell listened and then asked me if I've ever seen the movie *Letters to Juliet*. Before that question came up, I had been resting on my stomach, speaking to him through the headrest. But as soon as he uttered those words, I grabbed the sheet and turned to make eye contact with him, equally shocked and annoyed at his spot-on movie reference. "Darrell, seriously?" I exclaimed. "What are you about to say to me?"

He continued, "Melanie, I think you should go. I don't want to see your future the same as the old woman in the movie."

I told him that this was by far the most bizarre thing yet and explained how that very film is what made me accept David's request to visit in January. I promised Darrell I would no longer fight the signs and just go with my gut from now on.

October 20, 2010

A few days later, I was on a run, stressing a bit about waiting for David to send me the much-anticipated itinerary for his visit in January. I decided that if the timing was right and my mainland work trips confirmed a location on the east coast, I would run the idea by him of me visiting Spain. No sooner did I get home from my run when I saw the email from corporate informing me that my upcoming meeting would take place in Orlando, Florida in the first week of December, what timing! One more piece of the puzzle in place. As I opened my personal computer, I saw a message from David informing me that he had not yet booked his trip. He is very intuitive, and I think he picked up on something that ultimately prevented him from booking. I immediately offered to come to Spain instead. He was delighted that I wanted to visit him and agreed to the dates I proposed in early December. I felt great, but something was still nagging at me. I couldn't imagine showing up on David's doorstep, and then telling him about Luke. I had asked for brutal honesty from him and felt it only fair to give it in return. I wrote him an email explaining that there was someone in my life and I didn't want to hurt Luke, so I would understand if he didn't want me to come visit. It took forever to hit the send key because I felt that, yet again, I was putting it out to the universe to decide my fate. If he rejected me, I would simply have to accept that our destiny was not to be together. I pushed the send button and waited.

Hi David,

I asked for complete honesty from you, and I promised you the same in return. So I'm keeping up my end of the bargain...

Shortly after I mailed you "the book," I reconnected with an old friend. Recently, our relationship has changed and we are now dating. My relationship with him is still young and I don't see him much as he lives on another island. However, he is a good person and I would never want to intentionally hurt him, as I know he cares for me. I'm trying to be as fair as possible through this, so I wanted to be honest with you about my situation.

My thinking is this... I want to see you again. I want to hear what you have to say. I want to see your life and get to know you better. But please understand, I have no expectations of you and I want to make that clear. I am completely aware that we may decide that we are best just being friends. Or maybe we will explore a deeper relationship. We just don't know and I don't think we will know until we see each other again, but of course, that is just my opinion :)

What are your thoughts on this? Do you still want me to visit you in December? If so, I got approval from my boss on the dates (December 3 - 12). We can discuss further on Skype if you want. I will understand no matter what you decide. xoxo

Love,

Mel

David's response came the next day, and it spoke to the

character of the man that he is. Once I read it, I knew I was going to Spain.

Hi Mel:

This night i answer with more time when I can sit in front of my computer.

But I only want to said that I understand you, sincerely, I know its normal that you make your live and its my fault for not answer before, I know.

I want to see you again too, but I don't want that you hurt your boyfriend. i´m worried abaut your boyfriend.... in my experience, to me, my heart was broken and i can undestand the position your boyfriend.

I know that is a difficult decision, but you are the unic person that can said

Love David

Once I booked my flight for Spain, David and I started to communicate on a daily basis, as if to make up for the years that communication was misunderstood and sparse. This once distant man seemed to be available at my beck and call. Suddenly that attentive, loving, kind man who cared for me in Chicago had returned. I could talk about anything and often filled him in on my work and hobbies. I had signed up to take another wine education course through the Guild of Sommeliers the year prior, and the time had arrived to start. I had been preparing for an exam that was to take place on Maui after the two-day course. I was staying in my friend's hotel and trying to focus all my energy on my studies, but of course I brought my computer to speak with David in the off chance we could connect, which we did. I had tried to explain to him many times before what I was studying for, but our language differences interfered. When I showed him the course material via Skype, his eyes lit up and he said, "Is class about wine?"

"Yes, it's the introductory course you can take prior to obtaining the official sommelier certification," I replied.

Thankfully, I passed the exam. Upon receiving the good news, the instructor informed us that, in so many words, the certification was worthless. We wouldn't be able to claim sommelier status, as that was another level up, so if we were interested in achieving this status we would have to spend more money for a second test. Being that this was a hobby for me, I quickly decided I had fulfilled my spending quota for wine classes over the past few years.

Prior to reconnecting with David, I was introduced to Josh Grobin's music and was captivated by a few songs in particular, especially the ballad "Si Volerias A Mi." I would listen to it over and over, moved by its powerful energy that would make my hair stand on end and bring tears to my eyes. After reconnecting with David, I decided to try to make sense of the lyrics. I found a website and worked on the translation. I was speaking with David one morning and asked him to translate a few of the phrases: *como saltar sin red*, *me despojaste la piel*, *desataste un huracan* and *esclavo de ti*. He roughly translated these to mean: "how to do I jump without a net?," "you removed my skin," "you unleashed a hurricane" and "slave to you," and then asked me if I was trying to interpret a love song. I said yes and asked if he wanted to hear it. As I played the soulful piece for him over Skype, I could see the emotion in his eyes as the notes filled the air. I felt like I was watching his heart actually breaking as he listened. When the song was over, I could've sworn I saw a tear in his eye. He barely spoke and simply told me that the song was very sad. His energy had changed and I sensed that he wanted to be alone. He excused himself from the conversation and we said our goodbyes. The song had stirred something in him. The name of the song in English is "If You Return to Me." This was the man I couldn't forget, the man I knew existed under that closed and protected exterior, but I felt there was more to his sadness in hearing those words… that there was something that he wasn't telling me.

I left for a work trip in Colorado and had decided to extend my stay to spend time with a good friend from Hawaii who had recently moved there. She knew of my complicated history with David, so I was more than happy to share the story of our reconnection and how wonderful it was to have him back in my life. The next morning I awoke to the following email from David:

November 6, 2010

Good morning my cowgirl!

How are you? I'm in the winery, again, and I'm thinking in

you and preparing your travel.
The last night I saw one film: Letters to Juliet, and I think a lot of...
I would like if you can see this film, and I would like know your opinion.

Thanks

David

I couldn't believe what I had just read and our strange mutual connection to this movie. I thought about keeping my history with the movie to myself, but I figured that complete honesty had worked well with David thus far so I shared the "coincidence" with him.

David,

The short answer: Right now I seem to be playing the role of Claire who had to take a risk and follow her heart...

The long answer: The strange thing is that I saw that movie about three days after I received your first email asking if you could come and visit. I was babysitting my friend's daughter and she picked the movie. Prior to watching it, I was still upset that it took you so long to respond, so I wasn't sure what I should do — follow my head or follow my heart. Then I saw the movie and figured it was a sign that I should see you again, so I emailed you. However, I was still struggling to feel that I was making the "right" decision. I was telling a friend about my struggles. He asked me if I had seen "Letters to Juliet" and said he didn't want to see me end up like the old woman in the movie who waited to be with the man who was always in her heart. Neither do I. I now know that, regardless of the outcome, I am making the right decision.

I've often felt there was something in the universe constantly pushing me towards you.

I miss you too!!!

Love,

Mel

The following morning I awoke to a link David had sent via Skype. It was the video of the Taylor Swift song "Love Story" from the movie. As I listened to the song I felt my heart overflowing with love and joy, as the man of my dreams was proving to be everything I had hoped he was. He could bring me to tears in a matter of minutes. How could he stir emotions in me that no one else seemed to be able to evoke? What was it about this man in particular? I grew more eager to see him with each passing day. The time couldn't pass fast enough.

When I returned home to Hawaii, Luke was planning on visiting me the following weekend and I knew I had to end the relationship. I wasn't sure if I should talk to him over the phone or have him incur expenses for a flight, only to break up with him. I struggled with the dilemma for days and finally decided that he deserved an explanation in person. I also decided that I would not give him all the details and rather just say we weren't compatible. I wanted to spare him any pain and I figured going into details would only be hurtful.

I knew with all of the changes happening so quickly in my life that I needed to talk to my mom and let her know what I was doing. I almost dreaded calling her because I anticipated her response, which might sit well with the practical side of me, the one that considered Luke a safe option, but would be in total opposition to my heart, which knew David was the riskier choice but wanted him still. I was just waiting to hear how leaving a perfectly good man who was right in my backyard for a dream man in Spain was a risky venture and a big mistake. I braced myself for the call. She answered and we made small talk for a while before I actually got the nerve to tell her the news. To my total dismay, she didn't chastise me at all. I heard her take in a breath and release it, then in a calm voice she said, "Melanie, I never know what to expect with you. You are my dreamer child. You have talked about David for years now and maybe it's time to pursue him and see what happens." I about dropped the phone. I was prepared to argue my point or at least sit there and politely agree to disagree, but I didn't have to do any of it. Somehow, she knew that this burning question inside of me had to be addressed before my life could move forward.

The week seemed to crawl by and every day was filled with worry and stress about hurting Luke. Friday eventually came and I picked him up from the airport. We decided to go to the bar at Ruth's Chris Steak House in Waikiki for happy hour, which was ironic because I was dreading every moment. We took a spot at the bar in the back corner of the restaurant and I tried to sit away from people so we could talk. After ordering a drink, Luke reached over to be affectionate with me, but I stopped him in his tracks. I told him that something had been bothering me and I wanted to discuss it. He leaned in with a concerned look, as if he was ready to do whatever he could to fix the problem I was about to share. The look in his eyes showed he had no idea what was coming, and I wanted to run and hide under a rock and die. I regained my composure and tried to get it out as convincingly as possible, explaining that I thought it was time to sever our relationship because I didn't see a future with him. He gave me a look that told me he wasn't buying it and replied, "Mel, I don't believe you. We get along great, like the same things, we don't argue. Tell me the truth, what is this all about?" I stuck to my guns and tried to come up with as many excuses as I could. I told him over and over how sorry I was and how I didn't want to hurt him. He gazed at me with a face of concern like a parent would look at their child and said, "Mel, you look so stressed. Don't worry about me, I will be fine. I'm just worried about you and I feel like there is something you're not telling me, but I can't figure out for the life of me what it is. Let's just enjoy the night." He hugged me in attempt to console me, and I was reminded once again what an amazing man he is. The way he handled the news made me feel that much worse about what I just did. I could feel that he wanted to ask me a thousand questions, but he didn't. He asked me if there was something he may have done to cause my decision, and I told him no.

Luke is such a good person and I wasn't sure who this hurt more, me or him. I told him that I didn't expect him to pay for a hotel and that he was still more than welcome to stay with me. He agreed to stay, and I trusted him and knew he would never cross any lines or make me feel uncomfortable. He slept on the couch, and I'm sure part of him was hoping that the night would be different, but there was no intimacy.

When morning came, Luke informed me that he was thinking of changing his flight to leave a day early, on Saturday. I let him know he was welcome to stay and the decision was his, and I made every effort to avoid awkwardness. I needed to run some errands and Luke said he would join me. As we drove around Honolulu, I could tell he wanted to talk about us again. I said, "You can ask me any question that is on your mind." He glanced over at me and responded, "Mel, I know there is more to your story and you're not telling me something. Don't worry about hurting me. I just need to know the truth."

I looked at him and sighed, knowing he deserved honesty but dreading having to speak it. I offered more apologies as I began to tell him a very abbreviated version of my history with David. I told him how I pined for him for years, how I finally decided to make closure with him by writing him in June, and how he responded so late after two months. I apologized profusely for the poor timing, explaining that I would've never started a relationship with him had I known David would respond to my letter. For the first time, Luke got defensive. I could tell he didn't respect the fact that I was taking a huge risk walking away from our "perfect" relationship to meet up with a man who took months to respond to my letter. "Mel, I don't want you to get hurt and this seems like a bad idea," he said. "Who is this guy? Do you really know this man? What if he hurts you? And why did it take him two months to respond? That doesn't sound right."

I could feel myself getting defensive as well, but fought the urge to argue my point, knowing that he was fighting to keep us together. Luke decided to leave that night, and before he departed, he told me he would be in touch and that he would allow me time to get David "out of my system." He made sure I knew he would be waiting for me when I returned from Spain. He made me promise that if things didn't turn out the way I planned, that I wouldn't let pride get in the way and I would call him. No one had ever been so selfless before, so willing to take his pride and put it aside to spare the relationship from total demise. My heart ached. I knew he was special, one of a kind.

When Luke left I cried, not for the loss of him, but because I truly recognized and respected his beautiful spirit and felt so fortunate to be in the situation that I was in. Tears fell once I realized how it had taken me so long to figure out that when you follow your gut and do what's right, the universe rewards you. I was glad it turned out this way, but his kind, mature reaction made the journey ahead that much more difficult. I was risking losing a good man who was stable, caring, and kind for a man who had consistently disappointed me over the past few years. While my intuition still told me to go forward, my head was screaming for me to ignore it. I started to wish that Luke had been an asshole so I could at least lose respect for him, and then the bar for David wouldn't have been set so high. I was plagued with the lingering question, "Will this man disappoint me yet again?"

CHAPTER 10

December 2010

Finally the time for my Spain trip had arrived. I was headed to Florida first for work, and then on to beautiful, mesmerizing Spain. I had no clue what the plans were, and I was totally in, along for the ride, open to anything. I had mentioned a few things I wanted to do to David, but had no confirmation from him about how we would spend our time. I was going in blind and was giddy with anticipation.

I landed at the airport in Madrid and nervously searched my surroundings, as David was supposed to be there waiting for me. I walked out past customs into a sea of people, not one of them David. I scanned the crowd, wondering if he was late and started to feel extra anxious. I noticed a figure walking slyly behind the crowd, and we made eye contact. It was him! I ran to David with my arms extended as if we were family members who had let years pass without seeing each other and he held me close. He seemed surprised at my affection, and I kissed him on the lips. I knew at that moment that despite all of the emotional turmoil, I had made the right decision. I felt at home in his strong arms.

David and I headed towards our hotel in Madrid. As we pulled up, I noticed a familiar landmark — Hotel Laura, the very same hotel that had caused all the confusion the first night we met. The place where we made plans to see each other again, where he held me in front of the hotel after a long night out. Everything was just as I remembered it — the modern décor, the bright colors. I was thrilled to be back. We arrived at our hotel room and David proved to be a perfect gentleman once again. He excused himself from the room so I could shower and get ready in private. It was all a lot to take in so I was grateful for the time alone. My romantic life was suddenly moving at an alarming pace.

After I finished getting ready, I met David in the hotel restaurant, and we headed out to explore the streets of Madrid and take in a museum, Reina Sofia. I would later find out he hated museums and took me there because I had asked to go. I would have never guessed this as he guided me through exhibits effortlessly, pointing out all of the famous Spanish artists. The next stop was the Mercado de San

Miguel, a gastrophile's dream and a real cultural experience where you can find all sorts of local Spanish food and drink. We enjoyed a few tapas and David introduced me to *vermut de La Rioja*, an alcoholic concoction that I knew would at some point turn me red. David started in with a line of questioning about my life and the situation with Luke. Other than telling him that Luke was in my life back when he reached out to me, I had shared little else up to this point. I didn't want to spend our time together speaking about another person, but now he was asking, so I told him the story. I shared that I ended the relationship with Luke a few weeks prior to my departure and how Luke had surprised me at how well he had handled the news. When I mentioned that Luke said he would wait for me, David looked at me in utter disbelief and asked why I turned so red once I shared that story. I explained that it was the alcohol, and also the fact that we were standing under a heat lamp. He didn't believe me and I was hurt that he thought I would lie to him. I wondered what kind of person he must think I am to make up such an outrageous story. I was offended and insulted and saw a very distrusting side of David that I had never seen before. I wondered what had brought about such a cynical belief in others. We got through it for the moment and put it behind us so as not to ruin the day, though my concern lingered.

We continued on and I decided it was my time to find out what he felt he needed to explain to me about his life. What did he want to tell me that he had never told me before? As we walked the streets of Madrid, I told him it was his turn to share his side of the story as to why his communication after Chicago was spotty. He looked at me and said, “You know.” But I didn’t. I didn’t have a clue what he was referring to and asked him to elaborate. He insisted that I must have known, and after some hesitation he said, “I met someone else when I returned to Spain after Chicago.” My heart sank. It felt like he had taken a knife and drove it straight through my heart. If anyone ever tries to say that the emotion of love can’t be felt physically, they’ve never been in love before. My body was overtaken with shock. I stopped in my tracks and stared at him as if he had just told me someone died. The world around me stopped, and suddenly there was only him and I in the middle of city. I started to cry. He seemed surprised that I didn’t know. In all the time that we had been apart, he never once alluded to having someone in his life. He had always made it sound like work was the reason he didn’t have time for me.

David asked me to stop crying and tried to console me. I pushed him away and started to walk away from him. I needed to process my thoughts. I knew I was being very irrational, yet I didn't know how to control it. Suddenly I had so many questions about him and his life over the past few years. I was angry that he had just made me feel bad during the Luke story, but at least I was honest with him! He, on the other hand, had never once mentioned anything about another woman and I felt he had kept this information from me to keep me on a string. Furious, I tried to take some deep breaths to contain myself, and then I remembered my dream with the gum and the woman's underwear in the trash can. Was it a premonition? My head was spinning and I knew I needed to calm down so we could talk. I had no other option.

David explained that he did not meet her immediately after Chicago and that he was working a lot. Their relationship was an unhealthy one, yet he couldn't seem to end it, so she did — by cheating on him. This explained his distrustful reaction to my story about Luke and why he didn't respond to my letter right away. Cynthia had called it when she said, "He received it, but something else was going on in his life." He had just ended his relationship with this woman after she cheated on him and probably wasn't in a place to address my letter. In fact, he shared that he avoided opening and reading the letter for a while after. I could feel he was still hurting, which made me worry that he still cared for her.

I wasn't sure if he still had feelings for this woman or was just worried about getting hurt again… but I needed to figure it out for my own peace of mind. It took most of the day for me to process this new information, and I knew that in order to make this work, we had to push through these situations and put them behind us. It was the first day of our time together this trip and we were just beginning to discover things about each other's pasts and who we are as people.

That night he took me back to the restaurant where we first met. It was late and we were tired, but he knew I wanted to retrace the steps of our first meeting. As we sat in the restaurant, he looked into my eyes and told me how he never dreamed we would be here again. After many years of little contact, I had started to think the same thing, yet here we were and I wouldn't have changed a thing. The restaurant seemed a little different the second time around, but things always do. Our memories are always altered to a degree; the way we want to remember things rarely reflects their true nature completely.

The next day we jumped in his car and drove to Barcelona, which was a four-hour drive from Madrid. During a Skype session, I had told David about a trip that I had missed out on to Barcelona through my company. They were going to stay in a nice hotel and go to Gaudi exhibits and see other types of incredible art. Along our drive, I asked him if we could drop by the hotel my company had booked, the Arts Hotel, so I could check it out and see what I missed. I had heard a lot of good things about this spot and was curious. Although we had a pretty full schedule, he said he would try to fit it in.

We talked for most of the drive. David loved to talk about his country and seemed to have a wealth knowledge of the various areas along the way. He described the colors of the soil and explained the composition of different types of soil, clay and sand. He marveled at how even slight changes in things like soil composition and climate could affect the grapes. He told me to remember so I could compare the soils of his vineyards once I saw them. I was happy that my previous wine studies were helping me in the current moment. I had always loved how David seemed so connected to the land, and I could listen to him talk for hours.

At one point, I asked him if he had any music we could listen to. He said he had something that he thought I might enjoy… Michael Bublé started to play and I recognized the album that I had sent to him on his birthday two years ago. He gave me a pleased look and said he never forgot about me. Tears welled up in my eyes and I leaned over to kiss him. For years I was certain that everything I had sent to him was forgotten, along with his memories of me. But the more he revealed himself to me, the more I understood that I was always in his heart, just as he was always in mine. He told me that he had kept every card I sent, every letter I wrote, and he even had a file in his email that saved every message I had sent to him over the years. He put on the Sara Bareilles song for me, and we went back and forth playing songs that reminded us of each other over the years. In his mind, I was the one who didn't share my feelings with him in Chicago, and while I thought he could feel them, in the end he needed to hear me say it. He felt that he had shared his feelings with me and maybe he did, but I wasn't in a place to accept them. He played a song in Spanish for me from Julieta Veneta that was very telling of how he perceived me over the years. The story tells of a wolf (i.e., me) that becomes very strange and moody over time, representing my unpredictable emotions with him over the years. The name of the song was "Lemon y Sal" and symbolized his continuing love for me no matter how strange I had acted over the years, he always loved me regardless.

Through the years of my internal struggles over David, I had always taken for granted his comprehension of the

English language. I knew his English wasn't great, but because we had always communicated in English, I assumed he understood more than he actually did, which was in part why we had so many misunderstandings over the years. Yet there were still so many questions in my mind about why it took him so long to respond to me in the past, especially my heart-wrenching confession he now jokingly called "The Book." He had partially explained things, but I needed more answers. Other than recently ending a relationship, our language barrier was once again at fault for this as well. He shared that when he received the letter, he opened it and tried to read through but couldn't quite understand the content. His best friend Sergio understood English much better than him at the time, and so he asked him to interpret the letter. As he translated the first page, Sergio started to understand how personal the letter was. He told David that he couldn't help him, as the letter was too personal and was only meant for David's eyes. He told David he would have to interpret the letter on his own. And so, without help, this took time as both the language and the deeper meaning of the words was a lot to digest.

As we pulled up to our hotel in Barcelona, I noticed the sign "Hotel Arts." David didn't want me to be sad that I had missed the incentive trip through work, so he decided to recreate it for me and booked the hotel for our stay. It was a phenomenal hotel, a five-star accommodation with every luxury you could imagine. We checked in and decided to soak up the room for a bit before venturing out for the evening. I had noticed how David was more sensual than most men, and I attributed it to the fact that his livelihood was based on senses, most notable, his sense of smell. He was always telling me how much he loves my scent, and when he would get close to me, he would inhale deeply as if to breathe me in and evaluate the distinct aroma of my being. He said no matter what I do, he could always smell me… even when I was showering. If he walked into the bathroom, he noticed my smell lingering amongst the perfume of soap. It made me feel a little self-conscious, but it seemed to attract him to me, so I just went with it.

That evening as I was getting ready for dinner, I walked out of the bathroom and David was on the bed watching TV. There was a Chanel ad playing, and after it ended, David looked up at me and said that he loved this commercial. He tossed me on the bed, breathed me in and explained that the 30-second story was about a man who finds a woman by her scent. "Melanie," he said, gazing into my eyes, "in the years we apart, I never forget your scent." I was a bit concerned but figured my smell had to have been pleasant to him, so I eeked out the meager response, "Oh, that's sweet." In one of our many misinterpretations of each other's language, he assumed I was saying that I smelled sweet, so to clarify his point, he said, "No, it is not sweet, it's animal." Later on I shared this story with a gay friend of mine, Spencer, wondering how I should interpret what David had said and worried that maybe I smelled like a wet dog or something. My friend responded, "Absolutely not! He meant the exact opposite and it is the highest compliment. He's talking about pure primal attraction. Woman, you should have ripped his clothes of immediately!"

That night we had dinner in one of the hotel's restaurant, Enoteca, a spot graced with the two Michelin stars. We ordered the tasting menu paired with wine recommendations from the sommelier, a friend of David's. As we worked our way through the menu, I was able to try one of David's very small production white wines, Thousand Milks. It was divine! Complex with structure, yet not overpowering and soft, just like it's maker. This was the first of David's artisan wines that I had ever tasted, and the experience confirmed my belief that David put his heart and soul into his wine.

Our time in Barcelona was full of beauty, both in the process of getting to know each other more deeply and in our surroundings. David's favorite architect was Gaudi and he knew I wanted see his work, so we combed the city to find all of his masterpieces: La Sagrada Familia, Park Guell, Casa Batillo. His work was truly breathtaking and unlike anything I'd ever seen. Our nights were spent perusing the streets of Barcelona, running from tapas bar to tapas bar, which I always found challenging as I wanted to spend time and relax in each place. But the culture demands quite the opposite: You have one tapas and one drink, and you are off to the next location. The Spanish were relaxed in almost every way except when it comes to tapas. We were falling more in love with each experience together and each new discovery we made about each other. I never wanted it to end.

After leaving Barcelona, we stopped for one night to spend time with a friend who lives in Sant Celoni, a small city outside of Barcelona. David had brought a bottle of champagne and two bottles of his wines to enjoy over lunch with Marc, whom he hadn't seen in a while. In true Spanish tradition, the lunch was late and long, observing *sobre* mesa — long conversations at the table after the meal has ended — and we consumed a lot of alcohol. Everyone else had cleared out of the restaurant, yet there we sat continuing to enjoy our drinks. The chef emerged from the kitchen, I assumed to politely ask us to wrap up and get out. I quickly discovered she was a friend as she pulled up a seat next to David while he poured her a glass. I was three sheets to the wind by this point and bright red from the alcohol, ready to take a siesta, dreaming of lying in a cozy bed and drifting off into a alcohol-induced sleep. We sat there for another 40 minutes or so, and to my relief David informed me we were going to check in to our hotel. We said our goodbyes and zipped off to our temporary home. As we entered our room, I collapsed on the bed ready to sleep in a matter of moments. I heard David questioning my actions, and as I opened my eyes I saw David ready to go with keys in hand. This language barrier was about to kill me. I had no idea that he only planned on dropping our bags in the room. I needed to sleep! David pulled my parched body out of bed, and the only thing that slightly motivated me at this point was the thought of water, which the typical Spaniard drinks sparingly.

We proceeded to join David's friends at a bar a couple of doors down from the hotel, and their first question directed at me was regarding my drink order. The thought of alcohol at this point wasn't the least bit appealing, so I ordered water. If I didn't know any better, I would have thought I said a vulgar swear word by the looks on everyone's faces. David tried to humor me, "You can't order a water! Would you like wine? Is 70% water." Of course, I didn't. I wondered what was wrong with these people. How could they not be just as thirsty as me? A beer was placed in front of me and, defeated, I took a sip. The next thing I knew, we were headed to dinner, and while I realized that it was after 9 p.m., I couldn't even begin to think of eating another meal. My stomach was still digesting the food from lunch!

Nonetheless, we ate more, drank more, found a club and danced, and by 2 a.m. I thought I might die of many things, primarily exhaustion. I kept telling David that I was tired and wanted to go home, and for the first time, I thought he actually appeared inebriated. He acted like he couldn't, or didn't want to, hear anything I said. He was elated the entire time and I felt that my presence at the party made his night. At one point, he told me he loved me, and while I wanted to be happy about those words, I responded, "If you love me you will take me home. I want to go home NOW!" I felt trapped, exhausted and angry.

Hours later, the group started to emerge from the club and I expected that sleep was near. We jumped in a taxi and started to walk down a small street to a door that did not look familiar. I was completely confused, wondering if this was a back entrance to the hotel, and as we ascended the stairwell, I realized we were in someone's home. I couldn't stand it anymore. I'm not one to make a scene, but everyone was so drunk I figured they would never remember, so I stormed up to David and demanded that he take me to the hotel. He looked at me with a look of confusion, and I couldn't seem to form one word in Spanish. Finally, I walked into the living room and snapped to one of the girls (who spoke no English), "*Dónde está el hotel*?" She pointed, "*Derecho*." At this point, I walked up to David and told him I was out of there, and the only thing I knew was that I was headed in the same direction the girl pointed, even though she pointed to what I saw were empty streets. Thankfully, something triggered in his drunk brain and he followed me. He didn't have a clue how far away the hotel was and it could've been miles down the road. I was exhausted and frustrated with him. The hotel ended up being just a block away, and had I known this I would've retired hours before. This was the first time I ever saw David drunk and I hoped it would never happen again, as it greatly amplified our inability to communicate effectively.

The next morning we emerged exhausted, and David was a little hungover. Our next stop would be the biggest challenge for us both — his home, Rioja — and my true test for David's intentions. I wondered, *Would he share me with his friends and family and present me as someone whom he is planning on making part of his life? Or would he choose to hide me from everyone so no questions arise about who I am and what the future may hold?*

We loaded up the car for another journey of discovery. David loves surprises and it was time for another one, so once again I was left guessing as to what was in store. He did mention that I would meet his mother, as she lived in his home, but he warned me that she speaks only Spanish, and so she might be difficult and apprehensive. That was just what I needed to hear — that his mother already didn't approve of me! I had butterflies in my stomach at the thought of meeting her. David told me he would have to work a little during this time as well, so I assumed I would meet his partners at work, but this was all conjecture.

When we arrived, his mother was home playing cards with her friend. While David was right about her not speaking English, he was wrong about her demeanor. I was pleasantly surprised to find her kind and welcoming. As I spoke with her, I couldn't help but notice the decorative candle that sat next to the TV. It was the candle that I had sent him for his birthday after our time in Chicago. A warm feeling of satisfaction came over me. We settled in for the night, ate dinner and unpacked our belongings. I looked at the bookshelf in his room and one in particular immediately caught my eye, "The Alchemist"! Once again, Darrell was right. It was then that I realized since reconnecting with David, my reoccurring dream, the one that haunted me for the past few years, had disappeared. I had spoken to several people about the dream, many of whom interpreted it to mean I had something I needed to get off my chest. The fact that the dreams stopped happening after I told David how I felt about him made it clear that the interpretations were spot on. Again, I wondered if my journey would one day lead me "home" to a life with David in Spain.

The next morning we headed to David's beloved vineyards. Small and unassuming, they had a stunning ambiance that stemmed from the fact that they were in a more natural state, which in modern agriculture isn't always considered a good thing. Compared to his well-groomed neighbors where the only thing you saw were vines, David's vineyards looked wild as he allowed natural herbs to grow and share the space with the vines. He claimed that when you taste the grapes and the wines, you can often pick up hints of the wild rosemary and fennel that shared the land. He didn't use chemicals or irrigation, and always spoke of the importance of his vineyards being full of life and energy and growing in harmony. Seeing David's vineyards brought back a memory of the time he sent me a photo of himself posing in his vineyard, a boyish grin on his face, standing next to a bird's nest that had grown into a vine. Now I understood that his smile was reflective of the simple satisfaction that life could happen in his land without danger.

David pointed out characteristics of the soil and how light it was in comparison to the dark red soils we had driven through to get here. He explained that many people don't understand the depth and complexity of Rioja, or how different the subregions truly are.

After visiting the vineyards, we headed to the winery, and he showed me the barrels filled with his wines while explaining some of the process. I could feel that he was proud of his small production wines and how they were created naturally, not by a machine, technology or chemicals, but through the natural method of hard work and passion. David introduced me to the owners of the winery, who allowed him to make his own personal collection of wines from his vineyards under their roof in exchange for his consulting services. David explained that before he arrived, they were potato farmers who knew nothing about wine. His work was to make their wines, teach them about the business and grow their reputation in the market. They were a husband and wife team who greeted me with smiles and a lot of Spanish at a very fast pace. I tried my best to keep up, but they spoke so rapidly that I understood very little. While I couldn't comprehend much of what they were trying to communicate, I got the impression that they were good people and were very happy to see David with me.

That afternoon I joined David in his office while he was doing some work on the computer. There was a large map of the world with pins in every state or country that had a distributor. Most of the states were the larger markets like New York, New Jersey, California, Florida, and then in the middle of the ocean he had a pin on Hawaii. I knew the total population of my state was just over 1 million and it must have paled in comparison to his other markets. I asked, "David, all of the states where you have distributors are major markets except Hawaii. Why did you decide to distribute in Hawaii since it is such a small market?"

He stopped what he was doing and looked up at me, smiled and answered, "This is a good question. Why do you think I distribute in Hawaii?"

I thought back to the first time I saw his wine on the

shelf, when I took a photo and sent it to him in Spain and he never replied. I would never have dreamed that he brought his wines to Hawaii just so I wouldn't forget about him. He shared how he attended a trade show in San Francisco and met Tom Gibbon, the vice president of a distribution company in Hawaii. He approached Tom and told him he wanted to distribute in Hawaii because there was someone special to him there. Just when I thought David couldn't outdo himself, he shared something new that put my head in a spin. Could this really all be true? All those years we tried to complete our lives with other people and things to fill the gap that was missing, but our egos prevented us from being honest about our feelings. I wondered, *If I hadn't written to him, would he have reached out to me and told me how he truly felt?* I once read that your soulmate can't see past you, and I knew that no matter how hard I tried, I could never get him truly out of my heart. I wondered if he struggled with the same issues as well. If I hadn't put my heart on the line, would we have both suffered in silence together, yet apart?

I started to get sick the last few days in Spain, but tried to keep my level of activity up knowing that time was passing quickly. One day David took me to Laguardia, a small medieval village in the heart of Rioja Alavesa. As we walked through the small stone streets, he spoke of his dreams, I suspected to see if I pictured myself in them. I felt he was digging to see if I would be interested in pursuing our dreams together. We scaled one of the mountains lining the horizon from Laguardia to his village of Elvillar, with the goal of capturing a view of Rioja Alavesa and its vineyards from a birds-eye perspective. A break in the forest appeared and David pointed out to the horizon at piece of land high on the hill and said, “One day I want build my winery there, outside my town Elvillar, and I also want own small hotel in Laguardia for friends and customers can stay when visit.” Funny, before I moved to Hawaii, I had always dreamed of opening a bed and breakfast there, so his dream fit perfectly into mine. I had studied the hotel business in college and worked in the industry up until the last five years. I could easily visualize my future with this man and couldn’t see any other future outside of him. It seemed everything in my life up to this point was preparing me for this.

The last full day of my trip, David wanted to take me to a wine museum a few villages over. We paid for our tickets and David requested a translation device so I could understand the exhibits. He looked at me with a surprisingly serious face and said, “If you want be part of my world, you need understand everything.” As we walked through the different sections, we didn’t speak, and before moving on to the next display, he would confirm that I understood what I had just learned and ask if I had questions. The museum went into great detail about the process — soils, corks, barrels, everything that is involved with turning grapes into wine. While his demeanor was solemn, I was happy to know that he was visualizing his future with me in it.

After we left the museum, David took me to Briones, a small village close by. On our last night together, we walked along holding hands and I could practically see the wheels turning in David's head. He started firing off questions, which after awhile started to feel more like an interrogation. The next thing I knew we were in the car fighting. I felt he was pushing me away, and part of me wanted to defend myself by running and putting up a wall, but something inside me told me to fight. At one point, in a hostile tone, he asked why I was there and what my expectations were of him, almost as if he felt pressured by my presence. I stood my ground and told him that, yes, I did have expectations and that I came here to see if we had a future together. I didn't let him manipulate me; I had a feeling this was a test to see if I would play games and lie about my feelings, but I didn't have the patience or time for manufactured conflict. We argued for almost an hour and then, seemingly pleased by my response, he agreed with me about the reasoning behind our time together in Spain. It was a first step to see if our visions were aligned and I had passed his test. I knew life with him wouldn't be easy. I had a feeling he would constantly test me to see if I had the fortitude to stay and fight, or if I would run at the first sight of trouble. He was unlike any man I had ever met.

The next morning we woke up before sunrise and drove into Madrid. Our departure, while difficult, wasn't as bad as it could have been as we knew in just one month we would be together again in Hawaii. It was clear that David still wasn't comfortable with goodbyes. He wanted it to be short and sweet with little emotion. As I passed through security, I looked back to find him and he was almost halfway down the corridor. When he walked away from me, he didn't look back. Looking back was too hard for him.

CHAPTER 11

January 10, 2011

The holidays came and went, and before I knew it, I was picking David up from the airport for his six-week vacation in Hawaii. We planned on living together under my roof as another test run of our compatibility, which provoked laughs from a few of my friends who insisted that any man would fall in love under the seductive charm of Hawaii. Perhaps I had a slight home field advantage, but the thought hadn't even crossed my mind.

I signed David up for an English class twice a week during his visit, since it was his mission to become fluent. We also made arrangements to travel to Kauai and Maui. It was nice having him at my house. On the days he didn't have English class, I would come home to a clean house, and he would run errands if I needed him to. He proved to be quite easy to live with — clean, thoughtful and loved to cook. David and I spent many hours at the beach, meeting my friends, going to dinner, and he even did an interview for a new wine-themed radio program. We went on multiple hikes during his visit, and he was able to see firsthand how hiking helped to ground me and clear my mind.

The very first hike I took David on was Makapuu trail, a short, paved path overlooking the ocean. Hapa accompanied us, although I knew from prior experience that the sun-scorched terrain was hard on his paws. We decided to explore another connecting trail that wound down the arid and hot rocks to beautiful tide pools that butted out into the ocean. I expressed my concern about Hapa's ability to handle the trail's steepness. He gave me a look of disbelief and said stubbornly, "It's a dugh!" in his thick Spanish accent. As we ventured down the side, I could see Hapa was starting to struggle. In addition to the hot sun burning his paws, he had surgery on his knee years ago and I feared he was susceptible to re-injury. By the time we got to the bottom, Hapa was done; he wouldn't go any further. He just lay down on the blazing hot, flat rocks and panted. I was distraught by his inability to continue on, so I told David that I didn't think he could make it back up the hill. David rolled his eyes, walked over to Hapa and, in a firm tone of broken English, encouraged him to get up. After a few minutes of coaching, it became evident to him as well that Hapa was going to need assistance getting back up the hill. His 70-pound stature was too much for me to carry, so that left David as courier. Luckily, he was an extremely strong man with thighs that seemed to be made to handle carrying a heavy dog up a steep and somewhat treacherous slope. Knowing he had no other option, David reluctantly picked Hapa up, threw him over his shoulders and asked me to lead the way. I couldn't help but laugh (mostly on the inside) at the unusual sight of David carrying Hapa like a sack of potatoes around his neck. I did my best to follow the markers to guide us up the hill. We got a little off course a few times, much to David's discontent, but eventually made it back to the top. While he was a bit annoyed at the fact that my "dugh" wasn't like the "dughs" he had in Spain, his only complaint afterwards was the fact that he didn't like feeling Hapa's penis on the back of his neck. This comment stated in his broken English made me laugh so hard, I had tears running down my cheeks. This was often the case — something that was funny to begin with would be amplified by his mispronunciation or a misused word: "He peni touch my negth!"

While everything seemed almost perfect, there were some issues that we struggled with as we got to know each other. For one thing, I was concerned about David's incessant questioning of my past and how that related to the person I am today. It was clear that the more he grew to love me, the harder it would be at first, because the road to trust with him was a long one. I imagined he had a devil on one shoulder representing his past insecurities and an angel on the other. The real David, the true man I adored, was buried deep beneath a challenging and often disappointing past. He seemed to be constantly wrestling with an internal conflict: One side of him wanted to know all of the details of my past, but when presented with the information, he would turn and use it against me. At times I felt I was dealing with a child and not a grown man. I didn't want to share my past with him in the first place and only reluctantly did so. I felt strongly that our relationship shouldn't be based on our past, but instead should focus on the current moment and, if everything worked out well, our plans for the future.

David proved to be more stubborn than me at times and we wasted a lot of hours arguing over things from my past that couldn't be changed. I had made a lot of mistakes in my rebellious teenage years and partied in college quite a bit more than him, but I couldn't understand what this had to do with us in the present moment. We were both in our mid-30s now. Why did he want to torture me for my past? He knew his perspective was selfish, but no matter how hard he tried, I could see the devil on his shoulder winning. I tried to avoid answering his questions. Rather, I would point out the fact that no matter what my answer was, it wasn't what he wanted to hear… I had experimented with drugs, I had dated other men and yes had even been married before. He wanted a perfect innocent virgin and that wasn't me. I tried to allow him to deal with his demons while I stood waiting on the sidelines, but sometimes no matter how far you feel you are from them, the demons escape only to come out and bite you.

I had told David about Cynthia, my very special chiropractor friend, and how she had uncovered my deep issues about him and prompted me to write the letter. I asked him if he wanted a session with her, set up the appointment and dropped him at the office with plans to pick him up an hour later. As I walked into the office to retrieve him, his expression read as if he had seen a ghost, but didn't want anyone to know. As we were walking to the car, he kept staring at me and I knew he had something to say. "Why do you keep looking at me like that?" I said. "How was your appointment with Cynthia?"

With huge wide eyes he replied, "She read my mind! I don't like. She could push arm and tell what is in my head. I do not like."

I was sure there were a lot of dark secrets in his head, so I laughed at his reaction of disbelief and fear. I could tell he was scared yet intrigued and wanted to go back. I had assumed her "gift" wouldn't translate with the language barrier, but it did. She had the ability to tap into truths that most of us don't want to face, but just like me, his fascination with her intuition had overridden his fear of facing his demons. We booked another appointment for the following week.

David was part of the 90 percent of people in Spain who were Catholic. While he mentioned several times that he never planned on getting married, it was clear that this was a thought that was planted in his mind and seemed to take root and grow, rather than something he truly felt in his heart. One issue that seemed to constantly rattle him about us was the fact that I was divorced. He seemed to be ok with the fact that I wasn't Catholic, but the divorce challenged his ideals. The Catholic Church is much more conservative in Spain, and if you are divorced, you simply could not get remarried in the Church. I didn't believe David at first and did some research on my own, which confirmed everything he had told me. Feelings of regret and hopelessness started to well up in me once again.

Towards the end of David's visit, we planned a trip to Kauai. We were excited to hike, go on a helicopter ride and enjoy the luxuries of the hotel. You would think that nothing could ruin such a beautiful trip, but David had been with me for over a month at this point and was starting to prove that he was able to turn even the most beautiful journey into something ugly. It seemed I couldn't do anything right. He would get jealous and suspicious of every man who had ever been in my life. No matter where I took him on the island, he would ask if I had been there with another man. My patience with his behavior was wearing thin. The sympathy for the bad relationship that caused him to turn into this jealous man was starting to surpass my own sense of self-respect.

After almost two days of arguing and defending myself, I felt drained. As we packed up our things and headed to the airport, I was looking forward to returning home. I was angered that I had devoted so much time and effort to showing him a good time only to have him make me miserable in return. I didn't say much during the long car ride. I had stayed and fought for us for long enough and I started to feel like it was not worth the effort. If his intention was to drive me away, he was doing a brilliant job at it… and I was about to crack. Suddenly, he became keenly aware of the difference in my energy. At first he decided to continue his antagonistic ways and accuse me of giving up on him, as if somehow I was a bad person for tiring of his relentless accusations and assumptions of my character. I finally exploded and told him that his behavior over the last few days was starting to make me think a life without him in it might be a better option. I could see the hurt in his eyes and I instantly felt bad for saying it, but it didn't change the way I felt inside. I asked him to give me some time to decompress by not speaking to me. Our flight back to Oahu was quiet and tense. If I had been wrong about him and this was not just a phase but part of his personality, I knew I couldn't last.

Things settled down over the next few days, partly because I think David realized he had crossed too many boundaries and was trying to make up for his bad behavior before leaving. Prior to his arrival in Hawaii, he had asked me to design a tattoo for him, something that would signify our time together in the islands. While I knew in my heart that I wanted to spend the rest of my life with him, other than his reference of marriage in the Catholic Church, he had never expressed desire for a future together. But the tattoo idea was a clear signal that he was thinking the same thing. It was only fitting to go with a Polynesian design, so I researched a number of artists and found a woman who studied Polynesian art and history in addition to being a skilled tattoo artist. I sent her some of the themes we wanted to utilize — simple ideas like growth, love, trust and rebirth — yet she rejected these themes, claiming that the words didn't translate well and that we shouldn't mix symbols from various Polynesian cultures together. After weeks of getting nowhere with choosing a design, David and I decided to stop by a tattoo shop that I had passed multiple times. We talked to the artist and explained the concepts we wanted the tattoo to represent, but he, too, explained that by mixing the different designs from various cultures, the symbols would lose their meaning. However, he did say that what matters most is what the artwork means to us. The artist wasn't a friendly or talkative guy, but we liked his direct nature and the work that he had done in the past, so we scheduled an appointment for David the day before his departure. David had to remove the hair from his legs, and rather than going the easy way of shaving, he opted for wax to get the job done. I joined him for a professional waxing session and actually enjoyed his exaggerated reactions to each piece of wax being pulled off. I couldn't stop laughing as he repeatedly cursed at our wax technician in the best English he could pull together: "You very pretty but I HATE you!" We women don't really enjoy these things either, but we certainly seem to handle it much better than men.

The next day David and I headed to the tattoo parlor. The waxing had made his skin more sensitive, and I had the feeling he was in for another painful ride. I decided to step out and kill time while David finished his tattoo, which was rather large and would take hours. When I returned to the parlor, David had a tear in his eye. I asked him if he was still in pain and he looked up at me and said no. He told me he had been thinking of his time in Hawaii and ran through the list of all the wonderful people he had met —"Cynthia, Dean, Darrell and your dirty hippy friend." He wasn't saying it to be funny or rude but I laughed at his childlike honesty. After he was finished, the end result was a beautiful and rather large tattoo that covered the front of his huge thigh. The design incorporated the Maori image of *kuru*, a symbol of rebirth that represented both of our efforts to shed our pasts and start a new life together. Within the *kuru*, the artist included *lauhala*, a Hawaiian plant leaf, to represent the binding together or our new family, as well as a Polynesian arrow to represent the strength that will be needed for us to endure the hard times. David looked at me with his deep, soulful eyes and told me that I was now part of him and would always be with him. I had always thought the idea of getting a tattoo for another person was silly, but with David, it confirmed what I already knew inside — he wanted to spend the rest of his life with me. I mentioned that I wanted to do the same thing for him and get a tattoo that symbolized our future. I could see the excitement and appreciation in his eyes, but suddenly felt scared to go through with it. It wasn't the idea of having a permanent mark for this man, but rather the pain that I would have to feel and the fact that I am probably the most indecisive person in the world. I was never interested in a tattoo before and figured I was too old at 35 to be considering such things. Alas, I attempted to make an appointment before he left, but in the end, the stars didn't align and it didn't happen. He took the news personal and was hurt.

The following day I took David to the airport dreading the long awaited goodbye that seemed to be constantly integrated into our relationship. We knew we would see each other again in a few months but that never seemed to mend the pain. I returned home alone and my house suddenly felt so empty… as though all those years without him in my home never existed and I craved his presence.

David had mentioned that since reconnecting with me, his business seemed to be slowly improving. During his time in Hawaii, a number of things started to happen, one of which was his entry into the UK. A distributor there decided to carry his wines, and not only did they place large orders, but they preferred his personal artisan wines over the everyday wine he made for the winery where he consulted. This was good for David's future, should he ever decide to initiate a venture away from his current partner. David started to call me his "lucky rabbit leg," aka lucky rabbit's foot, but I found the error so endearing that I didn't have the heart to correct him. When he returned to Spain, he was working on a new label for one of his wines that had previously been using a "making a wish" theme with the symbol of a dandelion that has gone to seed. He wanted to carry this theme through on his new label. One day I looked in my inbox and saw an email from him with the words, "This label is for you," accompanied by an image of a young couple kissing under a falling star. He had created this label to show me that our wishes had come true, that all those years we spent apart looking up at the stars and secretly wishing to be together one day were all part of our story. Now we were together and in love and he was proud of me, proud of us.

March 2011

David had plans to attend a wine trade show in Düsseldorf, Germany, in March. Since I love to travel and had never been to Germany, I decided to meet him there. Our communication was always a gamble due to our native tongue differences, so while I was taking a taxi from the airport to the hotel, he was driving to the airport to pick me up — another miscommunication that provided just enough time to shower and get ready before he arrived at the hotel. He walked into the room and we embraced and start kissing. I tried to be nonchalant, but I was waiting for just the right time to surprise him with the fact that I finally did it — I got the tattoo from the same artist. He was able to use the same elements of the *kuru* and *lauhala* from David's tattoo to create a smaller and more feminine version for me. I had kept it secret for over a month and was ready to reveal it. I tried to encourage him to remove my pants, but I couldn't seem to pull it off naturally. The next thing I knew I was telling him in a rushed, unsexy tone, "REMOVE MY PANTS!" He looked at me with a confused expression, knowing that the request was out of the ordinary, but he is man and made sure to complete the task quickly. As he glanced at my hip, I could see the satisfaction in his eyes. David looked at the tattoo with great interest and appreciation, touching it gently like a piece of precious artwork and examining every inch as if to take a mental picture so he would always remember it. Suddenly all of the awkwardness of the moment was replaced with an intense and passionate desire to connect our bodies once again. I had always been paranoid making love to him in my apartment for fear that the neighbors would hear me, but in our hotel room I was free to be as loud as I wished. My entire body craved him.

David had made plans to meet his friend Toni, his distributor in Germany, for breakfast within the hour, so we were rushing to get ready and head downstairs to join him. On our way out, we noticed the door was ajar. My eyes opened wide and a wave of embarrassment came over me as I realized that the entire third floor must have heard our ruckus activities over the last hour. I covered my mouth with my hand to hold back a scream mixed with a bit of laughter and looked over at David pointing to the open door. We tried not to bring attention to our exit and slipped out as quickly as possible. David and I worked to contain our laughter as we approached the table to meet Toni. We quickly learned that Toni was staying on the third floor as well, which meant he heard me before actually meeting me and seeing my face. I was mortified.

Our time in Germany was very rushed as it was centered on David's business, and we spent every night out dining with clients and friends. One night we hit the town with a group of David's close friends who are also in the wine business. One friend in particular was a woman whose family is also in the winemaking business, and she proceeded to ask questions about how we met. I was consistently amazed at how David would reveal his inner beauty at the most unsuspecting moments, and how his words could be so profound. His answer to her was, "It is a beautiful history. Melanie shares it better than I," so I began to tell the table the story, trying hard to keep it as short as possible. I got right to the point, explaining how I had pined for David and how he would reach out to me only occasionally, seemingly stringing me along, only to find out that he had a girlfriend for a good period of time. I could feel emotions of anger and hurt welling up inside of me as the words came out of my mouth, and my voice seemed to change as the details unfolded. It was a sensitive subject for me that still evoked feelings of betrayal, although I knew these feelings weren't exactly rational. I shot David a look displaying my pain and dislike at that part of the story. David looked over at me, and in that instant our souls felt divinely connected, and he knew exactly what I needed to hear. He said, "Sometimes we need to have a bad experience first in order to truly appreciate what we have now." It took all of my strength to hold back tears and restrain myself from jumping across the table into his arms.

CHAPTER 12

The time we spent together was easy. We loved each other, liked the same things, and laughed and talked for hours. David and I made plans for our next visit together: San Francisco in April for my birthday. He had to be there for work, but it happened to fall over my birthday and I was more than happy to fly over to meet him and celebrate. He was always full of surprises, so the day of my birthday he told me to change my clothes into something more comfortable. I hadn't packed for comfort, rather for dinners and nightlife, so he treated me to new sneakers and a jacket. When I asked him why I needed to be comfortable, David simply smiled. He rented a car and started to drive into the country. I kept asking where we were going and what we were doing, but he would only make odd comments in attempt to throw me off. As the landscape began to transition to fields and farmland, I started to seriously wonder what the plan was. We drove by a farm of horses and David said, "You like horses, right?" I let out a scream of delight at the thought of going on a romantic horseback journey. As we continued down the road, I daydreamed of running horses and picnics. David pulled into an airfield, looked at me and said, "You ready?" I looked up and noticed a small airplane dropping people with parachutes and realized my "horse" daydream had been replaced by the horsepower of an engine that was ready to drop us from the sky. His surprise was skydiving! Thankfully I was ready for a good adventure, so we jumped together and I knew that life with this man would never be boring.

April 16, 2011

The evening of my birthday (which was also the anniversary of the day we met), we enjoyed a long dinner and continued the evening drinking champagne naked in our hotel room and talking for hours. Weaved into the conversation was the discussion of our future and what that would look like. Our relationship had been the most romantic story, up until that point. Our talk of marriage was just that, a discussion of how we could make it happen. We agreed that he would return to Hawaii in late June and we would get married. He joked around that he was waiting for me to ask him to marry me, so I called his bluff and got down on one knee and asked him to marry me. Until this day, he still teases me that I asked him to marry me, which I still defend with reverence. I knew this was destined to be one of those arguments that we would continue to have when we were 80 years old. He loves to get a rise out of me and this is one area where he is always successful in doing so.

The issue of marriage in the Catholic Church reared its ugly head once again, and all of my fears of disappointing David because of my past were eating away at me. He made it clear he knew I was the one for him and he would do anything to be with me, but he still struggled to come to terms with letting go of his dream of getting married in the Catholic Church. We talked endlessly about how to handle this, and I told him I would do anything to make it right. Unfortunately, the one thing I couldn't do was change my past. He had to find a place in his heart and mind to move past this. Eventually, we agreed that we would get married in neutral waters outside of the church, and would say our vows on a boat out in the ocean. It was the perfect solution to put David's worries to rest.

While the story of our proposal wasn't romantic, the idea of marriage felt completely different this time around. The proposal of marriage from my ex-husband from day one plagued me with internal doubt that I always brushed off as cold feet. This time everything was far from perfect, rushed, uncertain, risky and despite everything, I felt 100% certain I was doing the right thing. I assumed some of those same emotions would arise in my psyche this time around as well and was ready to deal with them, but it never happened. I was excited about the thought of being connected to this man for life. We finally had clarity in our lives now, we knew where we were headed. I would pursue work on the east coast and eventually sell my home in Hawaii. I knew my life would be in full speed preparing for the wedding which was only four months away. Yet, once again the planning didn't feel like work, as it did with my ex-husband. This time I was looking forward to planning the celebration of my future with this man. Granted we wanted to keep everything simple, fun and as un-wedding like as possible. Rather a party with few formalities.

June 3, 2011

We had one last trip planned prior to David's arrival in Hawaii for the wedding — we would meet in Japan in June. I love Asian culture, which was a good thing, because Hawaii (especially Oahu) was saturated with heavy Asian influences. I was once again tagging along on another one of David's business trips. He had recently started a new relationship with a distributor in Japan and was going to Tokyo so the distributor could gain an understanding of the man behind the wine. He would visit his customers and view their high-tech inventory systems to get a feel for how they operated. Just as I had expected, David's Japanese importers were a joy to do business with — hard-working, loyal, honest and reliable. They had been in business for over 30 years and many of the wineries that they represented had worked with them since inception. They believed in offering their clients not only an understanding of the wines they carried, but also a history of the producers behind them. I will never forget sitting in the boardroom with the owner of the company, along with his assistant and manager, when the owner asked David to send personal photos from his professional life so they could interpret his character and his philosophy. David informed them that he sent a CD of photos that included a picture of him harvesting grapes naked in the vineyards! The culture in Japan is to save face and avoid embarrassment, and as they all laughed at this vision I kept thinking that they were probably questioning the sanity of the man sitting in front of them.

That night the owner and his team treated us to dinner at a Yakitori restaurant. David had some strange ideas about how to uncover the true person hidden under a protective or professional shell, and that usually included excessive alcohol. We had wine with dinner, followed by saké. The owner headed home while his assistant, a very non-traditional feisty Japanese woman, and one of the managers, who was young and very polite, entertained us for the night. David was on a mission to get them drunk, and I could tell he was well on his way there as well — which meant his attempt to do "research" was soon going to be a moot point. Honestly, it was all a game for David anyway, because it was clear to both of us that these people were all of great character. I adored the woman because she seemed strong in mind, and while not allowing herself to stand out, she was definitely not one to follow cultural norms if she didn't believe in them. David kept pressing on and telling them that we needed to drink more and go to a club. This notion came up after he and the manager had done tequila shots, and I knew from experience it was all downhill for David, as tequila was a game-changer for him. As he was pushing for the next location, Hisae, the assistant, agreed to take us to a club. I was shocked to hear that this strong woman had succumbed to David's pressure. She led us through the streets and when we arrived in the front of our destination, I burst into laughter. She didn't disappoint me after all; she had walked us back to the lobby of our hotel! The next morning, David realized his plan had backfired. He lay in bed groaning and barely able to move due to a severe hangover.

One of the last days of our trip, we decided to take a day trip to Kamakura, a small city located about 50 minutes outside of Tokyo by train. We both had wanted to see Kyoto but time didn't allow, and learned that Kamakura was also a beautiful location to visit temples and shrines. We had been spoiled by our contacts in Japan who were great resources regarding local hotspots and eateries, and when we arrived in Kamakura, we felt a bit lost without their help. After a full day of exploring the temples and historical sites, we felt hunger creeping up on us. As we shopped, we made a point to check out a few local restaurants, all of which seemed to be full of tourists and overpriced. We stopped in a small antique shop to purchase a keepsake of our journey to decorate our home. The store was run by an extremely friendly local man who spoke little English. David and I found a large jade Buddha head that we both loved, as well as a painting with Kanji lettering that, according to the store owner, was created as a blessing for a home. We chatted with the store owner about how we were going to get the 40-pound head back to the hotel in Tokyo, and eventually on the airplane, and he graciously offered to wrap it for us in order to protect it. We agreed on a price and purchased the art from him.

I figured since the store owner was from the area, he could tell us where to find a restaurant that the locals enjoy. He tried to explain the location of his favorite spot, but when he saw the confused looks on our faces, he decided to go another route. The next thing we knew, he was closing his shop in order to walk us to the eatery, which was hidden in the back streets away from the busy main thoroughfare. We would have never found it without his help, and when we arrived it was clear that it was not a tourist spot. No one spoke English and he knew we wouldn't be able to communicate or read the menu, so he spoke to the hostess, got a table and joined us long enough to choose our food and place the order with the waitress. He also confirmed the cost of the meal so we knew what to expect. We tried to stop him from going out of his way so much, but he was so grateful for our purchase that he insisted on helping us. When he finally left, David and I were elated to be in such a hidden gem filled by local Japanese patrons. Our beers arrived and we toasted to the good fortune that always seemed to find us when we were together.

My flight departed prior to David's, and as always, he was happy to escort me to the airport. This trip was mandatory for him as I was carrying a 40-lb buddah head in my carry-on and a painting along with my bags. Luckily, I had used points to fly first class, so when David and I arrived with my multitude of luggage, the agent checking me in gladly took everything off my hands, no questions asked. Our goodbye was the easiest by far. We had so much to look forward to and knew that with all the preparations ahead of us that the time would fly by. I boarded the flight and settled into the luxury of first-class, feeling at that moment like my life couldn't be any better.

June 26, 2011

After a lot of planning and stressing, David finally returned to Honolulu. David had decided to bring his mother along to be a part of our special day. He hadn't spoken to his father since he was young and wanted to have some representation from his side. Due to the short notice and cost, she would be the only person from his family to attend the ceremony. He had always warned me about her volatile personality, but our first meeting in Spain was successful, so I welcomed her presence.

I picked them up from the airport and we headed

straight to my house. I had a two-bedroom townhome and they were going to stay with me until my house closed, at which time we would then move to my friend Dean's house. David and his mom settled into the house, she obviously wasn't used to sharing her space with an indoor dog and proceeded to pepper David with question about me, my house and my work. From her perspective, coming from a culture and time when the women didn't work and owning a house meant inheritance or a man to support you, my situation was rare. When David explained I had earned everything on my own, she showed little emotion. I wasn't sure if she was impressed or skeptical. I couldn't understand much of what she was saying, so I had to read her emotions, but overall she was sweet and seemed to want to chat and get to know me. I was excited to spend some good one-on-one time with her and looked forward to understanding more about the man I love through our interactions. Our time with her started off fine; she appeared enthusiastic about Hawaii and we had a lot of plans to keep her busy and happy. We took her to the beach, went out for lunch, got our nails done together. David clearly enjoyed seeing his mother and me get along, and snapped photos of the two of us in our pedicure massage chairs sitting next to each other trying to communicate as best as we could. David seemed to cater to her a lot and informed me she wanted a new bikini. Since she was a short, stout, rather large woman, trying to find a bikini proved to be quite a challenge. We hit three different stores and ended up at Macy's in the Kahala Mall. All of the women who worked there kept suggesting tankinis and one-piece suits, as there were no bikinis available in her size. I had even asked them to call other stores, but they had nothing. I was scrambling around searching for something that might work, when suddenly Lali snapped and screamed at me in a high voice right there in the middle of the store. Of course, my interpretation was spotty, but I knew she was more or less calling me stupid because there were fat people all over Hawaii and yet I couldn't find a bikini for her. With this explosion, David took the reigns and we left the store empty handed. I was in utter shock. Never in my life had someone gone off on me when I was trying to help them, and I couldn't understand what had happened. Did she think I was trying to embarrass or hurt her somehow? I felt bad not knowing what I had done to offend her and wondered why I was the target of her anger. After my shock wore off, I felt worried and when we arrived home I started searching the Internet hoping to find something that could be mailed to the house for her — an idea that David quickly shot down, not wanting to cater to her bad behavior. Hours later after passing the evening with her and witnessing her snide behavior for a duration of hours, my worry wore off and I was angry to discover this was part of her personality. David had warned me about her, but I never believed him because I had only seen her good side up until now. She had finally shown me her true colors and it wasn't pretty.

As David's mother became more comfortable with me and started acting more like her true self, the dynamic between her and I began to shift. I had been bending over backwards to make her feel comfortable up to this point, and rather than expressing gratitude, entitlement was the dominating character showing up. I noticed a split in her personality that would change, depending on who was around, usually with the goal of getting attention. She would be charming and pleasant in front of my friends, but morph into a different person when they left. It felt as if she was competing for their friendship, which I found odd. One evening, Dean and I were with Lali by the pool and she was sharing some stories about his childhood that involved his father. I was happy to hear something about this mystery man and I mentioned that we had passed some people in Laguardia one day who David said were part of his father's family. In Spanish, she quickly and rather defensively asked if we spoke with them. When I answered no, she said, "Good, because…," as she dragged her finger across her neck signifying that she would slit David's throat if he ever crossed that line. Dean and I looked at each other in utter disbelief about the behavior we just witnessed. I was all too familiar with this type of personality and now I was worried.

That night in the hotel room in San Francisco when we were discussing marriage, we started to grasp just how difficult it is to marry outside of your country, and we realized help was not only valuable, but also necessary. David and I hired a lawyer to work on processing the immigration documentation, as marrying a foreigner in the United States and allowing them to immigrate by means of marriage is not for the faint of heart. We had heard many horror stories of couples who had been through hell with the complexities of immigration, and thankfully we had no misconceptions about residency papers magically showing up at our door. I had a thousand things going on in my life, due to the upcoming changes, and we wanted to simplify our lives wherever possible. We had decided that for a few years, I would remain in my job, but sell my house in Hawaii and move to Boston in order to make the distance between us more manageable. So between training for a new division at my company and learning a whole new set of products, selling my house, buying a house, planning a wedding and entertaining guests, I was at full capacity.

In order to complete our immigration documentation, we had to have our marriage paperwork submitted immediately. We agreed on a marriage ceremony vs. a civil union, and that meant finding someone who could perform the ceremony and sign our paperwork beforehand. It's amazing how the universe works. Years ago when I first met David, I always visualized Darrell conducting our wedding ceremony, as he was a Hawaiian priest and such an integral part of our journey. At the time, all of my visions were only a dream and now here I was, asking Darrell to perform the wedding of my dreams. He gladly accepted and life was unfolding in front of me just has I had envisioned.

The paperwork to make our union official was completed before the ceremony rather than after, as we had to submit it for our immigration package. We met Darrell for lunch at Tango, a small little bistro in Kakaako. We signed the marriage documents over a meal. It seemed so simple until we arrived at the point when we needed witnesses. We had totally forgotten about this aspect! I quickly called a close friend, Lynley, who worked at Queen's Hospital down the road to see if she could slip away from work to sign for us. She agreed and was there to meet us in a matter of minutes. While we laughed at how utilitarian it all seemed, it was still important to have friends and not strangers acting as witnesses. I placed another call to Dean, who was allowing David's mother to stay at his house as a favor to us, and letting us use his boat and house as venues for our wedding. He was like a father to me and I wanted him to be our other witness, but he informed me that he couldn't get away from work to sign for us. Technically, the witness is supposed to sign in the presence of everyone, but clearly we were not following the rules to begin with, so Darrell agreed to let me obtain Dean's signature that night and then mail the paperwork in myself.

My last two months with David in Hawaii seemed to pass in a matter of minutes. As the date for the ceremony drew closer, at the last minute we decided to fly in his cousin from Spain to attend the wedding and to keep his high-maintenance mother company, as Dean was growing weary of entertaining her and my patience with her bad behavior had expired. In the days prior to the event, my sister arrived, as well as Anne from Chicago, Jeff from Portland, Sharon from California and my friends from Maui, Debbie and Mike. I also brought out my old friend Shane from Ohio and his girlfriend to photograph the wedding. The only person that was going to be missing, other than my mother, whom I had excused as she had recently been in Hawaii and I didn't want her to incur the cost of another flight, was my best friend, Keli. She was struggling with cancer, and I hadn't been the best friend to her throughout a personal situation with her husband, which meant I wasn't around much for her cancer treatments and this had taken a toll on our friendship.

I had asked Keli to join the ceremony on the boat, and she was the only friend from Oahu that was invited. I had reserved the ceremony on the boat for my guests who travelled either from other islands or outside of Hawaii, but she took it personal that her husband wasn't invited along and told me that she would not be attending my wedding. I was hurt, but I wasn't going to argue with her, as I could only imagine how many times I had hurt her over the last year. I knew she had been going through so much with her health and her husband, and the last thing I wanted to do was make it worse for her, but my hands were tied. There simply wasn't enough room on the boat.

The big day had arrived. We had planned to marry on Dean's Boston Whaler, followed by a reception in his house. I remember getting ready and feeling absolutely no doubts about the man that I was going to spend the rest of my life with. I spent the morning upstairs primping, and when I came downstairs to find David and start the celebration, the look on his face made me feel like I was the most beautiful woman in the world.

The boat was small and we managed to somehow squeeze 14 people onto it. The water line was almost up to the top of the boat, and it would rock when someone simply took a breath, but to us, it didn't matter; we were entranced in each other's eyes. Darrell conducted a beautiful Hawaiian ceremony and we received all of the little blessings that denote a sign of good fortune — a sprinkle from the heavens, a magnificent sunset, a perfect rainbow and an abundance of love from our friends. I couldn't stop smiling. I knew this was the happiest day of my life and I was marrying my soulmate, the man of my dreams. Just as he had done years ago, he looked into my eyes to make sure he could see his reflection in them, and he could, I was certain of it. The entire day, it felt like the two of us were in our own world. We were constantly looking into each other's eyes with amazement at how fortunate we were to have found each other and finally be together. We were totally in sync, both feeling there was no one else in the world and no matter what happened, we would be one after this day. I wondered what would have happened if I had had the courage to follow my intuition a few years earlier. Would everything feel as perfect as it did in this moment? Or, as David had said in Germany, did we need to go through our separate experiences in order to appreciate each other for who we are today? In the end, none of that mattered now. We were happy.

We headed back to Dean's house for the reception, and when we walked into the door, I was overwhelmed at all of the faces there to support us. These people had become my family in Hawaii and I didn't want to leave them. As I started to say thank you to everyone, I could feel myself welling up at the thought of not being close to them once I left the island. David quickly picked up on my emotions and took over for me so that I wouldn't completely break down into tears. We celebrated the evening with food, wine and friends. I had tried to learn hula for David, but didn't feel comfortable dancing in front of everyone. I convinced my friend Liane to dance her beautiful hula for both of us and for our guests. It truly was a perfect day.

A few days later, reality wiggled its way back in. David and his family were going back to Spain, and at the crack of dawn, I dropped them off at the airport. I kissed David goodbye and said a farewell to his cousin, Maitane, but his mother didn't say a thing — no "thank you," no eye contact, just a few grunts and she was off. Oddly enough, I realized I had grown accustomed to her behavior, and day by day I was learning more about the person she truly is and accepting her, knowing change with her was futile. I was to meet David in Spain in less than a month after I completed my training for my new job in Massachusetts. We were on to the next stage of our relationship, ironically starting our new life together very much apart.

CHAPTER 13

September 2011

When I arrived in Spain it was harvest season, David's busiest time of year. Our days were long and he worked constantly. I tried to help out when I could and was constantly asking him to give me jobs so I wouldn't get bored. One of my tasks was to push down the caps in the barrels every morning. I absolutely loved this chore and would speak to the barrels as if they were my children, telling them how much we loved them and how we expected great things of them. I would occasionally get caught by David, who would just look up at me with a wide smile and an expression that encompassed adoration and affections for my abnormal behavior. He seemed to accept me for exactly who I was, strange qualities and all.

After a week in Spain, I had to return to the United States to close on our new home in Massachusetts. When I arrived in Boston, there was a chill in the air and I knew it would only get worse with each passing day. I was about to experience my first winter in 10 years, and to make matters worse, I would experience it alone.

I had turned my life around completely, moved across the country, sold a home, purchased a home, started a new job and got married. With so many big changes, you'd think I'd be accustomed to transition by now, but my adjustment to Massachusetts was difficult to say the least. I hated the winter, wasn't familiar with the area, didn't have any friends and hated my new job. The people were different from Hawaii locals; their energy seemed to be so low and no one seemed happy. Or maybe I was just seeing in them what was happening within me. I missed my husband and I didn't want to be there alone. I also really missed Hawaii, so much so that I couldn't look at photos or even think about my island without coming to tears. I felt so far from friends and even further from nature. When I was upset or stressing in Hawaii, I would go into nature to ground myself and get connected to my emotions. I could remember hiking up to the top of Koko Head Crater and looking out at the ocean and the surrounding beauty, feeling as if all of my worries didn't exist in that moment. When I would return home, everything seemed somehow better. I didn't have that in Massachusetts and felt stuck and out in the cold. I tried desperately to find good in all I had — a wonderful husband (albeit in another country), friends (in other places), family and a good living that let me support myself — but something was missing and I continued to experience a nagging feeling that I had made the wrong decision.

When we committed to me moving outside of Boston, David and I thought that he would be able to visit at least every other month, if not more. Gradually, we were discovering that this notion was rather idealistic. It was much too difficult for him to be away for such a large chunk of time, so I spent much of my days alone. All of the good habits I had formed in Hawaii — positive thinking, exercise, balance — seemed to be thrown off by my plethora of life changes. When David would come to visit, life was bliss. We would cherish every moment, laugh, eat dinner together, do nothing and everything and be content in our unconditional love. But when he had to leave, he left a huge void in the house. I missed his presence and his warmth. I was able to appreciate that we were now together on paper, but I wanted more and started to seriously doubt that I could make it through more than a year without him.

As time passed, I started to settle in a bit more. I wasn't as upset all the time and sensitive to everything around me. I also got to know my neighbor, Colleen, who ended up being a godsend! She was a kind and generous person, and would help me when I needed it, whether that meant keeping me company, advising me on home issues since both of our homes were literally in the woods or watching my animals when I was away. I wasn't interested in making lots of friends in Massachusetts, and while I complained of being alone, I really wasn't interested in going out and being around people, unless it was with my husband. I didn't feel like I had a great deal in common with a majority of the locals that I met, and I knew that my time there was limited, so putting any effort into relationships seemed unnecessary. My only problem was making good use of my time alone. I spent most of my hours working or watching TV (something I had never done in the past), neither of which filled my soul. Thankfully, I had my animals to keep me company.

All I could think about was moving to Spain, yet it simply wasn't an option at that point. David was stuck in a dichotomy of sorts; he worked endlessly, morning to night, only to live paycheck to paycheck. His salary at the winery was menial, barely enough to pay the bills and support his mother, who didn't work or collect retirement benefits. Yet from the outside, people saw how his business was thriving and had no idea that despite his success, he was struggling to make ends meet. He had almost doubled his production of wines and was selling in 10 countries around the world. However, he and his business partner had totally separate visions for a business model. David was creative and enjoyed being able to produce small production artisan wines from not only his family vineyards, but also from various regions around Spain (and even a project in Germany). When he was free to do what he wanted, he produced beautiful wines that reflected his soul's passion for wine and life. His business partner, on the other hand, was in it for the money. He knew that producing table wine or young wine was the way to bring in a quick profit, and he operated with a one-track mind. Conflict stemmed from the fact that David's projects caused money to be spent on producing artisan wines, which are not cheap, while his partner spent even more money growing the young wine side of the business. Rather than growing at a slower pace and reaping some of the benefits, his business partner was constantly investing the profits into new vineyards and looking for opportunities to expand the winery, so in the end, money was always an issue and neither he nor David ever felt "ahead" financially.

David would speak to me about feeling burnt out and say he needed a break. It was clear that his energy was being squelched due to the tension of doing what he loved vs. making wine to make a living — and the fact that he was barely able to stay afloat didn't help matters. I encouraged him to pursue his dreams and separate his projects, so that he could do what he loved and make fine wine without having to answer to anyone. Everyone around him seemed to admire his work and believed in his abilities, and while he knew on some level he had an innate talent for winemaking, it seemed he didn't quite understand the depth of his potential. On one hand, this made him the humble man that he is, but on the other hand, it prevented him from taking risks that were necessary for growth in his career and his spirit. He had attracted a lot of attention over the previous nine months, which seemed to help him gain some confidence. I constantly tried to point out how much people respected and how his friends loved him, yet somehow the wounds from his childhood prevented him from truly believing in his worth. His mother had gone through bouts of severe depression and often thrived on other people's misery, and his father had left when he was an adolescent. Though he held his demons close, I was constantly amazed at how wonderful he had turned out. Despite all of the challenges growing up, his heart was as big as any I had known and his spirit was beautiful. He was the first and only man whom I had ever described as beautiful, and though he clearly was attractive on the outside, it was his inner beauty that shined most brilliantly, especially when he was in touch with his loving nature. Often times I had to be extremely centered in my dealings with him, as he could easily revert back to his mother's cynical and mean nature if triggered. It wasn't who he truly was, but rather a reaction to the environment in which he was raised.

I felt trapped in Massachusetts. I couldn't move to Spain because I was committed to a new job, and even if I wanted to move, David could barely support himself and his mother, much less me and my dog and cat. I would sit around wondering what the hell I was doing there and fantasize about finding ways out. I wondered, *Was I here going through the motions to financially support David until his fine wine business was separate, at which time I knew it would thrive, or was there another reason?* I struggled to find answers. After my job settled down a little, I started to compile all of my journal entries that began when David and I met. I was often amazed at the synchronicity that had occurred in my life with him and how painful those years were without him. I had spent so much time grappling with uncertainly and disbelief about what I was feeling for him back then, and wondering if those feelings were real or imagined. And then, in what felt like the blink of an eye, there I was, married to the man of my dreams. The fairy tale doesn't feel like a fairy tale when you are living it, it feels like life. But from the eyes of everyone around me, it was a story to be told. At least 30 people suggested that I should write a book and after a while, I decided it would be best to make good use of those nights at home alone and start writing the history of our romance. If, for nothing else, it could be a story to share with the children that we hoped for in the future, the tale of how their parents found each other.

Meanwhile, things seemed even more promising for David. The negotiations with his business partner were proving to be successful, and he was slowly separating his artisan and single vineyard projects away. He would still sell the young wines, but in essence would not be invested in the project, only pull a commission from sales. This would allow his creativity to ignite. But now he was faced with the problem of how to procure a winery without any money. I had a savings account, but it wasn't enough to sustain a business for much more than a few months. Something inside of me knew that if he just took the leap, the net would appear. He had searched around for investors and wineries and was starting to get frustrated when his luck suddenly began to change. People in the wine world started noticing him and his projects. He was receiving both national and international attention for his work, and it seemed that every week, something new was popping up about him and his projects.

Other than his family vineyards, which he cherished, David didn't have much to start with when he first began in the business. He used financial aid to get through college and worked part time in wineries in order to pay for his living expenses. He was a self-starter, unlike many of the other large wineries in Rioja that were family owned and thus had a hand up in the market through name recognition, history or inherited wealth. David was starting from scratch. And unless you have a lot money to invest in a winery, it is typically not a profitable startup business, at least not for several years. Look at the majority of the wineries in California — most are started by people with extreme wealth, because that is usually what it takes to survive in this business. Plus, a great deal of the free publicity from the large trade publications are directed towards their advertisers, and just as in any other business, these magazines tend to follow the money — at least so we thought.

March 2012

I called David on the way to work one day in tears telling him that I needed to see him. He still hadn't committed to visiting in April and I had only seen him for a few short weeks in February. I was miserable. He consoled me and told me not to worry and to check my email after we hung up. I did and to my relief he was planning on surprising me with a visit in April, but my emotional outburst forced him to leak the surprise. The news lifted my spirits immediately and now I had something to look forward to.

What seemed like days after hearing the news about his visit David broke more news and informed me that shortly after arriving in Massachusetts, he would need to return to Spain almost immediately, as he had some important business to tend to. My first thought was that he was leaving me *again*, however, he explained that he was expecting a visit from the magazine *Wine Spectator*, which was a huge deal, and he wanted me to join him for the interview. He said it was such an important time for him that he couldn't imagine being there without me. We used my airline points in order to enjoy a celebratory weekend in Spain for my birthday and his big interview.

He arrived mid-April and within days we were off to Spain. Our flight from Boston to New York was delayed, which caused us to miss our plane to Spain. When we inquired about alternatives, the only option available was a flight the next morning. We didn't have that kind of time.

David's interview was on Saturday, so taking a Friday morning flight was cutting it too close. We argued that we needed a flight out that night and we didn't care if we couldn't get to Bilbao; we would find a way to Spain if they would only take us to Europe that night. Thankfully, the airline found us a flight to Madrid that arrived the next morning! From there we needed to rent a car, and as part of my birthday surprise David had made lunch reservations (Spanish lunch at 3 p.m.) at Kaia-Kaipe, a fabulous seafood restaurant in Getaria near San Sebastian with an amazing selection of old Rioja wines. We were fortunate to find a rental car and drove directly to Getaria. I was exhausted and slept most of the way. David had the amazing ability to stay awake, and through my heavy snoring in the car, he got us there and even managed to take a few photos of me knocked out with my mouth wide open, which did not please me.

David and I could feel that his little business was about to experience a major growth spurt. He met with the editor of the magazine the following day, and I'm sure David's presentation was a shock. David picked him up in his banged-up truck, drove to the vineyards and allowed him to taste the wines. No frills because he had none to offer. When the interview was over, he dropped the editor at the hotel and noticed a black Mercedes pull up to whisk him off to his next visit, which was sure to be luxurious compared to David's farmer experience. But it was who he was; he was a farmer. He didn't have a beautiful winery and he wasn't rich, but at least he was authentic. We could only could hope the editor appreciated his authenticity.

A few days after the interview, we were ecstatic to learn that *Wine Spectator* decided to showcase a 500-word story on David, which would end up being a half-page with photos. Best of all, they would cover only his fine wines, his real passion. He would be featured next to famous wineries in Rioja, and the title of the article was "Six Winemakers Leading the Way in Rioja." It was just what he needed, not only to boost his self-esteem and confidence, but also to propel his work into the spotlight where it deserved to be. We spent the weekend celebrating with our friends in Spain.

The long weekend soon came to an end and it was time to return to Boston. Our flights home were long as we had two layovers — one in Munich and the other in Zurich. In Zurich, we had time between flights and decided to grab a quick bite to eat. The hours passed faster than we expected and the next thing we knew, the flight was about to board. We rushed to the gate, David made a quick last-minute run to the restroom, and we found our seats. As the plane took off,

David looked at his hand and noticed that his wedding ring was missing from his finger. In a panicked tone, he told me that he left his ring on the sink in the bathroom. I felt anger rising in me, but then I remembered how I am always pointing out the fact that he never wears his ring and assumed he was teasing me. I looked into his eyes for clarity and saw right away that he was serious. I could feel the regret and fear rushing through him as it hit him that he had just left a Cartier ring on a public restroom sink. The most important gift I had ever given him, a symbol of our marriage, was gone in a flash. I tried to contain my disappointment as I could see the pain in his eyes, and asked him why he took the ring off in the first place. He was always telling me that the edges of his ring were sharp and he couldn't wash his face with it on his finger. He wanted to rinse his face before the flight and had set it on the sink. I could've killed him, but the guilt on his face was so heartbreaking and he was apologizing profusely. I couldn't bear to make him feel any worse than he already did. I leaned over, hugged him, kissed his head and told him it would be okay. I could see his eyes were welling up with tears. We informed the flight attendant, but knew that we would never see the ring again, and at this point we couldn't afford another one. We took off in silence, both wondering why this had to be the ending to what we felt was a glorious weekend.

We enjoyed the simple pleasure of just being together, just the two of us, and the rest of his visit was tranquil for the most part. One point of contention that remained between David and I was the issue of my dog, Hapa, moving to Spain. Hapa always had a lot of health problems, one of which was allergies, which not only gave him a distinct smell but also made his white fur shed more than normal. This drove David crazy, but he was like my child and I loved him unconditionally, smells and shedding and all. I had gone through the grueling work of moving Hapa and Kitty from Hawaii to Massachusetts, and in my mind there was no question that they would both follow me to Spain one day. David often told me that it wasn't going to happen, which upset me. He knew I would never leave Hapa behind and that telling me such things bothered me beyond words. I felt it was his way of ensuring that I stay in Massachusetts to work in my soulless job that provided us with a decent living so I could continue to support us. I hated doubting his character, but when he purposely said things to upset me, I couldn't help myself. We had many arguments on the subject and I tended to be the one to end the discussion as my move wasn't in the immediate future anyway and I didn't see the point in fighting about it.

On the way to the airport with him once again, I started to get that painful feeling in my heart at the thought of him leaving me. David could sense it and he hated to see me troubled. He looked at me with comforting eyes and told me for the first time that Hapa would live in Spain with us one day. He continued, saying Hapa would have a beautiful history: He was born and lived in Hawaii, and his story would end in Spain with us as a family. I knew the moment he said those words that I was moving to Spain sooner than we had originally planned. He was softening, and it was just what I needed to hear. I had peace with the Hapa situation and was again reminded that he was a good person inside and could think outside of himself.

CHAPTER 14

May 2012

It was the end of May and I was headed back to Spain, this time for a much-needed vacation. Although I had only been in the job for seven months, when you aren't working a job that is your passion, it drains you and makes you feel lifeless. I was ready for a break, but when I landed in Bilbao, we hit the ground running. My visits to see David weren't vacations in the true sense of the word, as there was always plenty of work to be done. It was the time of year when the vines needed some TLC, and because he was working on separating the businesses, we couldn't afford to hire anyone to do the work for us. David always told me he preferred to do the work himself. He hoped that in the future his business would grow and stabilize enough to allow him to devote 100 percent of his time to working in the vineyards and making the wines, rather than focusing on administration or sales.

When pulling up to the vineyards, it was obvious which

ones were David's. First off, they were almost always old vines. Secondly, he followed the philosophy of biodynamics, which is an ecological and, in many ways, spiritual approach to farming. He didn't use chemicals, so all throughout his vineyards, there were weeds that needed to be pulled. This was the time of year to *espergurar* in the vineyards, which is thinning and pulling the green sprouts from the bottom in order to allow all of the energy of the plants to be focused on top where the grapes grow. We would work with our hands from sunrise to sunset. It seemed I touched every vine, talking to them as if they were eager children and asking them to please help their father produce a beautiful wine. I was sure the energy of my words would help to fight off any fungus or pest that might invade them and always enjoyed sharing my strange techniques with David to see his reaction.

I noticed a change in David when he was in his element. You always hear how when people are doing what they love, it doesn't feel like work. David was living proof of this, and I adored witnessing the alignment of his creative energy. I would tell him that he presented his wines well when he's selling them in the United States, but his true passion could only truly be seen when he was working in his element in Rioja. This man of few words could talk for hours about the region. He could tell you all the different soil types, microclimates, histories, weather patterns… He knows every little dirt road that winds around the vineyards in Elvillar and, for that matter, every region in Spain where he makes wine. When he's "in the zone," he opens up and all of his senses are elevated. When we step out of the car into the vineyards, his demeanor changes into a Zen-like state. He looks out over his vines with an appreciation that is almost palpable, as if these vines, which he worked alongside his grandfather since childhood, are his friends from youth. He takes a deep breath as if to evaluate the health of the land, and I can feel his inner peace. When he is taking it all in and setting his focus on the work ahead, it is clear to me that this is where he belongs.

We spent hours working the land, and to me it felt like doing yard work. After a few hours, my body would adjust to the manual labor and my determination to make every vine beautiful and healthy would strengthen. One evening we finished for the day and David asked if I wanted to stop and eat a *pintxo* (northern Spain's term for tapa) in Laguardia. It was a rainy, overcast Sunday and I looked sloppy from working all day, but I love Laguardia and figured the chances of running into someone I knew were slim, so I gladly agreed. As we pulled up, the streets were full of cars and packed with people, and David explained that there was a festival that weekend, the *Dia Del Gaitero*. We parked outside of the city walls and walked into the gates. Every time I return to this place I'm reminded of two things — when David shared his dreams with me and the absence of his father. The first time he took me here, we were in a bakery, and as a couple walked by, he pointed out that they were part of his father's family. The words were stated in a very matter-of-fact manner, yet I could tell that below the surface, he was sad.

As we meandered the now familiar streets, David once again took me to the place where, he said, just beyond it lay all of his dreams. Every medieval village has a church with a square in the front. David looked up at the church and commented on the beauty of the area. As we headed back through the small streets, we passed a couple in their 60s. David said "*hola*" to them and they greeted him in return. I thought nothing of it and we continued on. As I caught up to David, he grabbed my hand and told me that the man was his father. I had to stifle a scream and instead said, "What? Oh, I didn't really take a good look. I want to see him! I can't believe it!"

"Melanie, that was the first time I've ever said 'hello' to him," replied David. I looked at him with satisfaction and said, "Good, you *should* say 'hello.' He is your father. Maybe you should introduce him to your new wife?" We laughed, and while part of me was serious, I knew it would be awkward going from "hello" after 23 years to, "Hi Dad, remember me, your son? This is my new wife." Plus, we had worked all day in the vineyard and I wanted to look more presentable when and if I ever did get to meet him.

His father's side of the family was a well-known winemaking family in Laguardia, and as we headed down the block, David stopped in front of a window to point out his cousin's wine bottle display. I looked to the left and noticed his father approaching again as they had circled the block. My heart was racing. David didn't seem to notice and continued down a perpendicular street. I followed behind, looking back to catch a better glimpse of his father. I looked in his father's direction, and as our eyes met for a split second, we both realized we were doing the same thing and simultaneously looked away. I was surprised at how handsome his father was and how well he carried himself. I ran up to David and said, "Your father circled the block. I didn't want to say anything, but when I turned around to check him out, he was looking at us! When our eyes met he looked away. This is crazy! One day I want you to speak with your father!"

This was not the first time we had this discussion. David rarely spoke of his father and only recently had started to share more with me on the topic. I respected his privacy, so I tried not to push the issue, but I when the subject came up, I would always encourage him to forgive, not knowing what that might look like to David. Forgiving could just happen internally, or through written or spoken words with his father. It didn't matter to me, I just wanted that wound inside him to heal. After hearing the little bit of information that David shared and listening to the way his mother spoke of his father, it was clear to me. David's father didn't leave David, he left his mother… but by leaving her, he had no choice but to lose contact with his son. She and David were a package deal in her mind and I'm sure she made that clear to both David and his father. Over the years she had done what so many parents sadly and selfishly do — in their own insecurity, they paint a horrible picture of the other parent, which only serves to create feelings of pain, abandonment and guilt for the child, as they often feel it is somehow their fault.

I thought back to one afternoon in Spain when David's mom was showing David and me photos of her son as a child and came across photos of him and his father. One was of

David on his father's shoulder. I saw it and laughed and told David how cute he looked with his father. The next photo was David crying with his father, as if his father had done something to tease him and hurt his feelings. His mother, picking up on our interest in the photos, made a remark about how David often was unhappy with his father. Even though David was a grown man, she still tried to plant negative thoughts after all these years! I tried not to do the same thing with David and his mother by speaking negatively about her to him, as it served no purpose and my words would only hurt him. But inside I was angry with her for being so selfish and hateful all these years by keeping him from his father. It was clear to me that even though her son was a grown man, she was still trying to manipulate her son and paint an evil picture of her ex-husband. From an outside perspective, her actions were so transparent and only now was David starting to see through her lies and misrepresentations.

That night after seeing his father in the street, we were watching TV on the couch. David's head in my lap, he looked up at me and asked, "Do you think my father wanted to speak with me today?"

I could feel a lump in my throat forming as I quickly held back tears, "I don't know, honey. I find it interesting that he circled the block as if he was trying to run into us again purposely."

Suddenly, this strong man of 36 years felt like a child in my arms. His words enraged the protective emotions within me, and I wanted to tell him all of my very strong opinions on the matter and protect him from all of the pain in suffering in the world. I longed to go back into his past and fix anything that had ever hurt him. His words broke my heart. I wanted to reassure him and make sure he knew that his father left his mother, not him, and that all of the hate and resentment needed to be put aside. I brought these feelings up to him one morning as we were headed out to the vineyards. He agreed with me and, for the first time, actually showed some sympathy towards his father's situation: "You see how challenging she is when she's 'happy.' You can only imagine how difficult it had to be for my father to handle her when things were bad." He shared that they were going through severe financial problems when his father left. We agreed that should he ever form a relationship with his father in the future, his mother should never find out.

I just accepted the fact that his mother would be a challenge in my new marriage and I would have to rise above and be the bigger person in the relationship. Growing up with her, David had always been the adult. Now I would have to follow suit and be the bigger person. I appreciated that fact that she brought this wonderful man into the world, but I wondered how he would have turned out without his mom's negative energy trying to hold him down. I remember when we first reconnected he would say, "My mother is the only one who's ever been there for me and hasn't abandoned me." I later found out he was repeating his mother's words and I often wondered why some parents feel the need to control their children by planting insecurities in their little minds. David had such beautiful gifts and talents, but I suspected that the many years of hearing negative comments about the world prevented him from tapping into his gifts. He had been raised not to believe in love, not to trust, told over and over that he was unlucky, that the world was hard and the only one who truly loved him was his mother. Ideas like these prevent people from reaching their full potential and seeking what their soul desires most. Thankfully, through everything, David had at least pursued work aligned with his true talents, and I knew that with time, he would be rewarded for this.

As we traveled through Spain, I could feel the energy around David changing. He started to gain a following, and despite all of the challenges he faced growing up, his so-called "luck" was about to change. I sensed that things he had struggled with in the past wouldn't be a problem and doors would open up that had been closed before. His future was bright and together we could achieve all of our dreams. I could feel it in my gut, but at the time I didn't know how or when. I had faith that all of the stars would align in the near future. I just needed to be patient and have faith in this process that would ultimately allow us to have all that was meant to be.

David and I often spoke of children. I was 36 years old when we married, and while I never truly felt we were stable enough in our lives to start a family, I looked around and saw people with much less than us making it work. I stopped taking my birth control before we got married, but practiced the natural method one of my hippie friends used to refer to as "pull and pray." I started to wonder if we should just throw caution to the wind and stop worrying about being able to provide for ourselves and doubting our ability to provide for a child. David had always said that we would start trying once I moved to Spain, but I started to worry that waiting would jeopardize my health and put our potential child at risk. Once again, I had to find that centered place inside to remind me that I can't control these things and if I am meant to have children, they will come to me. I had always felt the energy of a son, which was perfect because one child, a son, was exactly what David wanted. I was fine with that, because I figured at my age, more children meant more work than my years would allow. One thing I was sure of was that my child wouldn't be deprived of any family, and he (or she) would have a grandfather, if he wanted to be involved, of course.

It was time to return to Massachusetts. I didn't want to leave, but then again, I never did. Not only would I miss the beauty of Spain, but I dreaded being away from the man that my soul had searched my entire life to find.

CHAPTER 15

June 2012

My routine life continued upon my return, however, this time the unrest in my soul seemed different, more intense. I felt as if the two-year timeline that I had originally set for myself in Massachusetts had to be shortened. The only thing keeping me from that drastic move was fear. David feared that he couldn't financially support his mother and me, and as things appeared at that moment, he was right. We both knew that, for the moment, my income was necessary. His negotiations were going well now, but developing a new business was still a work in progress. He was certain that he would rent a winery for his work during the harvest season this year, which would allow him to keep and eventually sell all of the fine wines he produced over the year. To keep an operation like that going, he needed to be able to pay rent and this was where I came in. We had spent many hours discussing what made the most sense for our future, and while my heart wanted to run to him immediately, I knew he needed financial security. After much deliberation, we decided to sell the house in Massachusetts. It was meant to be a home for our future family, but due to all of the changes in David's work that prevented him from being with me, we knew it would continue to be a large, empty home. Living in a smaller space made more sense — less maintenance, fewer bills and, most of all, less unused space. I contacted my realtor and set up a time to discuss the market and the right time to put the house up for sale. I seemed to be fixed on the month of August, but I wasn't sure if my intuition was telling me that something else was going to happen in that time frame. Regardless, I knew that in order to find out what was behind my focus on August, I had to just let go and be patient, and adopt a "wait and see" mentality. I reminded myself how the universe seemed to work in my favor when I stopped trying to control situations like these.

I met with my realtor the following week. After reviewing information about the market and timing, we decided that late August or early September would work fine. But before the sale could happen, I needed to tend to a few matters, including how I was going to ship all of my household goods to Spain. Up until sale time, we decided I would minimize my living expenses in order to have additional funds to help David cover rent.

I spent the next month pondering over all of the details and trying to decide what made the most sense financially for our future. June seemed to fly by and, once again, I was headed back to Spain. My visit seemed to be separated into two very distinct halves. The first part of the trip focused primarily on David's work in Rioja. He had told me about a winery in Elvillar that was the perfect solution to our problem, a winery and house in one! My heart skipped a beat at the thought of finding a real answer to the financial obstacle of David having to pay three mortgages — one for his mother's house, one for the winery and one for a home for us. Before I knew his mother, I had offered to live under the same roof with her until we could find another solution. Thank God for his insight on this matter; he knew such a thing was not possible and would wreak havoc on our marriage.

David had arranged to meet with the real estate agent on Monday morning at 9 a.m., so we headed to his village to take a look. From the outside, the stone façade had a significant amount of curbside appeal. As we walked into the house, it was clear that it needed a lot of work. Reminiscent of the 80s, the house was full of old furniture and in desperate need of updating. As we walked around the property, I became intrigued by the idea of a work-in-progress, but at the same time felt scared of all the work that was needed in the winery, which in its current state was an "illegal" winery that required many upgrades, to say the least. I wasn't sure what to think after leaving the structure, knowing that our future could hinge on the decision and we didn't have the money to waste if it turned out to be a bad move.

That same evening David left me alone at home, as he had dinner plans with a client that didn't include me. Before he took off, he pulled me close to him, wrapping his arms around me, and gazed deeply into my eyes as if it was the first time he'd ever seen them. He said, "Melanie, this night think in the home and tomorrow we will discuss it." I agreed and told him I would think it through. His mother eventually came home and I knew it would make her happy to feel included in the decision, so I sat down with her and made a list of pros and cons, and then translated them into Spanish. I didn't want the decision to be based purely on emotional reasons, and after looking at the list, it was clear that it wasn't. It made sense financially and I enjoyed doing minor renovations in homes. Plus, it had a nice yard for Hapa and a potential garden.

The following day we drove six hours to Galicia to

meet with a potential distributor for that region. The long car ride gave us more than enough time to discuss the home and whether or not it was right for us. David was putting a lot of emphasis on my opinion, and was clear that it was his desire to make sure I would be happy there. We discussed it until there was nothing more to say and on the drive home, I decided that I wanted to see the home once more before I left. I thought it would be good to walk through it when I didn't have so many people in the house like the first visit. This way, maybe I would feel a connection with the energy in the house and know that it was the right place for our future. We called the agent, who to our chagrin was unable to show us the house. David tried to explain that this was my last chance to see the property and that it was very important, but the agent was insistent that he couldn't leave the office. I proposed that we show up at his office and ask for the keys to go look without him. In the United States, this would never happen, but something told me it would work in Spain, and it did. We got the keys and were making plans for one of David's best friends, Chema, to join us. Chema was an engineer whose primary focus was wineries, and we wanted him there to give us an outside opinion and to advise us on the conversion of the winery to see if it was feasible.

We stopped to pick up Chema and were off to see if the

home was to be in our future. As we pulled up to the house, I tried my best to clear my mind so I would be ready to see any blazing signs that I might have missed on the first visit. As we moved from room to room, Chema offered perspectives on the structure and potential changes that could enhance the design. While he and David discussed the details, I used the opportunity to escape and spend time around the house alone. I calmed my mind and tried to just let my feelings flow. This home that had felt sterile during the first run through was suddenly full of life and possibility. I felt comfortable there and could picture David and I living a wonderful life together. I could even picture our son running through the hallway, a vision that made me smile wholeheartedly. We descended to the winery and I left the guys and slipped outside to roam. Quietly in my mind I consulted the energy of the house for insight on whether or not the home was for us, and if it wanted us to be there. The next thing I knew, under the blazing sun and 85-degree day, every hair on both of my arms stood straight up. This was a feeling that I knew well, from the many times when I thought of David and asked for guidance beyond the material world to give me a sign that he was "the one." On these occasions, I felt this same sensation, every hair on my body confirming my belief, so I knew this house would be ours. The man who built the house died at a young age during the actual construction, and

I knew he wanted us to continue what he had started but was unable to finish. We would love the home and bring it up to its full potential over the years.

CHAPTER 16

When we arrived back in Boston, our life was in full trajectory. David seemed to have a newfound confidence about him, a certainty about our future. All of his fear and worries about finances seemed to be replaced with a knowing that together, we could beat all odds. In the weeks following, it seemed all of the stars aligned in our favor and the universe was finally championing my entrance into Spain. David was meeting with all the right people, he had a photo shoot for *Wine Spectator* with the issue due out in October and he had put an offer in on the winery. I was beaming with anticipation, and then the news came: While the owners wanted more than we were willing to pay for the sale of the home, they were willing to rent it to us for 200 Euros less than we expected to pay! David and I discussed it, and we were fine with foregoing the option to buy. It actually worked out perfectly since we had even bigger dreams to one day build a brand new home and winery situated amongst vineyards and beautiful vistas overlooking his little town of Elvillar in the distance. David had taken me to a couple of locations where he was interested in building, but we both knew that these dreams wouldn't be realized in the immediate future. Upon hearing the news, I told David to sign the contract and take possession of the house in August in order to have the necessary work done on the winery prior to harvest. We were both jubilant about our future together. If I hadn't been a spiritual person prior to these events, I think I would have been transformed into a believer. I truly believed David and I had a team of angels working to bring us together. The events seemed to unfold with harmonious timing as we pursued our future, further reinforcing my belief that a higher power has no choice but to favor you when you work to make changes that are your true soul's desire.

One of David's major concerns was losing my income. At times, I would let his fears creep into my head and I, too, would start to ruminate over the "what ifs." It took a lot of quiet meditation and awareness to control the worrisome thoughts that would cross over from David to me. But I knew my life in Massachusetts wasn't my soul's desire. I was supposed to be with David, so I decided to tell (instead of ask) him that I was moving to Spain in February of 2013 and insist that he prepare both mentally and financially for this change. The news, of course, struck great fear into David once he realized he would need to provide for himself, his mother and now me. In order to relieve some of his anxiety, I told him I would not quit my company, but rather take a leave of absence. By doing so, they would hold a position for me in the company for three years. This was more for David's mental health than mine. I knew I was done with the pharmaceutical game. It had provided me with many wonderful friends and experiences, but it wasn't for me. The job too often left me feeling stressed, frustrated and unfulfilled. I wanted to take care of people and have them view me as an asset, not as a selfish, money-hungry representative.

It was time to start tying up loose ends in Massachusetts, which consisted primarily of selling the house. I had signed the contract with my realtor, who agreed to list the house in mid-August. My mother came to visit me one last time to help prepare the house for sale. I had maintained the house quite well, so there was little to be done, but we were determined to get it in prime selling condition. I had set my intention that the house would sell for a price that was fair to everyone involved, and I aimed to make back my investment plus the 5% cost that goes to the realtor. The timing was to be left up to the angels who seemed to be leading my journey. This involved a degree of letting go, which was still a very difficult concept for me. When anxiety would creep up, I would repeat in my head, *I lay the foundation for events to happen and then allow them to fall into place as planned.* From experience, I knew that when I actually executed "letting go" successfully, it often seemed to come with the biggest payout. So when it came to selling the house, I was determined to have faith in the process and avoid the temptation to control how it would play out.

David arrived in Boston with his cousin, Maitane, in the middle of August, right around the time that we put the house on the market. We paid for her trip so she could experience the east coast while I was living there. We were busy with open houses and realtor showings during his stay. While I so wanted to trust in the unforeseen forces, too often I found myself having expectations and wishing for the house to sell immediately. I had been enjoying a string of amazing luck, but I knew that expecting everything to happen exactly as planned was a bit too idealistic. The house had only been on the market for a little over two weeks when I had to depart once again for Spain for a two-week vacation. We hadn't had one offer yet on the house, so concern was growing, but I decided that the trip was a good idea. My dog Hapa would be out of the house and it would be easier to show the home during that time. The three of us flew back to Spain together and I used the flight to Spain to refocus my energy on the bright future that lay ahead, rather than worrying about the timing of my life. I had a lot of work to do on the house in Spain, primarily painting and cleaning to ensure that it was in move-in condition when I was set to return for good in February.

August 2012

David was busy working on the winery and preparing for harvest. For a few short weeks, it seemed as if our new life together under the same roof had already begun. We would wake up early and immediately start our day, usually working on separate projects in separate places, only breaking for meals and the occasional exchange of affection. I started to get a feel for how our new life would look, and the potential obstacles we might face in the process. I sensed a couple of things that would cause us a bit of stress once I made the move, for instance my poor grasp of the Spanish language and my inability to understand the road signs (and therefore drive) in Spain. David loved to speak English and I constantly catered to his ability to learn, but soon he would have to stop being selfish and speak to me in Spanish. I could tell he was trying to help me more, but too often he would either find my speaking errors cute or just allow me to slip back into English because it was easier. We had to tackle driving as well. David wouldn't believe me when I told him that I knew how to drive a standard transmission car (a common European stereotype of Americans), so the only way I was going to be able to prove it to him was to force him out of the driver's seat.

One evening we were driving along some of the vineyards dreaming about which plots we would buy and how our future would look. As David was maneuvering around the country roads, I asked him to stop the car and allow me to drive. There wasn't a soul in sight, so he considered it a safe option and handed over the driver's seat. It had been years since I had driven a standard, and while I knew I wouldn't drive perfectly, I didn't want to stall or jerk the car and give David reason to lose faith in my driving ability. He's the type of man who is too impatient to teach you how to do something, yet when you try it for the first time in front of him, if it's not perfect, he's immediately annoyed. Fortunately, I managed to pull off my claimed mastery of the standard transmission and drive us home safely. Both the language and the driving would have to be resolved rather soon once I moved to Spain because David was used to his extremely independent wife who gets things done. My transformation into a needy wife who can't function without the help of her husband would quickly grate on his nerves and mine, but that problem was months down the road and we could work on it later.

I had worked so much on the new house in Elvillar during the first week and half — painting, unpacking, moving furniture, shopping — that the remaining days were spent reading and relaxing. David and I would spend hours gazing out the windows from the living room of our home overlooking the beautiful Sierra Cantabria Mountains in the background surrounded by rolling hills of vineyards. The views were surreal and the energy was perfect. It was nice to have an entire month with my husband, uninterrupted. The only thing missing in Spain was my animals. I knew once they were there, I would be fully at peace.

The night before my flight home, my neighbor sent me a frantic email about my cat that had escaped from the house; she was unable to find him before her departure down to the Cape and was worried. My cat was not an outdoor cat, so I was panicked and spent the entire night texting and emailing, trying to find someone to rescue Kitty before night set in. Other than my other neighbors, who were not animal people, the only other person I knew was my realtor. I begged her to go find my cat. As I lay in bed, eyes wide open, I tried to sleep but was on edge, waiting for the sound of my phone to deliver the message of my saved cat. Colleen had called friends and neighbors, and everyone seemed to arrive at the same time on the mission to save Kitty. My realtor arrived first and told me that Kitty seemed lonely during the open house the week before. He had sat by her side the entire time wanting attention, and I knew if Kitty would come for someone, it would be her. I was right — by the time everyone got there, he was safely inside. I finally got her good news email telling me to get some sleep. Between the separation from my husband and my animals, I knew I couldn't stand it much longer. I needed my family to be in one location.

The next morning my heart sank as I stepped on the plane and away from my husband. This go round it was especially hard to leave because, for the first time, we had a home together, instead of his flat where every time we arrived, we were greeted with his mother's negative energy sitting on the couch watching reality TV. This place was ours and ours alone.

CHAPTER 17

September 2012

When I returned to Massachusetts, I could still feel David's energy in my home… this home that I needed to sell, yet was scared to leave. When it did sell, I planned to live with my neighbor Colleen. She was wonderful and I wasn't worried about us getting along, but I had lived alone now for many years, and I knew that living with a friend could be tricky. At first, the showings were few and far between, but I was optimistic that it would pick up. As September came to a close and October arrived, I started to worry. While I was trying to have faith that it would sell when the time was right, I started to wonder if something was wrong. I spoke to Darrell about what was going on, and he advised me that the house wouldn't sell if I had any conflict with letting it go. I knew this on some level, but needed to hear it from him before my conscious mind could process and accept it. He also told me that the house's energy seemed anxious and heavy and recommended I bless the home with a sea salt and water mixture before the next showing. That evening I did some digging into my soul and focused on truly letting the house go. It was time to take this step. This home, while too big and too much work, had become safe and I was attached. I always preached to David about abandoning fear, and now I needed to do the same for myself. It was time to cut the line and let another family enjoy the home. I smiled when I pictured a larger family utilizing the entire home, rather than just a small section. I internally said my goodbyes and gave the house my blessing.

The next morning was spent exercising, cleaning again and clearing the energy of the house once more. This was it! It had to be perfect for the next viewing. The browsers came and went and I didn't hear anything. Another family came through and, again, nothing. One evening I received a phone call from my realtor advising me that the first couple had made an offer — $80,000 under my asking price. I was starting to panic and the thought of an offer this low sent shock waves of fear through my body. I rejected the offer but started to wonder if this house was a worse investment than I had thought. I wondered, *Why didn't we have streams of people coming to look at the house? Did I get screwed when I purchased it, and in the end will this house suffocate me and keep me in Massachusetts for longer than I intended?* If the house didn't sell before Thanksgiving, it probably wouldn't sell until spring, and I couldn't wait that long. All of the good things in my life felt distant, and the only thing I could see right now was doom and an eternal life without my husband.

I reached out to Darrell for help. I tried not to do this very often as I didn't want him to be a crutch in my life, but I needed to get to the root of the issue. He told me that my energy had a strong sense of ownership regarding the house and ran me through some mental exercises to help me release the home and welcome its new owners. I was amazed at how focusing my energy and breathing deeply could relax, calm and reinvigorate my intentions.

In order to drive traffic, we decided to lower the price, have another open house and host a broker's open house the following Tuesday. It seemed there was a lot of interest but still no offers. I was struggling internally in a way that felt uncomfortably familiar. It was the same feeling I had after I had spent time with David in Chicago and our communication started to dwindle. I was in "control" mode, determined for everything to go my way, and the more it slipped away, the more desperate I felt. I had to have faith that the universe had a plan that was in place for a reason. I had to understand that if things didn't happen on my terms, I would be able to survive a few more months than I had planned without my husband.

Another month passed and my realtor recommended another open house to try and generate interest before the winter set in. The people who had initially made the lowball offer came back to see the house a third time, yet didn't want to raise their offer. After a week or so, they returned with an offer that was at least a starting point, but they made it clear it was their final offer. Worry was plaguing my thoughts. Fortunately, my mother had come into town to help me prepare for another open house and provided a nice sounding board. I told her of my concerns about the couple and their low offer and all of my "what ifs."

One evening we were walking Hapa along a trail behind my house. As I was going on about the house and the offer my mom said to me, "Melanie, let those people go. Sometime you have to let the half Gods go, before the full Gods can come in." Usually she said this in regards to men, but now that I had my "full God" partner in my life, it seemed to apply to many other areas of life as well. It was scary, but I decided to take her advice and, again, walk away from their offer. I also took my mother's advice and avoided lowering the price further, against my realtor's recommendation to drop it by another $10,000. I had considered a reduction of a couple thousand, but my mom advised me to hold firm and something told me she was right. Following my realtor's advice put me way too close to what I paid with very little room for negotiation. Not only that, but David made it clear that we weren't going any lower and if it made my realtor's life more difficult, "tough shit." This was always her tactic for a quick sale; my tens of thousands of dollars meant little to her as it would only change her commission by a few hundred dollars. I knew this was typical in the real estate business and in life — when the action doesn't have a direct effect on the person, it's much easier for them to suggest the easy way out.

The day of the open house, I decided to stick around the area while my mom and stepdad went out to explore. I was hanging out at my neighbor's house with Hapa, which was in clear view of the comings and goings of the sale. As the end of the open house approached, I checked my watch and figured it was safe for us to head home as it was a couple minutes before the hour and there wasn't anyone in the driveway. My dog had slowed down significantly over the last year, so he was dragging behind me taking his time. I picked up the "Open House" sign for my realtor and walked into the home, briefly looking back at Hapa to make sure he was ok. He was at the bottom of the stairs in the front of the house looking up as if dreading having to climb the eight steps with his old bones and, as I would soon find out, his weak heart. I decided to go in without him and allow him to climb the stairs in his own time. My realtor and I were talking in the kitchen about the various people who seemed to be seriously interested in the house when we noticed a few figures at the door. A cute Asian couple was standing with Hapa at their side. They apologized for being late and wanted to know if they could still take a look around. I made apologies for Hapa as his stature was big and could easily scare someone who didn't like dogs. They seemed fine with it, so I decided to switch places with them and let them look around while I stayed outside with Hapa. I took a seat next to the stairs near Hapa and talked to him in my animal voice, calling him my "old man," commenting about the fact that my once spry dog now could barely even make it up a flight of stairs. The thought always made me sad, as I knew his aging body wasn't going to get any better in the years ahead. The couple seemed to be in and out of the house rather quickly and we chatted on their way out. They asked me about Hapa and I explained we had been together for 10 years and that he was getting old. They agreed, explaining that when they arrived he was tackling the stairs one step at a time with a pace that looked painfully slow.

The following Thursday I received a call from my realtor asking me if I was sitting down. I had received an offer for $10,000 over what I paid for the house, which meant I wasn't going to lose as much money as I thought! I hung up the phone and cried tears of joy. All of the stress and anxiety had finally come to a head and soon it would be over. I called David to share the news and remind him how blessed we are, then immediately called my mom to tell her that the full Gods had arrived.

November 2012

Time seemed to pass at an outrageous speed once I received the offer on the house, and David was set to arrive a week before Thanksgiving. I had been going through the process of getting Hapa's papers in order for his international flight next year. I didn't want any last-minute glitches and I knew from the experience of getting the animals out of Hawaii, this was no easy feat. During the process, my vet had informed me that Hapa's heart disease was worse than they thought and they wanted me to come in for an echocardiogram to potentially adjust the cocktail of medications he was on. I didn't have time to wait at the vet for him and go get David, so I dropped him off and headed to the airport. On the way home, I swung by the vet to pick up Hapa and hear the prognosis. Dr. Tichy informed me that his heart failure was much more advanced than initially thought, based on the X-rays alone. I asked them what this meant for his flight to Spain and she explained that they would still sign off on a health certificate with the understanding that he might not make the flight. A tinge of pain rippled through my heart at the thought of that. I wasn't sure how that would change my plans. If he got progressively worse over the next few months, would I have to stay longer? Or would I risk flying him and potentially killing him? What if he got so bad that I had to put him to sleep before I left? I didn't want to think about it and hoped that the answers would become clear over time.

The next day David and I planned to go into Boston to submit the paperwork to the Spanish Consulate to finally make our marriage legal in Spain. When we returned home that night, Hapa had thrown up seven times. I spent the night cleaning the carpet and tending to my sick dog over the weekend. On Sunday night, he came into the bedroom as he always did to sleep with us. When David wasn't home, Hapa slept in the bed with Kitty and me. Most nights I had Hapa by my legs and Kitty by my chest, a comfortable arrangement that caused me to not emerge from bed very early many mornings, as this was our snuggle time. As Hapa entered the room that night, I could tell something was wrong. He didn't whine, but I could tell from his small noises of discomfort that he was suffering. He was shaking and lurching forward in pain, slowly clawing his way across the floor. I knew my husband wanted me in the bed with him, but I couldn't bear to see Hapa suffering, so I lay down on the floor next to him in the hopes that somehow my presence would magically relieve his pain. Neither of us got much sleep that night. I figured this is what mothers go through with their children — they share their pain in attempt to make it better.

At one point during the night, Hapa seemed to want to go outside and relieve himself. I was always hesitant to let him out late at night when he wasn't feeling well, because after 20 minutes or so, I would have to pile on clothing and a flashlight to go looking for him. He did exactly what I feared, but this time it felt a little different. He headed to a different area of the woods, and rather than calling for him and feeling annoyed, this time I desperately pleaded for him to come home. Reluctantly, he trotted back, but the pain continued. The next morning I looked up the symptoms of heart failure and assumed the pain was due to that, but I couldn't let it go anymore. He was shaking and seemed non-responsive, almost comatose from the pain. I let him out once again in the morning and he headed to the same area of the woods that he had visited the night before, which was strange because he had never really favored that spot. I could see the despair in his face and it was killing me. I felt utterly helpless. The woods were cold and his look told me to leave him in nature to pass naturally, but I couldn't do it. I pleaded with him to return as I had the night before, but this time he was resolute and proceeded to lay down. I had already dressed for work and was trying to avoid going in after him, but he gave me no choice. In tears, I thrust myself through the cold and wet brush to retrieve him, begging him not to die, insisting that I wasn't ready for him to go. I had heard about animals going into nature to die and while he seemed ready, I was not. I had to practically carry him back into the house with me. The last thing I wanted to do was work, but I had no choice. I had an appointment over an hour from the house that I couldn't cancel. I left Hapa under David's care and cried for two hours straight on the drive there and back, barely managing to keep my composure during my meeting.

When I arrived at home again, Hapa still hadn't eaten and was on his side shaking from pain. I thought I would do him a favor by letting him go if he was ready, but I wanted to be by his side. I let him out and followed him through the woods as he ventured into an area once again unknown to me. We got about a quarter mile away from the house and Hapa decided to lay down next to an old abandoned building. As I talked to him and petted him gently, I realized that he was not going to pass at that moment, but he was suffering immensely, in the freezing cold, no less. He weighed around 75 pounds and normally I could carry him, but not through this terrain. Reality set in and I went running back to the house to enlist David's help. He carried Hapa back home and we set a blanket down outside for him. My neighbor witnessed the retrieval from the woods and came over to offer help. David stood in the background taking everything in, while she and I discussed the inevitable in tears — taking Hapa to the vet to have him put down.

We arrived at the vet and, to our surprise, the doctor informed us that Hapa was going to make it. It wasn't his heart, at least not this time. Apparently, he had eaten a bone, and the object was causing excruciating pain and gas. I was relieved and grateful for the good news that I wasn't going to lose my best friend after all. They gave him fluids and painkillers and sent us home. He still seemed to be in quite a bit of discomfort, even with the drugs, but I was relieved to have him return home with us. At this point, he was on more medications than most humans I know, six in total. The next day he ate and was nearly back to normal, so we decided to keep our plans and take a road trip to North Carolina for David's work. Everything felt copasetic, at least for the moment.

After a few days of peace, Thanksgiving Day threw us for a loop again. Hapa was throwing up, not eating and noticeably weak. Adding insult to injury, we were at our friends' house in Philadelphia and I didn't want to ruin their holiday by rambling on about my dog, so I had to leave him to suffer alone in their basement. I would check on him every hour or so, but I felt like I was neglecting him in his time of need. Not a moment went by that I didn't want to excuse myself from the table and go lie with him. That evening in the middle of the night, I grabbed a pillow and blanket, left my husband and curled my body around Hapa once again, assuming it was the last chance I had to comfort him. If he wasn't eating or going to the bathroom by morning, I would have to take him to the vet again to put him to sleep. To my surprise, the next morning, he drank water and wanted to go outside to the bathroom. I was thrilled! We drove another six hours with Hapa sleeping in the back. He ate baby food, but only when it was served out of my hand. After checking into our hotel in Charleston, we got about 10 feet from our hotel room when I noticed Hapa starting to pass out, one of the signs of heart failure the vet had warned me about. David had to pick him up and carry him into the room, and his health was off and on during the entire trip.

We arrived home on Sunday when Hapa started to display other symptoms — he was limping and his left front paw was cold. Yet another sign of heart failure, I thought. David was leaving the next day and we had planned on having him take the cat with him. I had all of Kitty's paperwork completed, or so I thought. I returned from the government office that is supposed to issue pet passports empty-handed. I was told that one of my forms was missing a date from the vet's office. I knew I didn't have enough time obtain what I needed from my vet and return to the office before it closed. When I arrived home and explained my frustration to David with painful eyes, he looked at me and said, "I think there is a reason Kitty can't come with me. I think you are going to need him." I knew what he meant — that Hapa's time was coming — and fell into his arms in tears. We left for the airport to drop David off, and as I was driving back to the house, something told me to get a shot of pain medication from the vet. Hapa, the dog that previously ate medication like it was candy, was now fighting me at every turn. I knew an injection was my only option. I could tell he was getting weaker by the minute, so I decided that it would be smarter to sleep with him on the couch rather than carrying his 75 pounds upstairs. Normally, we would both squeeze onto one couch snuggling and sometimes fighting for space, but I knew he wouldn't be comfortable, so I pushed the chaise lounge next to the couch to create a big bed where we could both sprawl out but still touch. Neither of us got much sleep that night. Hapa barely made any noise, but the pain was obvious through his heavy breathing and continuous stretching. I prayed for hours upon hours that evening, asking God to relieve him of hurt, to take it away and bring my baby back to me. His pain was acute until about 3 a.m., and I could only imagine what he would have felt had I not given him pain meds before bed.

The next morning I put his bowl under his head and he finally took a drink of water, but he wouldn't move from the couch. I decided to move the vet appointment up because I knew his time was near. My neighbor, Colleen, helped prepare the car, and I carried my Hapa to the car. When we arrived at the vet, they took X-rays of his stomach and reported that the bone wasn't passing well due to his weak heart and he was showing more signs of heart failure as a result of stress. He wasn't a candidate for surgery, so my only options were to let him go or take him home. I couldn't bear the thought of seeing him suffer any longer, so I decided to let him go. The wonderful staff carried him into a conference room so we could have some time together before he passed. I was amazed at how, through pain, anguish and struggle, Hapa never showed one ounce of aggression or temper, only love. As he lay there on the couch, my friend who was still there with me noticed how he was resting his head on her hand. She replaced her hand with mine, so my hand was cradling his entire 12-pound head as I had done so many times over the last 10 years. The vet gave him the injection and his pain ended… in my arms.

I've experienced loss, but never to this extent. When I arrived at home, I felt empty, and for the first time in my life the thought of my death didn't scare me. In fact, I almost yearned for it in that moment of feeling devastated. It wasn't that I wanted to end my life, I just wanted to be with him again and I knew the only way that would happen was if I, too, passed on to the other side. At that point, nothing else mattered; I had tunnel vision. I wanted to be with my four-legged companion, and if a broken heart killed me, at least I would be with him again. When he passed, he took a piece of my soul with him. I lay on the couch, solemn and still. I couldn't sleep, couldn't eat, couldn't even think. I just lay there with my eyes open and cried. I had lost the one living thing that loved me unconditionally, the one constant that was always there for me no matter what else was going on in my life. Hapa was my companion in the kitchen to help me clean the floors, anxiously waiting for me to drop food. He was my hiking partner, my company for car rides, the face that greeted me when I entered and always said goodbye before I left, the pillow that I cried on when my heart was broken, the "person" I talked to when I was alone in the house. So many things had changed in my life over the last 10 years — my friends, my ex-marriage and new marriage, my home, my location — but he was the one common denominator through it all. No matter my mood or behavior, he was there to comfort and protect me.

Like a child, I had to learn to do "normal" things all over again without his presence. I didn't want to cook because he wasn't there to join me. When I watched TV, he would lay on the couch with me. After a shower, he would be waiting for me in his bed on the floor. We slept together every night. Even getting the mail brought tears to my eyes, as I had never once went to get the mail without him. Thankfully, my manager was a dog person just like me and allowed me to take three days off work to mourn. Knowing that I was alone, she dropped by my house to check on me and give me a gift — a bracelet with a bangle of a paw print that I still wear today. After a few days of not leaving the house, I headed out to my first office, the question "How was your Thanksgiving?" brought tears to my eyes. Over time, the sobbing subsided and turned into occasional tears, which would come when least expected. I missed kissing his head before bed and telling him he was white because he was my angel… words that I believe with all my heart and soul. I didn't rescue Hapa, he rescued me and got me through some of the hardest times of my life. I will always be thankful for that and know he is looking down and guarding me every day in his true angel form. I learned more about love from him than I did from most humans.

At one point during my grieving process, I received a message from my friend Cynthia in Hawaii: "Hapa helped you through some amazing times and knew his journey was done because, in his heart, he knew you were going to be alright now and forever." Her words were so profound and, in hindsight, I felt they were so true. I was stressing so much about how to get him to Spain, stuck by questions like: *Was I rushing things? How much more money would it cost? Would the move compromise Hapa's health?* In the end, he took these decisions out of the picture for me so I would have one less thing to worry about. He truly was a selfless dog.

The void Hapa left was hard for David. He didn't like

to see me sad. He had grown accustomed to my perpetually happy demeanor, even when times were hard, and 90% of the time I complained or moaned with a smile. My occasional tear-ups were quick, and David could easily make a joke and have me laughing once again. But after Hapa's departure, David saw a very different side of me. He would Skype me to check in, only to find me with red, swollen eyes. He saw and felt my heartbreak and it made him feel useless. His normal tricks to snap me out of it weren't effective. My sadness turned to anger and a personal attack on him. He offered advice on how he handled these situations — "Just don't think about it!" — which angered me. I snapped back at him, "Maybe repression is how you've gotten through hard times in your life, but I prefer to experience, learn and eventually heal from my emotions," and hung up the phone. Over time he learned that when it came to profound emotions, it was best to allow me release them, and if he was near me to just hold me. I wanted him to give me that same unconditional patience, silence and love that Hapa had given me for years when I was hurting. To be a shoulder and an ear with no judgment or advice.

Darrell had reached out to me to see if I wanted him to conduct a ceremony for Hapa when I was in Hawaii. I had spoken of returning once more before my final move to

Spain, but hadn't confirmed anything when Hapa was still alive, as trying to plan a trip to Hawaii on top of everything else seemed impossible. After he passed, I took it as a clear indication that some time in my beloved islands was exactly what I needed.

Hapa seemed to be working immediately from the other side. On November 27, the day he died, I received the final paperwork for the closing of the house, which put me one step closer to my dream. We set the closing date for January 15th.

After Hapa's passing, I removed myself from the doggie daycare's email list, so as not to be reminded of the gaping hole in my heart. Less than a week had gone by when I received an email from daycare. When I first saw the message in my inbox, I was furious that they hadn't removed me from their list. As I went to delete the message, I noticed the subject: "Help an shelter animal by donating to your local Humane Society." They needed towels, cleaning supplies, beds, toys, all things that Hapa left behind that I couldn't seem to part with. I knew this was what he wanted me to do, to pass on all the toys and love that I had given to him to help another shelter dog. It was time to cleanse my life by donating or selling everything I owned and start over. I had to work in baby steps, moving his bed and toys from their normal spot in my living room to the basement for a few days, then to the garage. Eventually, I worked up the nerve to load everything in my car and make the trip to the shelter.

To effectively become a minimalist in preparation for the move to Spain and to transition to life without my dog, it took two garage sales, multiple postings on craigslist, a full trailer that my mother drove back to Ohio, two car loads of Salvation Army donations and three loads to the humane society. When I donated Hapa's bed, which was a high quality arthritic mattress from L.L. Bean with his name embroidered on it, the women at the shelter were raving about how it would be perfect for a dog that had been there for eight years. It was a no-kill shelter and she was unadoptable, they told me. It gave me peace to know that Hapa's passing could comfort another dog in need, and I knew he was smiling down on me at that moment.

December 2012

The next task of the big move was getting Kitty to Spain. I was planning on bunking with my neighbor after the house sold and she was scared of cats, so I arranged to send the cat to Spain two weeks before I would head there for the holidays. This time everything went as planned. With teary eyes, I said goodbye and sent Kitty on an international journey to his new home. Now I was totally free to organize my life. I had been in the process of making my traditional holiday photo card when Hapa had passed, but things were different now and I decided to change the theme and dedicate my card and letter to my faithful companion. I chose a picture of him on the top of a mountain in Hawaii overlooking the Pacific Ocean after hiking one of my favorite trails, Kuliouou Ridge, with the caption, "Wishing You More Wag and Less Bark This Holiday Season." The accompanying letter read:

> *This year's card is dedicated to my faithful and loving dog, Hapa, who passed on November 27, 2012. Hapa, an American bulldog/pitbull mix rescue dog, defied any misconceptions about dog breeds. As a close friend said after his passing, "He was a gentle giant."*
>
> *Hapa found me in December of 2002. I had volunteered at the Hawaiian Humane Society for over a year and many dogs had crossed my path, but Hapa instantly made a paw print on my heart. One night the*

volunteers who cleaned kennels and exercised the dogs failed to show up. So, instead of only working with my usual behavior-training dogs, I started cleaning kennels and walking all the dogs. That's when I met Hapa, a little white guy with huge ears. Every time I stopped walking he would sit and beg for a treat with eyes that I couldn't resist and, after leaving that night, I couldn't forget. That weekend, I stopped in to see if he had been adopted and, to my dismay, he had not. Feeling entitled as a volunteer, I bypassed protocol and took him to a play area without signing him out. Suddenly an angry volunteer asked me how I got the dog out. I explained that I was a volunteer and just wanted to check on him. She informed me that a woman (who had properly signed him out) was waiting to spend time with him. My heart sank as I left so the woman could interact with Hapa. As I watched from a distance, I was amazed at how Hapa's demeanor quickly changed. He had lost interest in receiving attention and seemed distracted. After about five minutes, she gave up, and as she left the area she said, "I saw the way he behaved with you. He's clearly your dog." I ran to the desk to sort out how I could adopt this little guy. He had been there for over two weeks and seemed just as excited as I was about our new life together.

I remember our first car ride home and how funny he looked sitting in the back seat like a human with his head resting on the window, taking in the sweet smells of freedom and the fresh Hawaiian air. This ended up being a signature trait of Hapa's that I called his "Zen moment." Over the years, I would watch through my rearview mirror as his face revealed a place that I aspired to reach... He was truly in the moment, taking in each smell and sight without a care in the world, totally content, emanating happiness in its truest form. At our first stop, Petland, he couldn't contain his excitement and proceeded to pull me through the store in search of nothing and everything, when suddenly he stopped. I was in disbelief as I realized why — he was literally projectile pooping diarrhea that just barely missed me by a leash length. I had never seen anything like it and quickly thought that our fated meeting was a HUGE mistake. I gave him time to prove me wrong, and he did every day for the rest of his life. He made me a better person by the words we so often see in regard to dogs: Never Stop Playing, Wag More, Bark Less, Be Loyal and Faithful, Be Quick to Forgive and

Love Unconditionally.

As far as my life moving forward, the loss of Hapa accelerated my next move. I sold my house in Massachusetts, Kitty and I will spend Xmas in Spain with David, I'll return to the U.S. to tie up some loose ends after the new year and give my notice at work, and then start my life where I'm supposed to be — with my husband in Spain.

CHAPTER 18

December 2012

When I landed in Spain, my husband and cat were anxiously awaiting my arrival. Kitty was quite jet-lagged and acting rather strange. Not long after I landed, I began working toward accomplishing my next goal of getting the house in order. It still needed some major TLC, so I worked day and night to ensure that David was comfortable and that I would have a home I enjoyed when I returned for good. I brought up the idea of taking a trip to Hawaii, just the two of us. I knew his schedule was going to be very stressed at the beginning of the year, but my heart told me I had to go. He balked at the idea, stating that not only was it too difficult for him to go, but that I shouldn't go without him. His resistance bothered me; I wanted him to say, "That sounds great!" or "I can't go but you should go and see your friends," but neither of these phrases were uttered from his lips. I would occasionally bring up the topic, asking why he felt this way, only to have him respond with defensive remarks. A few days before I had to return to the States, I was trying to decide how to tell him that if he didn't want to accompany me to Hawaii, I was going without him. I didn't want it to cause a fight, but I did want his blessing, so the entire day I searched to find the right time and the right words. We decided to have lunch with our two friends, Ana and Chema. During lunch, David asked them a question that shocked me — he invited them to come on vacation with us in February… to Hawaii! I looked at him with excitement and he winked at me, knowing how happy I would be to hear this news.

I knew it was a hard decision for David, not only because of the time the trip would take away from his business, but also because there were so many uncertainties that lie ahead. David's U.S. importer had recently caught wind that David was looking to place a wine that they didn't want to sell with another importer. And while to most people this wouldn't sound like a problem, his importer was completely threatened by the concept of David selling wines through any other importer. David had learned from experience that if they didn't want to sell a wine but didn't want it in the hands of another importer, they would agree to carry the wine with exclusivity so no other importer could touch it. The downside of this deal is that the wine would not be a priority for the importer, and as such would receive few placements. This time David was smart and when another big player approached him, he was open to moving one of the wines to another importer. His current importer was the master of manipulation and pretended to play nice by telling David it was fine to sell the wine through another channel and that he would write up a contract for David to sign. A few days later, David emailed me the contract, which was clearly a tool of control, with provisions that prevented another importer from selling in any restaurant or store where his current importer was selling wine, or working with anyone who has ever worked with his current importer internally or externally— essentially making David's wines impossible to sell. The exclusions were astronomical and unreasonable, so I suggested that David consult a lawyer. He couldn't afford legal fees, so instead he shared it with a few of his friends in the business and asked for their advice. They agreed that it was too restrictive and told him not to sign it. The contract was written for the benefit of a greedy corporation and not a farmer, so David didn't sign.

After a few weeks of the importer pushing him to sign and David's non-compliance, he received a letter saying he no longer had representation in the U.S. The owner of the company, whom David never fully trusted, went one step further and sent a letter to all of their distributors announcing that they would no longer be representing David's wines due to a "conflict of interest that threatened distribution in the United States." Reading this made my blood boil. Here was a man who claimed to be a man of God, who held a position of power in an elitist sect of the Catholic Church, yet his behavior was greedy, manipulative with no regard to the livelihood of others. Unlike all of David's other business dealings, David had invited me to sit in on meetings, only to have the owner, behind a false smile, make it clear that I wasn't welcome. All dealings were only with David behind closed doors. After some research on the elitist sect, I found out why: The organization is considered extremely sexist.

Not only did the importer try to sabotage David's business, but after the fall out with his importer, Jacobo, the winery owner, showed he had no loyalty to David and decided to follow the money and stay with the importer. I felt awful for David as he had taken the winery from nothing to a fully-functioning operation, only to be backstabbed in the end. Now Jacobo had a channel for distribution, brands and wines that David had created, but without David at the helm, the quality of the wines was sure to go downhill fast, although I suspected it probably didn't matter to the importer or the winery, as they were concerned with profit first and foremost. We were just thankful that David had already started to separate his personal projects from Jacobo's winery. Eventually, Jacobo would prove to be even more brutal in business than David's former importer. He broke the contract and stopped paying David commission for his sales (which was his only source of income at this point), and when the time came for David to collect his wines that were aging in barrels in Jacobo's winery, he wanted to charge David 45,000 Euros to buy back his wines, even though the grapes were from David's vineyards and David made the wine! While the equipment used during the process was Jacobo's, we felt he was trying to financially rape us. Thankfully, one of David's best friends owned a winery and agreed that the figure was unfair and offered to help. On behalf of David, he negotiated the price down, although I felt it was still too high. David had to take a loan out to buy back product that was his in the first place, but he did it just to put an end to everything and start over fresh. I was starting to worry that I had been jaded and this business was no better than selling pharmaceuticals.

Perhaps I was spoiled by David's presence in the wine world. Not in the financial sense, as he didn't come from money, and earning a profit with wines created like his is difficult due to the labor and amount of care given to the wines. Rather, I felt extremely fortunate to be around the type of people who work the trade out of passion. I knew my view of the wine world was a bit skewed because of this; my standards were higher. It was hard for me to see people making wine solely for profit and without soul, especially while my husband struggled to make ends meet making his artisan wines the right way — with depth and personality. At times, I felt a bit of jealousy for those who were able to earn huge profits in the wine business, but I preferred the authenticity of David earning a modest living creating honest and passionate wines. I didn't want a lavish life if it meant compromising the integrity of his operation and creating wines with no soul for the single purpose of bowing to the profit-driven demands of the market. The separation from his importer and his old winery was really a chance to start over again. This time we would align with people in the industry who shared the same values as us.

CHAPTER 19

January 2013

After New Year's, I found myself in yet another challenging situation. I was back in Massachusetts living with my neighbor and her 16-year-old son for a month before I made the final move. We got along well and it was nice to have someone to chat with about all of the upcoming changes in my life. I planned on taking fewer than 90 days for my leave of absence, as there were rumors that the company may downsize during the first half of the year. This would allow me to remain an active employee and qualify for a severance package, if I were to be reallocated. I had decided to give three weeks notice instead of two. I felt that I was keeping a big secret and needed to get the information off my chest, so I set a conference call with my director and a team leader in the wake of the sudden departure of my manager over the holiday. I broke the news of my leave and waited on eggshells for him to give me the go ahead. After a few days, I had my approval and the weight was lifted. No sooner than a few days had passed when we received notice of a company-wide conference call. The powers that be announced there would indeed be one of the largest layoffs in the company's history in early April. I prayed that I would be on the list of reallocations, but I knew that the decision wasn't up to me. Once again, I had to trust in the forces outside of myself that knew what was best for me.

The time seemed to move so slow during the final weeks of work, thanks to the anticipation of returning to Hawaii and being with David and our friends Ana and Chema again. While I had grown to appreciate some of the offices I called on, I sensed a cold and rigid nature from many of the people who had crossed my path during my time in Massachusetts, a provincialism of sorts. Granted, while few, I had made some wonderful new friends during my time in Massachusetts. But a grand majority of the people I had encountered seemed to be thoroughly unhappy, and I wondered what it was about this place that kept them here. When I made the decision to move there, I knew it would be a learning experience for me, but I always wondered if I made the right decision. I was able to travel to places that I never would have seen had I stayed in Hawaii, and meeting up with my husband was easier than traveling halfway across the world, but I felt that my soul had suffered for it.

When I returned to Hawaii, I realized I had become more impatient with people from my time on the east coast. Thankfully, the bright side of me returned in Hawaii: I said hello to strangers without it feeling awkward, I greeted people with a newfound pleasantry and found myself smiling more than I had in a long time. My soul was happy again.

David and I were busy entertaining our guests while trying to catch up with old friends, but at least this visit didn't have the negative energy of David's mother to bring me down. While coordinating was stressful at times, I enjoyed the trip immensely. On several occasions, when I found myself alone with David, there were tears in my eyes from all the wonderful memories Hapa and I shared in Hawaii. David and I hiked trails and lounged on beaches that used to be our old stomping grounds and I prepared to say a final goodbye to my best friend.

I was a mess trying to coordinate Hapa's ceremony with Darrell. I had brought some of his ashes, just as Darrell had told me to, but began to worry that we wouldn't be able to fit time into our schedule to do it right. I knew our friends from Spain would probably think I was crazy, and who would really want to attend a pet memorial anyway, so I tried to plan it around them. Thankfully, everything fell into place and we met Darrell at the Aiea Heiau one morning for the ceremony while our friends toured Pearl Harbor. I wasn't sure if David wanted to come or not, but I didn't give him a choice; I made it clear that he needed to come and support me. He surprised me and told me he wanted to come and was looking forward to it. My friend Liane joined and brought Hawaiian dishes to share with our friends after the ceremony was over. Dressed in traditional Hawaiian garb, Darrell said a few prayers and instructed us on what to do while we were inside the *heiau* (ancient Hawaiian place of worship). We were to walk in a circular path meditating on what we needed to let go of — specifically, the things that were keeping us from our goals — and then invite in all of the resources and positive energy that could help us accomplish those goals. I was told to place Hapa's ashes inside the *heiau*, so I placed him safely between a set of rocks that was protected by a tree. As I looked down upon the white ashes scattered between the black rocks, it was hard to believe this was once my best companion, my little white angel, and now I was returning him back to earth and back to the land that he knew and loved. Darrell blessed us with *ti* leaves and water and told us to keep the leaves with us for three days. On the third day, we were to find a rock and wrap the *ti* leaves around it, and toss it into the ocean to release what we were holding on to in order to open us up for any blessings that we wished.

Our two weeks in Hawaii were almost up, and David and I carried the *ti* leaves with us for all three days, as Darrell had instructed. Now it was time to decide where to throw them into the ocean. David and I were driving and he asked me where I wanted to part with my *ti* leaves. I assumed he was asking so we could coordinate something together. I told him how Kahala Beach was special since Hapa and I used to walk there every morning to watch the sunrise, and on the weekends we would lounge on the beach together because it was dog friendly. Feeling his intense stare, I turned to meet David's gaze as he said, "OK, I know where I want to part with the leaves."

I replied, "Oh, ok, I don't have to go to Kahala. What were you thinking?"

He responded, "No. You go to Kahala. I want to say my goodbye at the bottom of the lighthouse trail." As he spoke these words, tears filled my eyes. These little moments, to me, are God's way of confirming my faith in David as a person. I looked at him and he had tears in his eyes, too. That was the trail where Hapa, David and I went on our first hike, where David carried him up the hill because he couldn't go any further. David never told me he felt sorry for being too hard on Hapa or for not understanding his gentle nature, but I knew this was his way of asking for forgiveness. He had held on to the guilt for his actions for all this time.

March 1, 2013

The last day of our stay, David and I separated from our friends and set off on our journey to say goodbye, release the past and open our hearts to new opportunities in our lives. We hiked the trail, as if tracking our steps and reflecting on every moment that had passed since our last trek. We descended down the rocky, dry trail in silence, each of us recalling happy times with Hapa. The weather wasn't as warm this day; the trade winds forced the ocean to beat against the tide pools, which were pristine the last time we were here. When we arrived at the bottom, I didn't want to get too close to the water knowing that a rogue wave could arrive at any time. However, David was less cautious and more focused on ensuring Hapa's ashes were properly swept out to sea. He walked across the slippery tide pools and stood dangerously close to the ocean. Even though his back was facing me as he looked out to sea, I knew he was not only asking our little white angel for pardon, but also requesting guidance on our journey ahead. He stood there with a calm determination, waiting for the right wave to come and offer its blessing. The ocean calmed momentarily, and then out of nowhere a wave crashed against the rocks projecting water 30 feet over David's head, almost as if it were angry. David threw the stone with the ashes tied to it as hard as he could while I prayed it was only my vantage point that made it appear that David was going to be swept out to sea with the rock. I snapped a photo and yelled to David to please return to safer ground. The ocean settled again to a tranquil state, as if his pardon was granted. Tears came to me as I watched David's gaze fixate intensely on the blue water. The power of the moment was intense and I knew it was exactly what he needed… what we all needed.

Now it was my turn to make my peace with Hapa. The journey to the next destination, Kahala Beach, was quiet. At one point, David looked at me with a smile on his face and said, "I think he's forgiven me." I knew in my heart it wasn't Hapa who had forgiven him, as dogs are ever forgiving, but rather it was David who had forgiven himself. We arrived at the place where Hapa and I had walked together every morning before work to watch the sun appear over the ocean. I said my prayer, and as I tossed his ashes out to sea, I felt a release from the sadness that I had been holding. That was my wish, to finally let go of the negative emotions I carried with me over the past few months and allow positive ones to take their place.

CHAPTER 20

David needed to stay in the U.S. to settle some additional business, so my arrival in Spain would be solo. His friend Sergio would give me a lift from the airport to Vitoria, but from there I had to drive David's huge van to my new home in the small village of Elvillar. I wasn't comfortable driving in Spain, much less piloting a huge standard transmission van over the Sierra Cantabria mountain to Elvillar, but I survived. I spent the first two days settling in, unpacking and cleaning the house, and eventually a trip to the grocery store was in order. David asked that I check on his mother, so I figured I would kill two birds with one stone. I called Ana, my friend who joined us in Hawaii, and asked her to accompany me to the supermarket and to visit his mother since she lived in the same building. I thought, with Ana there, the odds of a successful, conflict-free visit would be greater. To my surprise, Lali's anger wasn't geared at me this time, but instead directed at Ana. I was in a state of shock as Lali immediately lashed out at Ana for reasons that I couldn't understand. Ana didn't fight back and tried to dispel the negativity being hurled in her direction. Although she was speaking much too fast for me to translate, I caught Lali mentioning Hawaii. She turned to me and attempted to be cordial, but underneath it I felt there was a lot of misdirected anger. We tried to make small talk and Ana would help when we got stuck, but by that point, I wasn't interested in making much of an effort to find subjects to discuss. The more time we spent in that house only meant more opportunities for Lali to find a reason to be upset, so we didn't stay long.

After leaving, Ana explained that Lali was mad because she didn't tell her she was going to Hawaii. But oddly enough, David had failed to mention Hawaii, too, but she wasn't mad at him or me. I wondered why she had chosen to attack her son's friend instead. Ana had always treated me with kindness and respect, much more than Lali ever had, so when I found out the reason for the attack I got quite upset. I called David and told him what happened and explained that I didn't want to see her again for quite some time. I told him I couldn't handle her toxic energy, and I didn't think I should have to. He understood, and after that day never pushed me to spend time with his mother again. In comparison, the things that should have caused me the most difficulty — adjusting to a new culture, learning a new language, driving in a new city in a new country and shopping for products in a foreign language at the grocery store — were a breeze. I reflected on the fact that the things we often think will be the most challenging actually seem easy after we master them, but people, on the other hand, can never be mastered. The challenge lies in mastering yourself and your reactions — a lifelong journey that I work on every day but sometimes struggle with.

My first few months as a resident in Spain mirrored the life of a child. Everything was new and exciting. The air smelled fresher. The church bells that rang every hour on the hour didn't bother me, and I actually grew quite fond of their reliable sounds. I welcomed the sight of old stone roads instead of asphalt. Outside my windows, I could see rolling hills filled with grapevines and, in the backdrop, large mountains cradling Rioja, keeping it safe. I felt like I had travelled back in time to a place where people still grew gardens and raised chickens for fresh eggs. Most villages have a bakery, but ours was so small that the bakery instead traveled to us in a van. You could approach the van as the driver passed by at approximately the same time every day, or you could put a euro in a bag and hang it from your front door, the signal to leave a loaf. We also had a fish truck, a textile truck, and every Wednesday an old man who fixes watches would drive through the village belting out a strange sermon of sorts in Spanish playing over a loud speaker. I couldn't understand what he was saying, but I mentioned to David that it reminded me of Nazi propaganda. He reassured me it was just the watch man's way of alerting the people that he was there. I imagined the man must have been bored after retirement and wondered how a village of 250 people could possibly supply enough broken watches and clocks to keep him in business.

One day David decided to go on a walk with me to show me the *dolmen*, an ancient sacred burial site from the Neolithic age that is situated just outside of our village. On the way there, he followed a path, scattered with large limestone rocks deep in the soil that cut through some vineyards. He mentioned that it was an old Roman road and that there are still many like it in existence in the area. I was awestruck at the thought of how many years had gone by since Roman times. In America, anything over 200 years is considered old. As we reached the top I noticed a bunch of animals, goats and sheep, heading towards us in the middle of the road. Through the herd I spotted a man holding a cane, similar to the ones the wise men held during the nativity scene in church. The animal lover in me was thrilled to encounter the shepherd in the village for the first time, a man named Daniel. David approached Daniel to say hello as I excitedly engaged the animals in my animal voice while snapping photos as they walked by. I could barely take my eyes off them while David introduced me, and I continued to repeat, "*Lo siento pero me encanta animals*" (I'm sorry but I love animals), hoping that he would understand my fascination with this foreign sight.

Naturally, we decided to follow Daniel for a while. David wanted him to show me how the dogs herded the flock and I squealed in delight as Daniel made a few directive noises. Suddenly, the dogs went running around the perimeter and proceeded to herd the sheep and goats into a tight bunch. Once they were finished with their work, he made a few more sounds and the dogs were sitting by his side. I had never seen anything like it before in my life; I had been so Americanized that it was hard to imagine how people still did this sort of thing. David told Daniel to advise his wife that we would like to place an order for goat cheese the following day. The next morning the doorbell rang and it was Pilarin, the shepherd's wife, delivering fresh goat cheese made that very morning! I decided at that point I wanted to start growing my own food. There was no reason why I shouldn't have a garden — chemical free, of course, just as all things we tend to in our family.

I got to meet David's grandmother, Mariuchi (Lali's

mother), who lived in the same village, and to my surprise, she couldn't have been a sweeter person. She was 87 at the time and good friends with everyone in the village. She couldn't get around much, so I decided that if I couldn't bring myself to keep his mother company, I would instead focus my energy on getting to know his grandmother and helping her when I could. I tried to visit her as much as possible, although my visits always caused me a bit of stress due to the language barrier. And that stress wasn't only when I was with her; I would feel it come on as soon as I left my house to walk through the village. Elvillar is a small village of approximately 250 full-time residents, and the population grows each summer as many of the homes are second homes for those living in the city. The average age must be around 70, as most of the full timers are elderly. People would see me once and remember me, the foreigner who sticks out like a sore thumb. But to me, everyone looked the same — elderly, generally short in stature, with short hair and average weight. I would leave the house and pass by someone, praying that I hadn't met them before and that the only words they would speak would be a simple, "*Buenos dias,*" or "*Buenas tardes*." If I had met them already, the fact that I didn't speak or understand much Spanish meant nothing to them. They would engage me in one-way conversations, going on in Spanish while I just smiled and shook my head with an occasional, "*No entiendo*." But all that didn't matter, since everyone I encountered seemed happy to talk to someone new.

As the days passed and my Spanish got progressively better, I started to engage more with the people. One day, I was headed to David's grandmother's house when I spotted her sitting in the street chatting with friends. They lit up when they noticed me and invited me to sit with them, although I had no idea what they were speaking about because, not only did they speak so fast, but also all at once. They started in on how much my Spanish has improved and then quizzed me about my understanding of certain words, common words that equate to swear words, like *joder*, which means fuck (among many other things). I quickly responded in Spanish, "I believe so," but it didn't make any difference, they wanted to tell and show me what it meant. I interpreted his grandmother's neighbor's explanation to mean, "It's kind of like love but…," as she made a pumping gesture with her hands. The group burst out in laughter at her description compounded by the appalled expression on my face. Apparently, it's quite common for the women in the village to have a perverted sense of humor. I noticed it in David's mother and aunt, only to discover it's not a family thing, but a village thing.

April 2012

My initial move to Spain was quite stressful in regards to my work, as I had taken a leave of absence and there was a small chance I would have to return to the U.S. to settle some work issues if I wasn't part of the anticipated layoffs. I prayed that I would be let go, which entitled me to a severance. David and I had a work trip to Galicia, about six hours drive on the west coast of Spain, planned around mid-April and we were en route when I received notice of a mandatory conference call from my company. Within hours I would know if I had a job or not. My heart raced as I spoke with the manager who was in charge of delivering the information. In typical corporate style, she read a drawn-out, verbatim script, instead of cutting to the chase. After five minutes of fluff and legalese, she got to the point — I was laid off! Never in my life had I been so happy to hear those words. This company that had sucked any form of pleasure out of my work since leaving Hawaii was finally going to compensate me for my years of loyalty. I shared the news with David and thanked God and my angels, as I always do in situations like these. It was a blessing and another sign that I was following the right path. With the help of my severance pay, I was confident we would be financially ok for the next year. I felt like a new person, as if a layer of skin had been removed, exposing the true being that had been hidden behind years of fear, doubt, worry and regret. I didn't know what I would do for work and it didn't even matter; I had faith that my future was bright regardless of what it held, because now there was one certainty that was clear: It would be spent with my soul's connection, my husband.

CHAPTER 21

May 2013

As I settled into my new life, I couldn't believe how much joy I derived from being a housewife. Never had I dreamed I would enjoy not working and taking care of my home and my family, which consisted of David and Kitty. I would occasionally help my husband in the vineyards or winery, but otherwise, time was mine to do as I wished. I knew it was a temporary situation so I soaked up every moment. It was exactly what I needed to refill my soul. David would wake up early and go to work, trying to be a quiet as possible so I could sleep as long as my body needed. He seemed to enjoy allowing me to sleep in, only to tease me about my life of luxury later. It didn't matter; he could tease me all he wanted. For the first time in my life, I was content. I had everything I wanted… well, almost everything. I still dreamed of a garden and chickens, and for these to come true, I needed David's help. Growing a garden wasn't on the top of his "to-do" list, so I had to wait for him to decide when the time was right. I was waiting on him and it made both of us crazy. He didn't feel it was a priority and was annoyed by my constant requests. Dependency on him or anyone for that matter was always a difficult thing for me. I had been completely independent all of my life and if I wanted a garden and couldn't do it myself, I could hire someone to do it for me. He was used to a self-sufficient wife who asked virtually nothing of him, and I was accustomed to getting what I wanted, when I wanted it, not on someone else's time.

One day, in typical David fashion, he told me to dress in clothes that I wouldn't mind getting dirty. We drove over the mountains to a little village where Sergio's family had their family home and a garden. David had decided to teach me how to garden by helping Sergio's family. The garden was a communal garden where, for centuries, the neighboring families have continued the tradition of maintaining and handing down specific plots. The water system was ancient, fed from a natural water source (which ran continuously) through a limestone fountain that provided fresh drinking water. The water then led to a stone tub where, I was told, the families used to wash clothes before there was running water in the homes. From the tub, another channel directed the water towards a large labyrinth of gardens, and the entire system was gravity fed. Small channels ran along either side of the gardens, and when it was your turn to water, you would direct the water to the channels closest to your garden by either removing or blocking other channels with stones and soil so eventually the water would feed into your garden. The families used the same system in the garden soil so the water would run alongside and feed into each row.

We learned a lot that day, and I eventually got my garden with the help of Sergio's parents, who loaned us some equipment to work the land. After I was finished constructing my garden filled with tomatoes, peppers, lettuce and zucchini, I immediately turned my focus to chickens. My stubborn determination did not please my husband, as I'm sure he was hoping the garden would keep me busy for quite some time. I began obsessing about how to build a coop, spending a good amount of time seeking out supplies that were much harder to find in Spain than the U.S. I couldn't go to a home depot and have a staff member greet me at the door and direct me to the proper aisle. Things just don't work that way in Spain, so I had to be more creative. Plus, I didn't want to spend a lot of money, so I decided I would build the coop out of old construction materials that were lying around the property. I started to compile my list: wood, chicken wire, nails. I found an old metal frame that I decided would work great as the structure for my coop, and I planned to disassemble old pallets for the wood. Everyday I would wake up, eat breakfast and spend a solid eight hours working on the coop. I'd never built anything in my life, but I was determined to see this project through to completion, even if it killed me. I came close to losing a finger or two many times, and I swore like a truck driver as I attempted to break apart pallets and get the pieces to fit. I was sure that the people in the village could hear my ranting and probably diagnosed me with some mental disorder. I maintained the appearance of a man for about a month building that coop. I would end the day filthy, sweaty, stinky and sore from all the hard work. I had more bruises and cuts than one could count, but eventually I finished with virtually zero assistance from David, which gave me great satisfaction. "Ha! Take that, David! I could do it without you." He loved and hated me for my tenacity. He looked at the final product and called it my "white trash chicken coop," then asked me how my "independent ass" planned on getting the 70-plus pound coop down two stories to the yard. I told him I would use the mini-forklift to transport it down the ramp, but I knew I wouldn't even be able to pick up the damn thing, much less control it going down a steep incline. Damn! I had no other option but to ask for help. This made for more tension between us because I knew I needed him, and he knew I needed him, but I didn't want to have to admit it. I decided to shut my mouth, see what happens and focus on yet another new project, the run surrounding the coop. I started digging the trench to install the fence. David wasn't thrilled about my one-track mind, yet one day I arrived home and found my coop placed in the center of the run, just where I had wanted it. I didn't have to eat my pride or throw a fit, he just did it one day with a friend when I was away from the house. He never did tell me how he got it down there or who helped him, and I never asked.

June 2013

I had my first visitor from the U.S., although she was actually living in London at the time. She was the receptionist at one of my doctor's offices in Hawaii and often took partial credit for David and I being together, as she was the one who directed me to Cynthia. Jenna was young, yet quite an old soul. She was telling me the story of her first son's paternal father, who always struggled with drugs and was in and out of prison. And how, while she wasn't involved with him, she never spoke ill of him or denied him time (supervised) with his son when he asked. Her wisdom surpassed her age, unlike many people I had met, and I knew I could trust her. I decided to share my feelings with her about the situation with David's father and get her input. I had written his father a note and included the issue of Wine

Spectator he was featured in, as well as some photos from our wedding. I had heard that he lived in Laguardia, but wasn't quite sure and didn't know how to get the letter to him. She confirmed that it was the right thing to do despite the trouble it may cause and wished me luck. I wanted her to go with me to ask around about his whereabouts, but figured word would definitely get back to David if I brought her along since she was Asian. If I didn't stick out enough already, she would certainly hinder my plan to stay incognito as there aren't many Asians in Spain. I decided I would tackle the job after she left.

I set off into Laguardia with my large envelope in hand and headed to the post office. I assumed the village was small enough that if he lived there, they would know him and give me his address, but I was wrong. Rather, they handed me a phone book to pick through. I couldn't find his name and decided to leave as I was getting nowhere. Defeated, I walked around the streets hoping that I might recognize him and hand him the package, but I had no such luck. I headed home and decided I would hide the package from David so he couldn't find it. The thought of connecting with David's father was almost as strong as connecting with him, and I tried to suppress it hoping it would go away, thereby confirming that it wasn't the appropriate thing to do. But his father entered my mind at least weekly and sometimes daily. I knew one day I would have to do something, if David didn't beat me to it, that is.

David had virtually given me the green light by putting my chicken coop in place, so I started asking around about how to obtain two- or three-month-old chickens. I followed a couple of leads that lead nowhere. His friend had recommended a farmer fair in Vitoria. Sounds easy, but again, in a foreign land, nothing is straightforward. I woke up early and mapped out my drive, with the intention of arriving early to find parking since traffic and parking stress me out in Spain. Everything was falling into place, or so it seemed. I found a parking spot right away, located the fair with no trouble, and soon found the animals that were for sale. They had cows, pigs, goats, sheep, horses and even ponies, but no chickens. I was defeated once again. On my drive home I noticed the fuel level was low, so I decided to stop at the gas station in the village next to us. The attendant was a friendly man and I enjoyed practicing my Spanish with him. He escorted me in to pay, and while hanging in the front of the station window, he showed me his caged parakeets. I mentioned that I was looking for *gallinas*, and he started telling me how his friend had some chickens, and then invited me to go across the street with him to see the birds.

They were all in cages, which made my heart ache, but I tried to fake enthusiasm for his efforts to show me the birds. I explained that I was not looking for adult birds, but rather birds that were just a few months old. He asked for my number and said he would give me a call after talking to a friend. I figured what the heck, it's only a phone call, so I handed it over. When I returned home, I didn't mention the conversation to David. Things were still tense and he was tired of hearing about my chicken project while he was busy trying to provide for our family.

The next day my phone rang. I didn't recognize the number, but picked it up anyway, bracing myself for the Spanish that would come pouring out, of which I would probably only understand half. It was Fernando, the attendant from the gas station. From what I could gather, he was instructing me to come to the gas station at 2 p.m. to see the chickens. I tried to clarify in my Spanglish and said, "So I come and look and if I like them, I can buy them?" I could tell he was thrown by my question, and I deduced that he was insisting that the chickens be a gift. I tried to tell him that I couldn't accept, but I knew I wasn't going to win the argument. I hung up the phone and reluctantly informed David about the conversation. His response was predictable: "What? Are you kidding me! What do you know about this man?”

“Um well, he’s the man that pumps my gas,” I said. “Seems like a nice man.”

“And? Where are the chickens from?”

In a meager voice, I replied, “One of his friends has chickens.”

“Are they healthy? Do they have diseases?”

“I don't know but I assume not.”

“And how old are they?”

“Well, I asked for two to four months, but I’m not sure if he understood me.”

“How much are you paying for these chickens?”

I was getting irritated with his interrogation: “I think he said they were a gift. But I’m not sure. Stop, ok? I didn’t ask him to give me chickens. I simply mentioned that I was looking for chickens and gave him my number. I didn't know he was going to give me chickens!"

We didn't speak much after that and the drive to the gas station was completely silent. We pulled in and I asked for Fernando. The employee directed me to the restaurant across the drive where he was having lunch, while David was doing his own thing and checking out the inside. I noticed Fernando sitting outside with a bottle of wine. He was dressed quite nicely, different from his normal work attire, and I sensed he was expecting someone. I approached him and he greeted me and offered a glass of wine. We started to chat and I learned that he wasn't a station attendant, but rather the owner of the gas station as well as the restaurant we were sitting in! He told me he also owns a fuel distribution company which serves his three other gas stations, and he owns more stations in other areas. David rounded the corner and I introduced them. David's energy shifted instantly; he became relaxed and friendly. After a few minutes, a truck pulled up and two men got out. Fernando introduced me to them, and the next thing I knew, I had four chickens in my trunk. In the car, David looked at me and offered his two cents, "This type of thing only happens to you. That wasn't the attendant, he owns this station and a few others in the area." I giggled and said, "I know! How crazy is that?"

We took the four girls home and introduced them to their first taste of freedom. I was delighted to have inadvertently rescued four caged birds. David put them on the ground and they lay totally still, as if they had forgotten all of their natural instincts, including how to walk. David had to pick them up and put them on the ground again to get them to use their legs. I had read about chickens and all of their natural habits, but these birds were nothing like the chickens in those books. They weren't perching, exploring or scratching. The only thing that made them comfortable was the small, dark coop that I had built for them. The first few days were stressful, because they seemed to be scared of me and refused to eat or drink. I was worried that their time in cages had killed all of their natural instincts and that they might die, but eventually they came around. Day by day, they started to become accustomed to me. They started scratching for food and making noises that seemed less stressed and more pleased when I approached. They seemed to develop personalities and would follow me around if I needed to work in the garden. I was enamored with my four girls and I never dreamed I could get so much satisfaction out of having chickens, but I did. I needed to build something for them that would provide a continuous water source in case I had to leave town for a few days. In my online research I found what was called a nipple system and it seemed easy enough to put together. It was a string of piping from a water source that leads to red plastic "nipples." They are bright red to attract the birds, who then move the metal nipple so that water comes out. Perfect! Now my problem was where to find the nipples. I decided the most logical place was the same place that sold the food. Rather than driving around endlessly, calling first seemed to make the most sense — that is, of course, if you can speak the language. I dialed the phone and a man answered. In broken Spanish, I tried to explain that I have chickens and needed something to give them water. I swear someone told me the word was *tetas*, so I asked the man if *he* had red tits for chickens to drink from. Suppressing his urge to laugh, he answered, "Excuse me? I don't understand anything." Apparently, *tetas* means boob and I probably should have used the verb *vender* (to sell), not *tener* (to have), which is more possessive. It reminded me of when I wanted to ask a man how many eggs his chicken laid everyday, but instead my Spanish translated to, "How many balls do you have?" His response, of course, was *dos*. After this conversation, I decided to order the nipples online from the U.S. and have them sent to my house in Spain.

At first I was a little obsessed with the safety of my chicken girls. There were many days that I thought I had lost them, only to find they had escaped into the neighbor's garden. I would have to lure them back into our yard, figure out how they had escaped and rebuild the fence once again. They became gutsy little things with a number of seemingly human traits. Give them an inch and they would take a mile. They went from not wanting to leave the coop to trying to escape from the yard. After discovering the neighbor's garden, they would get me in trouble by picking at his lettuce and tomatoes. On either side of my yard, both neighbors had gardens that they were quite fond of, but of course they always favored the garden of the grumpy old man who yelled at me to keep my chickens away and threatened to call the police if they entered his garden again. The people in the village used chemicals on the land as if it was sugar, and I didn't want my chickens in there any more than he did!

The girls were quite entertaining and they soon grew to love me. Or rather, they grew to associate me with food, so as I approached they would come running and cooing at me, which felt like love. I truly enjoyed the company of my four little chickens. They would follow me around and the yard making cute noises and checking me out. At first I stressed about them a lot and checked on them constantly, but after awhile I grew to trust that they were fine and I would often simply check on the chickens from my living room window rather than running outside every time. It gave me great pleasure to see them exploring the land, and even more pleasure when I collected healthy, fresh eggs every morning. David started to come around as well; I would catch him watching them play and he seemed to love the taste of fresh eggs.

July 2013

I started to have visitors right around David's allergy season, which was uncomfortable for everyone. He was grumpy and busy with work, so I was usually expected to entertain my guests without his help. While I was still contributing financially to our family, David was starting to have a lot of resentment that I was not working. While on one hand, I think he enjoyed watching me sleep in, the stress of having to provide for another person brought out an ugly side in him at times. It all seemed to come to a head when my friend Colleen arrived from Massachusetts. She was full of questions and David isn't a big fan of a constant line of questioning. David was good for the first few days and then started to erupt with anger and harsh words not only with me, but in front of her as well. He had zero tolerance combined with zero sense of humor. I had never been so disappointed in his behavior. It's one thing to get frustrated with me, but this was someone who had treated me like family when I lived in Massachusetts, when I had no one else to lean on. It was embarrassing and completely unacceptable. After she left, we had one of the biggest arguments yet. I tried not to yell, but was at a loss as to how to get across to David that you can't treat people poorly and personally attack them because you think differently than them or you don't want to answer their questions. I couldn't stand it when I saw him behaving exactly like his mother — judging and critical of others with no regard for anyone else's feelings. I tried to keep his mother and her influence in his behavior out of our arguments, but this time I went below the belt and ended up acting just like them by losing my temper and personally attacking his character. We may argue and have disagreements from time to time, but this was a full on fight. I was so angry I started to cry at which point David accused me of trying to manipulate him with tears. Once again assuming this stemmed from a game his mother may have played, I erupted with anger that I hadn't felt towards him in the past: "Get the fuck out of my face! If you think this is all a game to manipulate you, you are even more fucked up than I originally thought. Stop projecting the bullshit you have in your mind onto my actions. Now get the FUCK OUT AND LEAVE ME ALONE!"

I didn't speak to him for the remainder of the day. He knows I don't explode very often and he could tell I wasn't playing game. I can't say he apologized because that isn't his style. He has little ways of trying to make things right again: a kind gesture, cleaning up the house or doing something that is out of character. A few days later he told me how he wrote to Colleen and thanked her for everything she had done for us and told her she hoped she enjoyed her time in Spain. I was certain Colleen must have been confused by sudden kind words, so I explained it was his way of apologizing without actually having to say I'm sorry. She's such a kind soul, she wasn't looking for an apology or an explanation and took his words at face value and we never discussed it again.

David had mentioned a few months prior that he was thinking about getting a dog. While I was better, my heart was still a little broken from Hapa. I could still come to tears if I allowed myself to think of him too long, but the idea intrigued me. I wanted David to have a dog that he felt was his, unlike Hapa who was clearly mine. While David loved him, at times I felt he loved him like a stepchild. Having been a stepchild my whole life, my radar for this sort of thing was high. I wanted the idea to be David's, but he didn't mention it much. As with all things in my life, it seems that if it is meant to be and I'm hesitating, the universe sends me a sign. Sometimes it whispered, but in this case it barked. Two nights after David mentioned getting a dog, we were awakened by the sound of a barking dog at three in the morning. While stray cats would occasionally awaken us at night with their noises, this was never the case with dogs, so I knew something was up. After a few minutes, I got out of bed and walked out on the terrace to see if I could find the dog and check if anything was wrong. I was shocked to find the dog in our driveway behind our locked fence. He was barking down into our yard, which is why he seemed further off in the distance than he really was. I put on a coat and opened the gate to allow the dog out of our property, perplexed by how he managed to get though the fence since a dog of his size couldn't have fit through the metal bars of the gate. He was a shaggy, blonde Mastiff, or at least I assumed. Structurally he was a large dog, and like 85 percent of the dogs in the village, he looked thin and hungry. He seemed scared, but I talked to him in a calming voice and eventually he approached. The collar around his neck was attached to a thick metal chain that had been broken. He had escaped and seemed to have a limp. My heart was breaking for him. I hated the way that a majority of the people in our village treated their animals. If they were hunting dogs, they were kept in cages in the middle of nothing, only to be let out when the owners were ready to hunt. This guy appeared to be a guard dog from his stature, but after I earned his trust he was a love. I gave him some attention and then went back in to ask David what I should do. Clearly frustrated by my question, he responded, "Melanie, you can't rescue every dog and clearly this dog has an owner. Leave him alone. The owner will come looking for him tomorrow and he'll be fine."

"But he had a limp!" I said.

David told me not to worry and come back to bed. Lying there, staring at the ceiling, I couldn't sleep. I could hear the dog dragging the heavy chain around and attempting to get into our front porch. Eventually, the noise stopped. I hoped he had gone back to his home and was able to fall asleep again, but we were awoken once more an hour later to the sound of barking. This time David wanted to handle it. I knew he wouldn't hurt him but wouldn't use a soft voice either. He was frustrated that now we had a dog that he feared would hang out around our house looking for me. He went outside and I went on to the porch to watch. He shooed the dog away and he never came back, but I was convinced we needed to rescue a dog now. I would bring up the idea every once in a while to see if he would bite, but nothing really seemed to change until one afternoon. I was shopping with Ana and she told me that a friend of her boss was looking for a home for a Labrador puppy — and free, no less! David's previous dog was a Labrador, so I asked Ana to send me photos to show David. I always imagined I would adopt a dog, but from the few discussions we had on the subject, David had so many stipulations — age, size, breed, hair length, etc. I knew adoption would be a challenge, so I decided to run the idea by him and see what happened. To my surprise, he said he would like to look at the puppy. I immediately shared the news with Ana and asked her to set up the visit as soon as possible. I was excited at the thought of having a new dog, but at the same time, I was feeling a little guilty knowing that cute purebred puppies are much easier to place than a dog in a shelter. I was trying to justify it in my mind that it is still a "rescue" because it needs a home. David and I sat on the couch that night looking at the photo of the puppy over and over. A few hours later, I heard from Ana — the owners had already found a home for the puppy. While I was disappointed, I felt like it was supposed to be this way. She then informed me that they had another Lab that was due to have puppies in the next few months and that we would be the first ones they called. I didn't understand why these people didn't have their dogs fixed. From the photos, they clearly looked like upstanding people and the dogs seemed to be well taken care of. I had met her boss; he was a classy man and I couldn't imagine his friends were any different. I wondered why, then, did they have two dogs, neither of which were fixed? The state of La Rioja was notorious for having to kill several thousand dogs each year that don't have homes. David had told me that many times in this area, people give puppies as gifts for the holidays. However, when summer comes and it's time for vacation, many pet owners abandon their dogs. Hearing this, I felt as if someone had thrown a stake through my heart and I had to do something.

I started researching websites and found that there was a shelter in Logroño. I searched their very slow, poorly maintained website and found a few dogs that looked appealing, so I sent them an email. I never heard a response. A few days later I called the shelter to inquire about seeing some of the dogs. Their hours were tight, and if you called over lunch, you'd get a voice recording that wouldn't allow you to leave a message. They also don't work a full Saturday and not at all on Sunday. I finally got through to a live person who informed me that first I needed to come to the main office to fill out paperwork, located in downtown Logroño.

To put things into perspective, this is supposed to be a time of financial crisis in Spain, but they wanted me to drive to the center of town and spend money on gas and parking, only to fill out a paper about who I am and what I want. Ok, fine, I would do what they asked. To my surprise, their headquarters was quite nice — small, but nice. Oddly enough, there were no animals in sight. After completing the paperwork, I asked if I could see the animals, to which the worker responded, "Oh no, not today. We will give your information to a volunteer and they will contact you to set up a visit." Confused by the process, I responded, "Fine. When should I expect to hear from someone?" Expecting to hear the word "tomorrow," I was disappointed to learn it wouldn't be until the following week, as the volunteers were currently focused on an upcoming fundraiser. The American in me wanted to burst out of my skin and say, "Are you fucking kidding me? I understand you need money to keep this operation going, but your mission is to find a home for a dog. I am ready to take a dog home immediately, so please get your priorities straight and have someone contact me ASAP!" I didn't, of course. I had lived in Spain long enough to know that things operate differently here and throwing a fit doesn't change anything.

I awaited the call and heard nothing. David always tells me how doing business in the northern part of Spain, the

Basque country, is often easier as the work ethic grows stronger the further north you go. Since I hadn't heard from the association in Rioja, I start searching the website for the shelter in Vitoria. David and I found a few dogs that looked interesting. On a Saturday afternoon, David picked up the phone to call the shelter. Under my breath I said, "Good luck! It's Saturday afternoon, no one is going to answer." The next thing I knew, David was speaking with a man regarding the dogs. I could tell the man was short with David at first, but once David communicated that he wanted a dog that was fixed and that he would live with us in our home, the man softened and kept David on the phone for quite some time trying to help. They were closed on Sunday, but he offered to meet with David and I anyway, as he had to be there for a few hours to tend to the dogs. I couldn't believe it! One phone call and we were light years ahead of my attempts to adopt a dog from Logroño.

The next day at the shelter, the man whom David had spoken with was there to meet us. He handed us off to a volunteer to find our pup. I offered up all of David's restrictions — no adult dogs, no large dogs — but I did mention my soft spot for pit bulls and other "dangerous" (or as I like to say, "misunderstood") dogs. She showed us the puppies and they were cute, but I could love anything. David had to be the one to choose. After some time, the attendant said she wanted to show us an American Staffordshire Terrier with a “wonderful demeanor” that they had in for quite some time. She explained that he was partially blind and they had to operate on his eyes when he arrived at the shelter. I assumed this was part of the reason he had been there for so long, since most people don't want to inherit dogs with health problems. She opened the door to the kennel and out trotted this little bundle of muscles named Keko. I could tell that David was impressed by the strength and structure of the dog. We spent time with him and he seemed like a good fit, but he was almost three years old and I wasn’t sure if David was willing to bend. I could have taken him home right then, but I didn’t say a word and remained pretty reserved on the drive home as well. When we arrived back at the house, David finally asked me in an annoyed voice, “So you don't like the dog?”

“I love the dog, but I can love any dog, you are the one who needs to love this dog. I wasn’t saying anything because I didn’t want to push him on you.”

We discussed all of the issues with getting a dangerous breed and how long the paperwork could take, but decided to go for it and have them hold the dog for us. In Spain, you have to go through a huge amount of paperwork for these breeds and the government, surprisingly, doesn't move very quickly to issue such things. We had to wait over a month to receive anything, and during this time we had another surprise.

October 2013

I had missed a period, which never happens to me, and even though we technically wanted kids, I was kind of in shock and didn't know how to tell David. After about a week, I couldn't stand it anymore and uncomfortably delivered the news through nervous laughs. Rather than happiness or glee, David's response was negative: "What? No! We can't have a child right now, how will we take care of it? We can't afford it. I can't believe you've done this."

Did I just hear him correctly? Did he just blame ME for getting pregnant? The asshole that occasionally showed face had returned, and he remained for a week or so. We didn't talk much about it that first week because when we did, we argued. David was often reactive and was never good about employing a filter. But after about a week, a funny thing happened. He seemed to make a 180-degree turn and started becoming protective of me. He had been reading things about pregnancy and started telling me what I could and couldn't eat. But he also changed in a really good way — all of the back rubs and foot rubs I'd given him seemed to be returning to me. He was speaking to me in a kinder voice and giving me priority over things he hadn't before. I knew he had researched the process of pregnancy and was starting to get excited. He helped me make my first doctor visit and told me he wanted to join me at the follow-up appointment when they do the first ultrasound. Weeks went by and we were processing and visualizing all of the changes that were about to come in our life. It was starting to be a fun experience to share together. At this point, we hadn't told anyone except for one friend who is a doctor, as we needed to know the next steps. Despite our arguments and disagreements, the news of our joined soul seemed to strengthen our bond even more.

Outside of our excitement, our life continued as normal. David always warned me that something would happen to my chickens one day, that a predator would find its way in, and after three very short months, it did. One afternoon after David and I had awoken from a nap, I looked down and couldn't make out what white object was laying beneath the olive tree. I called to David, because I had a tendency to panic when it came to my chickens, and pointed down to the yard and said, "Is that white thing under the tree a sleeping dog and are those things on the ground dead chickens?" Upon seeing the chickens, his energy changed immediately into anger as he confirmed my fear. I ran to the front door, threw my shoes on and hurried downstairs to the garden. My presence startled the dogs and they awoke immediately. There sat two white dogs, a mom and her puppy, ribs exposed like they hadn't eaten in days. My heart sank as I looked at them and my four dead chickens scattered around the yard. I asked them in a desperate voice, "Why? I understand you're hungry, but *why* did you have to eat *my* chickens?" They were pacing in the yard nervous and unable to find an exit when David appeared with a garden hoe over his shoulder, running towards them and swinging. "No, David, no! They are animals and they don't understand what they did was wrong! And they look hungry." I moved from the stairway so they could escape and eventually they did. They cut through the pine tress that lined the side of the yard, so now I understood how they entered into our property. I headed upstairs to grab plastic bags in order to discard what was left of my chickens. I was stricken with feelings of guilt as I placed them in the bags because I couldn't protect them from the hungry dogs. In the midst of my tears, I looked up to see the guilty dogs peeking through the neighbor's garden. I knew they were looking for their kill, the food they had earned. As hard as it was, I followed them down a dirt road. Even though they had collars, they appeared to be scared of people and refused to come to me, so I threw one of my chickens on the side of the road for them. I knew they would return to collect their next meal, and who was I to intervene with nature?

I had been going to visit Keko at the shelter once a week to check on him and keep him company since we couldn't take him home immediately. One day we were in Vitoria and David asked if I wanted to visit Keko since we were close to the shelter. He had never joined me for the visits, so I was surprised by the gesture. I went through the regular routine of asking if I could play with Keko in the run area. David followed us there, telling me he needed to speak to the manager about the pending paperwork. I stayed in the run area with Keko, and as I was preparing to return him to his cage, David mentioned that it wouldn't be necessary this time. He received the approval without telling me and we were there to collect Keko, not visit! We took him home that day, and I left the shelter feeling excited and nervous to have another dog after Hapa. In the middle of dealing with our loss of our feathered family members, we had just gained another companion. I thought about my odd attraction to pit bull-type dogs and came up with a theory: I was drawn to these dogs because they are so misunderstood, like my husband. If raised in a hostile environment, they can be tough fighters, but when treated with love and care, the true soul exposes itself and becomes beautiful and passionate. The fighter in David still reared its ugly head too much. He needed to reconnect with his softer side, and my gut told me that he would find that side of him in his father.

In the domestic animal kingdom of our house, the softer side of Kitty was also slow to develop. I wasn't sure how Kitty would take to our new family member. He had been socialized to other dogs through Hapa and some four-legged friends who had visited the house in Hawaii, but years had passed and Kitty now was an only child, just as Hapa was when introduced to Kitty years ago. Kitty, the newcomer at the time, loved Hapa and often tried to cuddle and vie for his attention, but Hapa was never interested in forming a friendship with Kitty. He would tolerate Kitty graciously allowing him infringe on his space. Kitty, however, wasn't as kind to Keko's new presence in the family. The hierarchy was quickly established and Kitty, like David, was more interested in fighting, rather than showing his softer sides of grace. Keko excited to meet his new roommate, leaned in to take an introductory sniff only to be met with a quick and unexpected smack to the face. Surprised, Keko took off searching for a place of shelter from this monster. As he ran away Kitty whipped around and bit Keko's butt causing him to yelp in pain and hide behind my legs for protection. The obese cat was instantly the boss and not afraid to show it. David's aspirations to have a strong, tough-guy dog breed were dashed in an instant after seeing his little "bundle of muscles" dominated by a fat cat.

December 6, 2013

The eighth week had approached and it was finally time for our first ultrasound. The doctor started to search for the baby and proceeded to show us a little image on the screen. I looked at David and saw genuine happiness in his eyes. The doctor spoke to the other doctor in the room and I sensed that something was off. David's face hardened as he comprehended what they were saying, and I struggled to piece the words together. They couldn't find the heartbeat. I can be positive to a fault and had not prepared myself for negative news. The doctors gave us the information in a very matter-of-fact manner, telling us that it may be too soon and suggesting we come back in one week. I remained quiet as we headed out, and I knew David understood how upset I was. I didn't want to cry, but tears of surprise erupted and I gave myself a few minutes to let them flow. I looked at David and told him I was fine and I would use my positive thinking to start the heartbeat in our baby, and that next week we would receive happier news.

A week couldn't have passed any slower. I knew that the universe knew better than me, and if the baby wasn't healthy he would pass, and if not, we would have a nice surprise. One thing I had noticed during my pregnancy: Both my sense of smell and taste had become extremely strong, but over the last few weeks that had subsided. I decided to push that out of my mind and hope the ebb and flow of such things was normal. We arrived at the second appointment with nervous anticipation. The doctor informed us that nothing had changed and we had to go to the emergency room in Vitoria to schedule a D&C, the removal procedure. I didn't cry this time. I was prepared either way and had faith that these events happen for a reason. While I was sad, the experience seemed to bring David and I closer in the end. I knew the next time we would be ready when our little spirit decided to come back to us.

Part of me wondered if this came to pass because I hadn't set things straight with David's father. I had always wanted our child to have as many loving family members as possible, but worried that if I chose to wait to rectify the situation until a baby was born, it might cause trouble or put the child in the middle, and this was the last thing I wanted.

CHAPTER 22

I loved being outside and taking long walks with Keko. If the weather was nice, we would walk up to the dolmen, an ancient burial site about three kilometers from our house. I loved the energy there and often used it as my place of sanctuary or walking meditation. The thought of David's father always plagued my mind and I pondered whether or not it was right to give him the letter. Every time I approached the dolmen, I would ask my angels to please give me a sign to let me know if I was doing the right thing by even thinking of intervening in David's family matters. I wanted a sign like the barking dog, but it never came in that form. Rather, it was a nagging thought or goal that I just couldn't let go of.

We had secured a new importer in the U.S., and in February David and I had planned a business trip to the East Coast to visit with clients. While in New York, we were having dinner with our friend, Mike, who was telling us about his two sons, each from different women.

His oldest was 17, and he was concerned with the

deterioration of their relationship over the past few years. As he sat there and shared his story, I felt my heart breaking as I realized the parallels between David's situation with his father and wondered what he was thinking. David waited until Mike was completely finished with his story and then spoke: "I understand your son. I haven't spoken to my father in 25 years."

"What? Why? Is he a good man?" asked Mike.

For the first time in my life I heard David speak truthfully about his father. "Yes, I think he is a good man."

I could feel how personal this was for Mike as he replied, "Then why don't you talk to him?"

"My mother can be difficult… right Melanie?" David said as he looked at me and smiled. With a smirk on my face, I gestured as if I were zipping my lip and continued to eat.

"It made my life easier with her to not have him in my life," David continued. "I tried to run away from her for a few years, but eventually she got sick and I had to live with her again. Now that I am living with Melanie and am further from my mother's negativity, I think about meeting him to take a coffee in Logroño sometimes." David had opened up to me over the years about the situation with his father, and a very tiny bit more with friends, but this revaluation was shocking.

After the conversation was over and we sat there finishing our meal, I told Mike that I knew David confided in me more than anyone in the world. I let him know it was extremely rare for David to speak of his father, much less to friends, and that sharing something like that with him was a huge step. Later, Mike stepped out for a cigarette and David looked at me for a reaction. I kept a straight face until he said, "Well?"

I could no longer contain myself, "Oh my God. I am so proud of you. I still can't believe the words I heard come out of your mouth!"

Laughing, he responded, "I knew you would love it!"

We returned to Spain after our trip to New York, and after only a few days David was headed to Jerez for a week-long course to become a certified educator of Sherry. I stayed home alone and took care of business and the animals. Every time David went away for work, the first thought that would come to my mind was my role of "secret agent" in tracking his father down, as I still had the letter with the photos. Yoga used to be my form of meditation, but I hadn't taken the time to search for a good class. My replacement now was to walk to the dolmen. I took Keko on our walk to this spiritual site, begging for a sign that it was time to contact David's father. Other than a nagging feeling, I had nothing tangible to give me a green light.

The next day I promised myself I would go on a hike that I'd been wanting to do for quite some time. Afterwords, I would head back to Laguardia to see if I could track down David's father. This was the first time hiking the Leon Durmiente Trail in the mountain range close to our home, about 15 minutes drive. Now that I had Keko, I felt more willing to go out and explore new trails alone. I searched online to find a map of the trail and loaded Keko in the car. The village was a tiny town — perhaps even smaller than Elvillar — situated on the side of the mountain. It had one main road, so I drove to the far end of the church and parked, just as the map had instructed. As we climbed to the top of the peak, I started to have second thoughts, since some of the edges were cliffs and I tended to lose my footing on the way down steep trails. When Keko and I arrived at the top, we took a rest and admired the views of the vineyards of Rioja, the windmills of Navarra, and the forest lining the opposite side of the mountain facing Vitoria. Keko was making me nervous because I knew his vision wasn't 100 percent and he kept walking dangerously close to the edge. I had to stop looking at the drop-off, and the next thing I knew I heard playful sounds and glanced over to find him frolicking with a big black Labrador. The owner and a friend arrived a few seconds later. We started talking about our pets and they assured me that the dogs would be fine, telling me they have better senses than humans, and that lack of vision didn't equal my dog plummeting to his death. I asked them if I could join them on the descent, as I was a little hesitant about facing it alone. They were happy to help and we headed down as a group.

When we arrived back at the village, I was planning on saying goodbye and loading up my car. My new friends mentioned that they were going to walk through the village to see the old church that was there. I always seemed to be in a rush for no apparent reason, and decided this time I would take in a bit of the location and join them. There wasn't much to see — a crest on a building and the church. We rounded the church and stopped in front to gaze at the beautiful large door with another crest overtop of the door. The Lab owner stated that we were witnessing the crest of Saint Peter, otherwise known as *Sampedro* or *San Pedro,* symbolized by two keys (which I later learned represent the power to forgive). That was it, I had my sign! My husband, David Sampedro, needed to be reconnected with his father. And while I still had fear of what lay ahead, I felt I couldn't brush it under the rug another day. I headed home to start my mission, full of excitement and intense anxiety.

David had said for the first time in his life that his father was "a good man," but I still worried. He didn't speak with his uncle on his mother's side, but I never forced this issue, mostly because his energy was very much reminiscent of David's mother's negative energy. The first time I saw his uncle at his grandma's house, I had no idea who he was, and he didn't even have the courtesy to say hello or introduce himself. I had to ask about who he was, and the next time I saw him, I introduced myself. When I said *encantada* (nice to meet you), he didn't return the greeting — didn't say one word actually — and reluctantly allowed me to give him the traditional two-cheek kiss. What if his father was bitter like this too? I didn't want another person like this in David's life; he needed more positive, supportive people around him, not more adult children. My gut told me it wouldn't be the case, but I wanted to get some additional confirmation before potentially going out and getting my head chopped off.

The only people whom I felt I could trust were the shepherd and his wife. I had an excuse to stop by their home, as I had missed her weekly cheese delivery on this particular Wednesday. I walked to her house and rang the bell. When she greeted me at the door, we started with our normal small talk while I worked up the courage to bring up the touchy subject. "Is David's father a good man?" I asked finally, with a degree of insecurity.

The look in her eyes brought me relief as she raised her hand to her heart and said, "Yes, a very good man." I didn't say a word as she continued, "If you and David want to know him again, I'm sure it would make him very happy."

I was in complete shock, as I never expected such a response. I had always assumed everyone in the village had supported his mother and felt the same hatred for him that she had felt, but it was just the opposite. I could feel a deep sympathy developing for David's dad as she went on to describe him as a hard worker, the complete opposite of his mother who hadn't worked for the last 10 years and expected David to support her. I walked away with a great sense of relief. Once I arrived home, I prepared myself mentally to confront this challenge. Today was the day I was going to find his father, speak with him, and get to the bottom of this! But in an instant, I lost the courage and gave in to my constant state of doubt. I closed my eyes and focused on the crest of Sampedro that had presented itself to me earlier. I figured baby steps were a better option. I would at least take the package into Laguardia and walk around hoping by some odd chance I would run into — and actually recognize — his father.

I got in my car and was there within minutes, as Laguardia is the next village over. I walked around aimlessly with no results. My previous line of questions had produced nothing, so I figured it wouldn't hurt to ask the woman in the bakery if she knew David's father and if he lived in Laguardia. With another deep breath, I walked in and asked her if she knew most of the people in the village. She said she did, so I pulled out the envelope with his name and asked her if she knew him and if he lived in Laguardia. She confirmed my hope; he lived in Laguardia, but in the flats located outside of the walls of the village. She then pointed me to David's cousin Itor's bar, since he would know his exact address. Ugh… the cousin. Granted, Itor was a cousin from his father's side of the family but I knew if I asked him about David's father, there was no turning back. I was opening a door that I couldn't shut again.

During a previous visit, I had made friends with one of the waitresses in the bar at a hotel a few doors down. In my cowardice state, I tried to find her but the bar was closed. I had no choice; I would walk by the bar and if the cousin or aunt wasn't in plain site, I would leave promptly. As I entered the bar, the cousin was standing close to the door talking to a guest and as soon as he saw me, he greeted me with his typical friendly demeanor. I felt stuck and managed to translate the words into Spanish, "Is David's father a good man?" Once again, I was greeted with the face of heartbreak. He pulled me outside and started to tell me about his uncle, David's dad. He was so emotional; I had to slow him down because I couldn't keep up with his pace of Spanish. He told me that every time David's father came into the bar, his first question was, "Have you seen my son?" followed by, "How is he doing?" My eyes started to well up with tears and I felt my heartbeat speed up. I had no idea he had any interest in David and I was sure from everything I had heard before from David, it would be a shock for him as well. He eventually asked me if I wanted to meet him. I responded, "Yes! Of course! That is, if he will meet me?" He continued to tell me he would like me to speak with his mother first, and then phoned her to tell her that I was in the restaurant waiting with questions about David's father.

He sat me in a private booth attached to the bar so that no one could overhear our conversation. His mom walked in and took a seat to my left. I had met her before and she was always friendly, but this time she seemed a bit more reserved. She didn't start in immediately as her son had; she was more cautious trying to find out if I had bad intentions. It only took a few minutes for her to realize that I had good intentions. After sharing some of the history with me, she shared that David's father did everything with David in mind. He had stayed with Lali until David was a teenager, mainly because he didn't want to leave his son alone with her. When the day came for him to leave, he didn't abandon David, which was always what I was told. He gave David the option to go with him, but as most young children do, he chose his mother. I had a feeling that in David's case, part of his desire to go with her was natural and the other half was a result of her crafty manipulation. She continued with yet another contradictory story, saying that after the divorce, David would still have visits with his father, but over time this ended by David's choice. Once again, my mind was filled with rage at the thought of David's mother putting him in the middle, training him to believe that his father was a villain. These stories delivered blow after blow of new information… she also told me his father sent money to his mother even after the divorce to care for David, and that the house they had in Vitoria was for him. She claimed he had a hard life but never complained and said he "suffers in silence." The words resonated with me. Then she told me that David has a grandmother that is 91 years old, and that nothing would make her happier than to see her grandson again. His aunt remembered David's birthday and a bunch of stories from his youth. She shared that she, too, had a feeling that David wanted to come back to the family, as she noticed him coming into their bar more over the years. She had promised herself that one day she would try to bring David back into the family, but only when she felt the time was right. Then she posed the same question, "Would you like to meet him?"

"Yes, if he's willing," I replied.

She made a few phone calls, and within minutes David's father, Bienve, was sitting next to me in the restaurant. He had been working and left immediately upon hearing that I wanted to meet him, so he was still in his work clothes. We greeted each other and he started asking me questions that would confirm the extent of his knowledge of David. He had been trying to keep track of David through friends and the Internet, so he knew where we lived, and where and when we got married. I asked him in disbelief, "How do you know all this?" to which he responded, "He's my son." He told me about how when David was young it was he who spent a majority of time with his son, and it was he who would bring David to Elvillar. He talked about how David is his only child, how he loved David's grandfather on his mother's side and was truly heartbroken when he passed. He recounted when he offered to have David stay with him and how David chose his mother. He asked about David's vineyards and his work in an effort to catch up on all the years he'd lost.

After about 30 minutes, he called his girlfriend, Clara, to come to the restaurant to meet with me. A warm and friendly woman, she shared how they both put a lot of effort into searching for David online and trying to keep up with his life. She was more than his girlfriend, as they had been together for 16 years. Within a few minutes of her arrival, he asked if he could run home and change out of his work clothes. No sooner did he leave when I looked over to see her face covered in tears. I grabbed her arm to comfort her, realizing they were tears of joy. I turned to my other side to his aunt, only to discover that she, too, was sobbing. I couldn't believe that me of all people, who would tear up over a Kleenex commercial, didn't have the slightest need to cry. I was elated with joy at what was happening. When his cousin first told me that David's father still cared about him, I fought to hold back tears, but right now I just wanted to jump up and down with excitement. I hugged them both as I thought about how David had missed out on a lifetime of happiness. This was a normal family — everyone spoke to each other, supported one another, and cared deeply about the family bonds. This is what David needed all his life! He had no concept of a happy family. His aunt and grandma were the stable and caring people on his mother's side, but they often celebrated without David, as they had to choose between David or his uncle. They never got together as a fully functioning family during the holidays; it was always David and now me stuck at his mother's house with heavy, depressing energy. I would count down the minutes to the departure hoping that a fight didn't emerge over the course of the visit. Did this mean we now had a real chance at spending the holidays with joy and celebration, rather than dread and anxiety?

David's father returned and they were all very interested in knowing if this was my idea or something that David was championing as well. I wasn't sure. I knew my husband and how difficult he can be when it comes to emotional issues. It had taken him years to speak about his father, and even now when he spoke of him, he rarely gave details, I suspected because doing so would reveal emotions that were too strong for him to cope with. I remember when Hapa died and I was crying, David's advice was to "stop thinking about it," as if that would magically make all the pain go away. But that's what he and probably most men do — they don't think about it and never really heal. This is why David couldn't speak about his father, because if he spoke, he had to think, and thinking brought up all the emotions that he had stuffed down for all those years.

We stayed in that booth talking about everything for several hours. I realized I felt more comfortable with these strangers within the first few minutes than all the time I'd ever spent with his mother. We exchanged numbers and promised to keep in touch. His father and girlfriend walked me to my car, we hugged and I drove off with a heart full of promise and anxiety, wondering how David would react.

David returned home from Jerez a few days later. We had friends in town and I knew there wouldn't be an appropriate time to tell him until after they left. Holding all this new information was killing me and I needed to get it off my chest. One morning our friends decided to sleep late, and David and I saw the opportunity to get some exercise. He wanted to run and I wanted to walk, so we agreed to head in two different directions and meet in the middle, and then return home together. It dawned on me as I was walking to meet him that this may the perfect moment to tell him about his father. I start working up the courage to speak the words, nervous and unsure about what kind of reaction I would get. I assumed he would be mad at first, lose his temper, and over time forgive me and be thankful. This was how he processed most everything when it came to us. We met up and started down the road to home together. A few minutes passed and I figured, the sooner the better, as it would give him more time to process before returning home to a house full of guests. I went for it: "I have something to tell you but it may be emotional for you. Do you want me to wait until after our guests leave? It's about your father."

"You met him, didn't you?"

I couldn't believe how well we knew each other. "Yes," I admitted with a hint of guilt, "and he's a wonderful man."

I continued to tell him everything that unfolded. He just walked alongside me, listening and not making a sound. As we approached a crossroads, he interrupted me and instructed me to give him Keko's leash. He attached it to Keko's collar and took off running in another direction. I stood there watching him run away in shock. He didn't ask one question, just ran away. I assumed it was too much information and he needed to process it alone. Was he mad, scared, happy? I was in the dark about what he was feeling. As I arrived closer to the house, I saw him coming up behind me. I ignored him and continued walking, assuming that he didn't want to talk to me. I heard him yell my name, so I turned around to meet him. His face revealed nothing, as if I hadn't just told him a story that could change the path of his life. I asked him if he hated me. He ignored the question and gently touched my back. Later that day, he was extra affectionate with me, and I avoided bringing up the dad topic. I waited three days and finally asked him what he thought of the information I had shared. He didn't want to talk about it.

A week later we had to go to Barcelona for a wine fair and tasting. I brought it up again on the drive and he quickly shot down any chance of getting to the meat of the issue. Once again, I got an, "I don't want to talk about it." On our second day in Barcelona, my phone rang and it was Clara, his father's girlfriend. I hadn't reached out to them since our meeting, even though I wanted to, as I wanted to respect David's process. I was delighted that they were making an effort. She asked me how he responded, and I did my best to tell her in Spanish what happened and that I thought he wasn't ready. I assumed it would be easier to explain this in person, so I arranged to meet both of them when I returned to Rioja.

We decided to meet on Friday at the lake by Laguardia. The previous evening during a walk, as I was toying with the notion of inviting him to join us, David mentioned that he was headed to Vitoria the next day for a 3:30 p.m. appointment. I told him that I had made plans to meet with his father the next day at 4 p.m. and was hoping he would come. For a moment, he acted interested and questioned why I chose a time when he would be gone. When I offered to change the time, he accused me of trying to manipulate him. That was his defense and I wasn't going to fight it.

Friday arrived and Bienve and Clara greeted me in front of their home. Bienve immediately took Keko's leash from my hand, and I knew in that moment that I adored his father. The three of us walked around the lake together talking the entire time, and then we decided to go out for a coffee together. I enjoyed our conversations and noticed how easy these people were to be around. When I returned home, I texted a photo to David of his father walking Keko and wrote, "To be clear, THIS is manipulation." He arrived home less than an hour later and didn't ask a single question about my time with his father.

Two days later we had to work on hand-labeling bottles for a U.S.-bound order. David was on the couch when I left for the warehouse by foot, and he planned to meet me there with the car. I had just walked out of the house when I heard my phone. I looked down and saw "Sampedro." Wondering what David could want after leaving the house only seconds ago, I answered in a confused and slightly annoyed voice, "Si?" To my shock, it was David's father. He told me that he wanted to see David and asked me when it would be a good time. I think he called hoping that David would be there next to me. I promised him I would speak with David and see what I could do. When David arrived at the warehouse, I told him his father called and wanted to see him. To my surprise, he responded, "When?" Was that an invitation for a meeting? I told him that I explained our work situation so it wouldn't be for a few days, and I asked him when he would like to see his father. He said nothing more and asked no questions. Frustrated once again, I dropped the subject, but at least this time there was a little hope in my heart.

April 2014

David and I, both being dreamers, will often take long walks and talk about our vivid visions for the future. When my sweet Hapa passed last year, David promised me that one day we would find a white vineyard and name it after Hapa. One night on a walk, we found our Hapa vineyard! We marveled at the beautiful old vines on limestone soils climbing a hill where at the top you can find the remains of an ancient roman road. The energy was fabulous. David showed me how the current owners didn't take care of the property as they should and how at the top of the hill there is a small grove of trees. I realized that this was the same plot of land he had shown me years ago, one of the places he dreamed of building a winery. Sometimes we get so caught up in living that we forget to dream, but I was determined that this land and this vineyard would be ours one day, and it only made sense to have our winery near my Hapa vineyard. My ultimate goal was to one day donate a portion of the profits of the wine we created to an animal rescue organization. I made David promise me he would inquire about who the owners were so one day, when we had more money, we could contact them, even though I knew that day would be further in the future than both of us hoped. We were currently renting and within the next year, we would start looking at finding another winery. We liked the idea of continuing to live above our winery — it made sense financially and we wanted to keep our "children" (the barrels and tanks) close to us.

Another day passed and David still hadn't mentioned anything about seeing his father. Throughout this process, David often referred to me as being manipulative, and it enraged me because I knew he was comparing me to his mother. My patience was growing thin and I was starting to get angry at him for maintaining this attitude. It was unhealthy to ignore his feelings about his father, and more importantly, every day that passed without contacting him inflicted more pain on a good man. Now that the story was clearer for me, couldn't David see that his past wasn't entirely his father's fault? Yes, he may have left David by leaving his mother, but he didn't truly leave David. In actuality, it was David who chose to leave his father. By staying with his mother, David signed up for a lifetime of suffering, a lifetime of being the victim and feeling the world was against him. These were his mother's thoughts and feelings that arose from her own bad decisions, but when people reacted negatively to those decisions, it was never her fault. The words that David spoke to me when we reconnected in 2008 were etched into my brain, a phrase ingrained in his psyche from his mother: "The world is hard, I only have my mother, you can't trust people." His father, who probably never spoke like this and I'm sure didn't want to put David in the middle as a child, decided to let his son make his own decisions. I imagined his father hoped David would come around one day and eventually understand the full story, but I doubt he expected it would take 25 years.

If my husband wanted to refer to me as a manipulator, I decided to live up to the title, although it felt better to tell myself it was a "mini-manipulation." I was trying to help David right a wrong in his life, so I decided to tell him that we had dinner plans with his dad and see what his reaction was. To my surprise, he asked why I decided to bring them to the house, but I didn't get a flat-out no, so that was encouraging. I sensed he was worried about having them in our tiny village where everyone would be watching, so I told him the details weren't 100 percent set yet and mentioned we had also talked about meeting in Laguardia. After a few hours of letting the idea sit with David, I sent a message to Clara asking her if they would like to meet for a meal on Wednesday night. She immediately called me back and told me that they would like to invite us to dinner in Laguardia. I hung up the phone and told David the news. Within a few hours, reality started to sink in and he proceeded to chastise me, saying that he doesn't interfere in my family business and I shouldn't interfere in his. I knew he was scared, although he would never admit it. I can tell when he's really angry because he makes it very clear, but this time he was annoyed, nervous and troubled, but not truly angry. He was feigning anger, the only mechanism he had for expressing his feelings.

That afternoon David and I drove to Vitoria for our monthly vet appointment for Keko's eyes. Afterwards, we had a fight about money. We had gone to lunch and he said he didn't have money to pay for the meal, yet afterwards when he wanted to shop for sport clothes he asked me how much money he could spend and I replied, "Zero, but you can look." This was just enough, on top of me meddling in his personal affairs, to make him clam up and avoid speaking to me. Clearly, I had done nothing wrong, but he needed a reason to stop speaking to me. I got the silent treatment the rest of the night and the entire next day.

The day of our dinner, I took Keko on his daily walk around Elvillar and ran in to the shepherd with his flock. Daniel and his wife would forever hold a special place in my heart, because they had been the ones to confirm that David's father was worth reconnecting with. I had told Pilarin, his wife, that we were having dinner with David's father earlier in the day. She had apparently relayed the information to Daniel because, for the first time, he spoke to me with more honesty about David's father than anyone had ever done up to this point. He shared how Bienve had started a business and was a very hard worker, but David's mother was constantly sabotaging his success by spending outside of their means and causing financial problems for the business. He talked about her quickness to anger and her emotional outbursts in front of others. He told me how his father had decided when David was younger that he couldn't stay married to her forever and how he would only stay with her for David's sake and planned to leave when David grew older. He kept repeating, "It was her fault." When I asked why no one ever shared any of this with David, he responded, "Children don't want to think their mother is bad." He acknowledged that to go against her meant you had to deal with her wrath, and that a majority of people in the village didn't agree with how she handled the situation.

As I listened, even more things started coming together about the past. I thought about David's stories of how the people in Elvillar gossip and never want good for others. Maybe there was some truth to this small town mentality. Or maybe David viewed the people of his village through his mother's eyes, with the philosophy that a good offense is the best defense — a defense mechanism of sorts. *Make them the bad guys who only want to gossip so that if any painful truths come out, you can brush it off as jealousy from small-minded people.* Up to this point, her plan had worked perfectly. David held a lot of contempt for many people in the village, so anything that might come out would be quickly disregarded as false. So perhaps it was true that when his father's business failed and they divorced, Lali had to sell vineyards to pay off some of the debt, but it was debt that she helped create. She was accepting money from him after the divorce, while at the same time trashing his name in front of David. How could all of this information have waited so long to come to the surface, and why was I the one to be unearthing it? I still felt that no one wanted to tell David the truth, but it couldn't come from me or his father as it would probably just provoke an angry response. Sometimes to move forward in your life you can't look back, but was David's character strong enough to do that? I hoped with everything in me that he was ready to move on and forgive, to let go of resentment without placing judgment.

April 9, 2014

Our dinner reservations were set with his father for 9:30 p.m. David had left the house around 10 a.m. and hadn't returned the entire day. I sent him texts with the details, but no answer. I was working on my computer at 8:45 p.m. and still no sign of David. I was worried he wasn't going to show or would send an excuse, but I had already decided that if he cancelled, I was going to kick him out of the house for a few days. He could go stay with his mother and be reminded of what life was like with her, and I would only allow him to return when I was ready. The thought that my husband was a selfish person kept plaguing my mind and I didn't want to think of him that way. I prayed he wouldn't miss this opportunity and he didn't. He came home at 9 p.m., yet he seemed to be in no rush, slowly checking emails and finally getting around to changing his clothes. Luckily, Laguardia was only five minutes away, so we arrived on-time. As we pulled in to the center of the Laguardia, I peered through the hotel window and noticed his father and Clara waiting for us at the bar. As we entered, they walked over to greet us. David shook his father's hand, but I could tell his father was hoping for more. Bienve appeared nervous, talking a mile a minute, and at one point I heard him say, "I didn't kill anyone," in a desperate attempt to convince his son that he isn't a bad man. David wasn't exactly warm, but I was happy that he was willingly answering his father's questions. I had been around him many times when he chose not to answer questions positioned by family or friends, and I was grateful that he was being cordial enough to respond.

We enjoyed our dinner together as strangers and family. While I would have loved to see a softer side of David during the dinner, he did the best he could do at that moment and I was proud of him for taking such a big step in his life. We all struggle with our demons everyday, and those demons that come from the mind as opposed to the heart are especially challenging to overcome. But on this day, despite his brain telling him that he shouldn't go, he showed up. Just as I had done with him years ago, David was fighting his mind and trying to follow what his heart was telling him — that his father was worth fighting for. I had struggled with my demons about David for years, but in the end when I let my ego stop controlling me, I found my heart was right. I knew David had to find the same in his heart.

I remembered sharing my toils with Darrell concerning Luke and David and his premonition, specifically how I wrestled with my head vs. my heart. His advice then had been hauntingly accurate: “Melanie, regardless of which path you choose, this time, you will be okay. However, life with David will be harder, but in the end you will be happier.” Those words lived up to their promise; I had never been happier and more content than in my relationship with David, yet the issues I faced in just about every aspect of our life together continued to challenge my constitution on a regular basis. But the difference with David, the thing with him that I had never felt before, was my lack of ego. With David I was willing to fight for us and not for my ego. The marriage and my love for him would always win over my selfish desires. I needed David to find the same in his heart with his father.

We had plenty of arguments, but David made it clear that I was his heart and his family. While I appreciated the fact that he loved me, he stated these words in a way that made me sad. One night while sitting on the couch late night watching TV, he leaned over, kissed me and told me, “Melanie, you are my family now and the best family I’ve ever had in my life.” I was touched by his words, but I couldn’t ignore the fact that with each passing day, he was slowly diminishing the opportunity to grow his “normal” family by not reaching out to his dad.

I truly enjoyed the presence of his father and Clara, so

when time permitted, I made plans to meet with them. More often than not, David's schedule didn't allow him to join, but he made sure I knew he had no problems with my meeting up with them. As I got to know his father more, I grew to understand why he couldn't reach out to his son for so many years. His personality was easygoing to a fault. He didn't want to rock boats or cause trouble, but there is a time and place when you need to stand up for yourself and point out when you feel something is wrong. When he would go on about how he wanted to see his son, or how he's willing to help him in any way possible, my responses started to become very direct. I would simply state, "You should call him!" I noticed Clara encouraging her husband to do the same thing, to take action. I could feel how hard it was for him to talk about finally getting the chance to be a part of his son's life. He was the polar opposite of David's mother, who was more than happy to start a fight, tell you her feelings and force her agenda. His father was so far to the other extreme that he too had let many opportunities pass for fear of causing problems.

One day during a walk with Bienve and Clara, I had shared how I was going to get more chickens. He offered to get them for me and drop them off at the house. I was a little nervous to accept and unsure if David would be comfortable with his father coming to Elvillar, but when I mentioned it, he didn't have much of a reaction so I gave his father the green light. A few afternoons later, David's phone rang and it was his father! It was the first time he mustered the energy to call his son. He had craftily used the chickens as an excuse to talk to him, and they worked out the details over the phone. When they hung up, I told David I was sure that one little phone call was probably really difficult for his father and mentioned how proud I was of both of them. Within a matter of days, David's father, trying to do anything he could to win his son's favor, dropped off two new chickens for me.

CHAPTER 23

The relationship between David and his father was far from a fairytale, but it was definitely a step in the right direction. I'd hoped that my intuition was right and that by setting things straight with his father, positive things would start appearing in our lives — the universe's way of telling you when you are following the right path. Overt time, things seemed a little easier with our lives and the sales of our wines started growing. We sold out of four different wines and came dangerously close to selling out of our core brand. David had challenged me to sell out of all of our wines when I first started helping him with the business — a challenge that I promised to complete with arrogance while inside doubting my ability, as I was learning a new arm of sales and had relatively few (practically zero) contacts in the wine world. And while selling out of most of the wines left us in a good position, things were still a challenge, as we still needed the capital to bottle the next vintage. I dreamed about the future when money wouldn't be an issue and sitting on vintages would be a normal occurrence to be released at our leisure. Our cellar would be organized and full, dating back to the first vintage in 2007.

May 2014

Another pleasant surprise came to us in May: We learned we were pregnant again! This time, the news came with less emotion… good or bad. We were both more cautious now and understood the importance of getting to that 12-week mark. In the beginning, I was sure that I wasn't pregnant, that somehow I had a false positive. I had no symptoms and other than occasional bouts of exhaustion, I felt completely normal. I tried to convince David and my doctor of my theory and neither of them was buying it. My doctor tried to convince me that one miscarriage didn't mean that another would follow, but I wasn't convinced. It was my way of protecting myself from any disappointment and failed expectations. I shared the news with my close friends whom, when they found out that I had miscarried before, told me not to withhold information this time around. They all separately told me the same thing… that they were grateful I had shared the news early on and would send me and the baby positive energy to get us through a healthy pregnancy. It was nice to have more support, as just about every one of my friends who insisted I keep them in the loop had also gone through a miscarriage. I was enjoying having my own little entourage of advocates and well-wishers around the world, who would check in with me on a regular basis, constantly reminding me of how fortunate I am to be surrounded by loving people.

The dreaded eight-week ultrasound crept up on us once again. This time I was prepared for anything they threw at me and to our surprise, the doctor quickly said that everything looked healthy. He called David in to look at the ultrasound and there it was, what looked like a tiny bean that one day would be our child. The one thing we always wanted but were so scared to have. We were scared to fail, scared to loose our independence, but all the while knowing that looking into the eyes of our son would bring us more joy and love than the overwhelming love we had for each other thus far. It seemed almost impossible to imagine. And I now had peace knowing that our son would have a complete family, and that no friend or family member would be excluded from loving him.

David and I had planned to visit clients and family in the United States for two weeks in July. While sharing our plans with his father, he inquired about who would watch our house and animals. I could tell he was eager to help, and I knew that our friends whom we normally leaned on for this job would be grateful as well. I gladly agreed to his offer and gave him keys to the house. When we returned, we were shocked to find he had cleaned our entire backyard. The grass was cut, the clutter organized and the garden had been worked with great care and was flourishing like never before. I couldn't believe how similar he was to my mother. She would drop anything and work her tail off to help her children. The down side to this was the fact that the villagers saw him at the house and word got back to his mother. When we arrived home, David drove into Logroño to check on her and the wrath came down upon him. He never told me what exactly she said, and truly I didn't want to know. He was upset when he returned and said that with her knowing that his father was back in the picture, we could expect a lot of problems ahead of us. Then he threw in a jab about how it was my fault. Maybe it was, and if I thought I had done something wrong, I might have felt sorry, but I didn't. I simply stated that he's almost 40 years old and it was high time he started living his own life and stopped living under his mother's control. This wasn't about her; it was about our child, our family and David. My pregnancy hormones were in full throttle during the first few months and after a few more visits to his mother's house and coming home angry with me because she was upset by the fact his father was in his life again, combined with his angry reaction when I told him his father was going to stop by the house to drop off the keys, I completely lost it with him. I started screaming that the entire situation was ridiculous and that I was losing respect for him. "I told your father you were a good person," I yelled. "Well, you know what? I look like a fucking liar! You don't even have the heart to spend time with a good man, you'd rather cater to your mother's selfish motives that have controlled you for years. If you can't be kind to your father when he's in our house then get the fuck out!! You said you need to work in the vineyard, just go, LEAVE. I will spend the time with your father."

I can't remember if I cried this time but I was shaking with anger. He did what I asked and worked in the vineyards until sunset and his father had left. I didn't like the darkness that I felt inside, the anger and hatred because I knew when I let those emotions control me, I was the pot calling the kettle black. Thankfully, my hormones once again normalized and I realized that I could continue to have a relationship with his father, and that David could join us when he was ready. I stopped trying to control everything.

I prayed that one day, my husband would realize that he truly deserved to have a loving father in his life. I hoped that David becoming a father would make him compassionate toward his father. I was one hundred percent certain that he would be an amazing parent. He is a good man and a loyal husband, and behind his ego lies a huge heart. And yes, we have our problems. He's not perfect and neither am I, but the difference is the love never goes away. I knew David would have to go through the same emotions I did — eliminating the ego, forgiving the past, trusting in his heart that his father is a good man. I knew it wouldn't happen overnight and healing a century of pain was going to take time, but I trusted that my husband would eventually come around and follow his guides, just like I did. I saw a brighter future for us and our family because we were following the simple mantra: *When you do what's right, which usually isn't the easiest path, the universe rewards you.*

CHAPTER 24

Finances once again reared their ugly head. David had compiled tons of documentation to apply for help from the government and everything seemed to be in order. Our asking price was a fraction of what other wineries were requesting in assistance, 30,000 EU in total, whereas the large wineries, which already have money, request up to 100,000 EU for the salary of one export manager plus other requests for marketing and other expenses. Our figure included my salary, travel and marketing all in one.

No sooner did we arrive in Spain and David had to turn around head to China for a two-week business trip. China was not the market for our fine wines and David wasn't excited about going, but they had offered to pay for his flight. The subsidized money from the government was to pay for these things, so David offered to pay for his ticket and allowed the importer to pay for Sergio's ticket instead.

After the two weeks of travel through China, David arrived home and started in on the pile of paperwork that greeted him. One item was a certified letter that I had signed for in his absence. I had thought nothing of it because in Spain it seems everything from any section of the government is sent certified mail, whether it's important or not. Apparently, this time it was important. David approached me with the letter in hand yelling at me for not notifying him when it arrived. The government was notifying him that he had 15 days to set up an account for the funds, or the money would be retracted. Two weeks had passed at this point. We headed to the bank the next day to set up the account, but nothing moves quickly in Spain and they couldn't set up the account within a few days. In the end, even after David appealed by explaining the situation and begged the government for assistance, we received nothing. There is nothing worse than the sinking feeling you get when you made a mistake that you weren't even aware of and you are helpless to do anything to rectify the situation. "I'm sorry" seems so weak in moments like these. David wasn't happy with the situation but knew it wasn't totally my fault and that making me feel miserable wouldn't help our relationship, so we eventually moved past the subject.

Once things settled down a bit, it was time to check on the vineyards to see how they had progressed in his absence. We walked the vineyards together, often hand-in-hand because I was a bit more paranoid of a fall in my pregnant state and wanted his extra support. He gladly helped me through the vineyards while simultaneously mocking me for my sudden lack of independence. I knew he enjoyed being needed and offering me support. He has his little ways of showing me, often through sarcasm, but I know him well enough to know his heart is good. While we're walking he asks me if I ever dreamed we'd be walking together pregnant through the vineyards. Even though I had dreamt of such a thing, I simply smiled at him and said, "a beautiful thing, isn't it?" We'd had our moments and bad times. I had serious doubts about his character when his father returned into his life and he didn't respond how I would have liked, but now I know that David has to digest things on his own terms. I could accept that now and didn't push him when I wanted to spend time with his father's side of the family. Being able to accept the situation for what it was helped our relationship once again prove its beauty.

David would often joke with me about my "magical powers", noting that in the past if I focused on something hard enough, if it was meant to be, I would get what I asked for. We needed an extra push financially to build our dreams and as fate would have it, luck decided to pay us a visit. Our friend Dean was eager to see how things were moving along for us in Spain and was interested in investing in vineyards. Prior to doing so, he wanted to learn everything he could about Rioja Alavesa and our business because a potential purchase would be not only for his benefit but an investment in us as well, as we would rent the vineyards from him. We spent two weeks sharing our home with Dean and his son, who happened to be traveling through Europe at the time. It was important for Dean to share his findings with his son because his son would ultimately be the benefactor of the purchase. We spent our days exploring the region and sharing our ideas and many nights indulging in innovative and exquisite Spanish cuisine, which is surprising to first time visitors who are often unaware of the high quality food culture of Spain. After only a few weeks, Dean was eager to find a way to enter into the world of wine and decided the best route would be to take an even riskier route than previously planned. Rather than investing in vineyards, he wanted to invest in David by offering us a personal loan to help us grow the business. He would hold off on charging us interest and defer payments for a few years in order to help us establish ourselves financially. His help couldn't have come at a better time. Once again our angels surprised us – this time by appearing in human form, but of course David would attribute it to my magical powers.

September 2014

Over the passing months, David became more and more excited about our child. At the six-month point, we went to get the ultrasound and find out the sex of the baby. David was adamant about wanting a boy. So much so, I was beginning to worry that he might not love a girl, as much as a boy. He said a lot of things in jest, but sometimes it was too much and I worried there was truth behind some of his words. The night before the appointment, he had spoken into my growing belly to our child, "You must have a penis tomorrow. Do you understand me? I will be very upset if not." It was that same humor/truth that stressed me. I had always envisioned and at times felt the energy of a boy, but this test would reveal our fate.

We were called into the exam room and the process started. We were delighted to hear that everything looked healthy, and we could see the spine, head, arms, legs and little fingers and toes … check, check and check! The doctor asked us if we wanted to know the sex, and after an anxious *yes*, she moved the wand on my belly to expose on the screen what looked like a teeny tiny toothpick. *It's a boy!* David grunted a sound of elated triumph in my direction — a sense of satisfaction not only with the situation but with himself, as I had repeatedly reminded him that the sperm determines the sex and therefore any "fault" would be his in this case. I felt a huge sense of relief for many reasons — the health of the baby and now for the mental health of my husband. My stress was once again elevated when I found out that he wanted a boy only to help him in the vineyards and winery. I joked, "Wait, you only wanted a son for a slave in the vineyard, so you can work him like your family worked you?" His response was, "Yes! exactly." Suddenly, I realized that a girl might have had an easier life with David as a father. He has very high expectations in general and with his son, I can only imagine the bar will be very high.

David's gentle and loving side seemed to surface with each passing month. The larger my belly grew, the more he would tell me how pretty I looked. It seemed counterintuitive to me, as I saw a changing body softening and growing in all the wrong places, except for one — my breasts. I was never well endowed, yet for the first time in my life I actually had boobs. There were times when he would go from speaking to my belly with our child and work his way up to my breasts begging them not to return to their prenatal state, "Please, don't change! You are so pretty like this," he would say.

When we didn't have guests or plans for the evening, our favorite thing to do was stay home and watch movies on the couch. David would often take the position of his head on my lap pressed up against my belly listening for any movement. He would delight at feeling his head kicked by our son's growing appendages. We may have had many disagreements but everything was aligned when it came to our son's future. We both wanted to give him a better family life than we had. To make him feel confident and loved and teach him how to love by demonstrating our unconditional love for each other, examples neither David or I had growing up in divorced families. We had to learn how to love on our own, rather than by example.

As time passed and people opened up more to me about his mother's behavior and the things she had done in her past, the more I didn't want to know. They were histories that made me feel sorry for David having to grow up with a constant stream of lies and deceit. Knowing these things meant I was keeping a dark secret from David, and I knew there was no use in sharing my knowledge with him as it would only cause pain, arguments and probably denial on his part anyway. His version of the truth — his father left him — was almost easier to stomach than the actual truth. Interestingly, it was never his father who spoke negatively about his mother, even though it was he who was hurt the most, and from what I understood about him was that had been is pattern since David was a child. Nights when David would ask his father where is mother was, he would politely make excuses for her. But it was as if David has been reprogrammed, since he seemed to have no memory of such events. In the same way my mother had done with my father, he thought it best to keep his negative opinions of David's mother to himself — even though this act of grace allowed the wall between them to grow larger. Throughout the entire process of learning the truth about who is father is, somehow I had finally come to a place of where I could forgive his mother. A place of internal peace. I could now accept that David's mom was wrong and not let her actions now or in the past bother me. I didn't see her much and when I did, I no longer felt nervous or scared. Rather, I was cordial and for the most part silent, as there wasn't much to say. We had very little in common. But I know I will follow the same path as my mother and David's father, and regardless of what transpires with my son, I will not plant negativity about his grandmother in his mind. Nor will I allow anyone else to for that matter.

One afternoon I was spending time with his father when Clára showed me a picture of Bienve when he was 20 years old. I couldn't believe the resemblance, it was as if I was looking at an antique photo of my husband. I commented that there was no doubt he was his son's father. His father laughed and said how Lali always told him that David wasn't his child. I probed further due to the oddity of the statement,

"After you divorced, she tried to claim that David was not yours?" I asked.

"No. She told me that repeatedly while we were married," Bienve replied.

"What? That's crazy! That would mean she was with other men?"

"Why do you think I finally left?" he said, without emotion or judgment, but rather a factual statement as he continued to sort through some old photos.

CHAPTER 25

The harvest this year was different, more stressful as the weather wasn't on our side and I couldn't pitch in. My friend Liane was visiting from Hawaii and was eager to take part in the process. Reluctantly, David accepted her assistance and after finding that I knew what I was talking about and she really was a hard worker, he took her up on her offer multiple times. I spent more time watching than actually doing, being that I was seven months pregnant but occasionally I could pitch in. When it came time to foot crush the grapes, my extra baby weight would come in handy and I gladly offered assistance and inserted my round figure and bare feet into the barrel to start stomping. No better time than the present to expose our son to what lies ahead. The baby seemed to enjoy the life in the vineyard and in our winery and would show me his enjoyment with constant kicks.

Our rent was up on the house/winery and the owners wanted to sell, but time was running short on finding an alternative winery for the next year. Our current situation wasn't a viable option, since we needed to purchase not only the house but also the land next to our house to allow trucks proper access to the winery — but the owner didn't want to sell. We were finding that no one in our strange little viticultural village wanted to sell. If they didn't say no immediately, they would state the same thing in so many words by offering an astronomical figure for the land. In the start of my pregnancy, when I was highly hormonal the stress of uncertainty had me in knots. As my hormones normalized and I returned to myself, I started to find my faith again and know that the right opportunity would present itself in its own time, not mine. We'd spoken to many people about parcels of land, and I'd asked his father to search out some properties, but nothing seemed to be going our way. Rejection after rejection was a constant test of my faith and learning to let go of control was the only way to stay sane.

I had been trying to stay active during my pregnancy and over time my long walks started to shorten and occur less often. One evening, I convinced David to help motivate me by accompanying me on one of my walks. We headed in the direction of our *Abejera* vineyard, the closest one to our house. It was getting dark and David decided to direct us down a small road that I wasn't familiar with. As we proceeded down the road, we started talking about the location and how it could potentially be a good place to build our winery and home. David said he would inquire the following day to find out about the owners. I didn't think much of it, as this situation had passed many times up to this point, always ending in disappointment.

The next day, David returned home with "good news" that the owners weren't from Elvillar, but the next village over. He was hopeful they would be more reasonable to deal with, but I was getting tired of the dealings we'd had recently with the local people and was starting to think it would be better to just find a location completely outside of the village. It would make the marketing of our concept a little more difficult in the future, being that we had named our winery after the name of the village in Basque, but I would simply have more explaining to do and that was easier than fighting for a reasonable offer with unreasonable people. Later on in the day, he told me he was heading into Logroño and was gone for a few hours. He walked through the door and announced that he spoke with the owners and they were very nice, and more importantly, reasonable people that were open to selling the vineyards. He didn't have a price, but felt confident they wouldn't be crazy with a ridiculously high price, and so we waited. A few days passed and we had our figure. It was the most reasonable figure I'd heard in months. David felt it was still a bit high and wanted to negotiate a bit more. He prepared his paperwork to make his case and we met with them on a Sunday morning. David was right, they were lovely. The man was blind and I was in awe at his independence. He was a little late because he had gone on a walk and due to the heavy tractor traffic on the road had gone at a slower pace. When he discovered the time, he ran home without assistance. He had made a very normal life for himself despite his vision challenges. He had an energy about him and for some reason his look was a bit Hawaiian, so I was instantly comfortable in his presence. We walked out of their house twenty minutes later with a solid agreement on the price. It was surreal, and neither of us celebrated as there were many pieces that still needed to fall into place. For the first time in David's life, would he have his own winery? Not rented, not using the space of a friend or consulting at a winery in order to "rent" the space to make his wine. But his very own space. The property was surrounded by vineyards on the top of a hill outside the village. We called it our "mini chateau."

December 5, 2014

After weeks of waiting for the notary to tell us everything was in order, we were finally ready to purchase the land and transfer the property over to our name. We met the property owners at their house, drove them to the notary and made payments as if it was perfectly normal for us to purchase land and start building our dreams. That night during dinner I looked at David and said,

"It doesn't seem real. We purchased the land, the plans for the house and winery are practically set and we are acting as if it's just another day."

We had been disappointed so many times, that we were afraid to celebrate, but we both knew everything would fall into place. We knew it was meant to be. I told David we had to bless the land before we broke ground and he agreed. Moving forward we wanted to be sure the land was endowed with positive energy.

December 17, 2014

I had decided to have a natural birth with our son, who we had decided to name "Ian." It was easy to pronounce in both English and Spanish, and even more important, I had read it meant "gift from God" and "God is gracious." I wanted my son to learn grace, to learn forgiveness and not harbor pain and resentment as has parents had.

I didn't like what I had read about the utilization of drugs during the birthing process. After almost nine months of being told by family, friends and strangers about what I could and could not do with my body — *don't eat that, you need to get rid of your cat, you can't take the medication while you're pregnant* — suddenly the advice shifted. When it came to the most important day, I was told things like, *are you crazy, the pain is unbearable!* or *No award was ever given for not having an epidural*. In my mind, it translated to: *God forbid you live with a cat during pregnancy, but the day you give birth you should go for the spinal cocktail of local anesthetics and narcotics.* "Oh and don't worry, it's safe, it won't affect your child." I gave up unpasteurized cheese for nine months, but on the final day I get to take a narcotic or opioid? I had thought that I would not be in the minority with this opinion, but the more I asked around, the more I wished I hadn't. There were very few women who supported the idea of natural childbirth. I found support only in those women who had opted for a natural birth during their time. All others launched immediately into fear mode. I decided to reach out to Cynthia in Hawaii. We were both pregnant and only months apart. I had a feeling she would be pursuing the natural route and I was right. She recommend a book called "Hypnobirthing," the basic premise that fear creates pain. I was immediately hooked because that was one thing I hadn't felt when thinking about the birth of Ian. As a woman, my body is made for this and we were in this together, Ian, David and I. We had molded into a strong team over the last eight months; we could conquer all odds together. David was my rock and Ian would lead me safely through the process, if I could just stay relaxed and have faith.

I shared my plans with my mother, who was set to arrive on January 14th, only a few days before my due date of January 17th. She once again was my champion, telling me how she remembered the side effects that my sister experienced with an epidural and how she herself had given birth with relative ease with both my sister and I. She shared how she was playing cards in the lobby with my family during a large part of her first stage of labor. They say labor reveals how you view life. My mother was the strong, independent optimist. She wasn't there to be the center of attention or to be coddled, she was there to do a normal, natural thing and she did — without fear and therefore with ease. Of course in her encouragement she did what all women do and claimed that it may have been due to a higher pain tolerance. I know my mother and it was her relaxed and fearless mind that lessened her fight or flight mode and moved the process along as it was meant to be. I was happy to know that she would be there for me once Ian arrived.

January 22, 2015

Ian was due January 17th. My mother had arrived on the 14th just in case he was early and yet the day came and went. While I was ready to get the show on the road, he wasn't ready to enter this world just yet. I had been walking throughout the pregnancy but decided to step things up a bit to encourage him. I was trying every trick in the book, walking, spicy food, pineapple… but nothing worked. I wasn't even having Braxton Hicks contractions. There had been a few days when I felt something, but it was always a light sensation so I never knew what to think of it.

Five days after his estimated date I woke up at 4:30 a.m. with a strange sensation. Once again, nothing was intense so I wasn't sure if it was a contraction or stomach issues. All doubts were soon erased from the picture as contractions started that would bring me to my hands and knees without pause — or so it felt. I wanted to pass as much time as possible in the house, but it seemed impossible to time the contractions since from the beginning it felt as if I never had a break in between them. At 7:00 a.m. David became worried and forced me to go to the hospital. Snowy and icy roads were uncommon, however on this night in particular the roads were worse than David had seen in years. I was oblivious to everything as I had my seat laid down trying to breath through my contractions. We arrived safely at 8 a.m. and by 10:53 a.m. we were able to bring our little Ian into the world without the use of drugs, just as I had wanted. Granted it wasn't a walk in the park and even though I had given David a list of preferences for the medical staff, he didn't read or pay attention to one of them, so I had to tell what felt like 10 different nurses that no I didn't want the epidural. Another request was to not be forced to push. I had tried to explain the philosophy prior to David, and as I expected it fell on deaf ears and the doctor told me to push when my body wasn't directing me to do so. In a panic David told me, "FUCKING PUSH!" and so I did. They immediately laid Ian on my chest, umbilical cord still attached. I could feel how fragile he was as I lay there shivering from the shock of childbirth. In typical David humor his comments were along the lines of amazement at how it reminded him of his days assisting the shepherd. He said it was exactly like the birth of a goat. David with his olfactory hyperawareness commented that Ian smelled like a baby goat, too! We spent two days in the hospital, which is normal in Spain. Never in my life had I spent so much time staring at something or someone, but there I sat for hours on end gazing in awe at this sweet, fragile miracle we had created. I didn't sleep much due to worry, and at night I would lay him in his crib next to my bed, scared that something was going to happen to him if he wasn't next to me. I would then transfer him to my bed next to me, but then I'd worry I was going to fall asleep on him and put him back in the crib. Everyone says the love you feel for your child is unlike any other. I've even heard it's more than what you feel for your spouse. I felt the same profound love for my son as I did for his father, not this overwhelming gush that everyone had spoken about. I had been through good and bad with David, things weren't always easy but my love for him was unwavering.

As the months passed Ian grew to know his entire family, including his grandpa. Ian was my confirmation that I had done the right thing by contacting David's father. He brought so much joy into everyone's life. I had people coming up to me in the streets telling me how happy his father was to be part of Ian's life and they would always throw in a comment about how he is such a good person — a fact that I now knew, but it was nice to hear that the people in my small village appreciated him as well. And finally things were improving with David and his father. After months of his father offering to help, David finally accepted and they spent many mornings working together in the vineyards. I knew David well enough not to speak much about it or ask many questions. I didn't need to know the details. My heart knew the answers. We didn't have much but we had everything we needed. Things were moving and I had faith in everything that had brought us up to this point would lead us in our next journey as we started the construction on our new winery. Sometimes when I'm feeding Ian, he will stop, smile and coo while looking over my shoulder. I tell him to thank the angels for me… for us.

The roads of life our family travels on are never without challenges. We struggle every day and we also give thanks every day for all of the beautiful things that we've called into our life. We are building our dreams. We've started the construction on the house and the winery and have many dreams that we would like to fulfill with the land when it's all finished. We want a horse to work the vineyards, we want to cultivate bees, maybe some chickens again. We'd like to prepare all the biodynamic treatments for the vineyard at our new property, and we've visualized part of our home to be used as small exclusive hotel of sorts for clients or visiting wine lovers. The list was endless. Life with David will never be easy, nor will it be boring. It will be challenging and filled with arguments, but it will also be filled with deep, passionate and enduring love. I see it when my husband looks at me, and now I see it when he looks at Ian.

About the Author

Born and raised in Ohio, grown and stretched in Hawaii, Melanie Hickman now lives in Elvillar, Spain (Rioja Alavesa) with her husband, son (and another on the way), dog and cat on their "mini-chateau" surrounded by nothing but vineyards and mountains as far as the eye can see. A perpetual dreamer and lover of nature, animals, laughter, kindness, travel and most importantly, food and wine, she is Level 2 Certified with the Wine & Spirit Education Trust (WSET). www.strugglingvines.com

Made in the USA
Charleston, SC
10 May 2016